Yearbook of Legal Practices and International Organizations 2026

Yearbook of Legal Practices and International Organizations

VOLUME 1

The titles published in this series are listed at *brill.com/lpio*

Yearbook of Legal Practices and International Organizations 2026

Edited by

Peter Quayle

BRILL | NIJHOFF

ISSN 3050-550X
ISBN 978-90-04-76566-5
ISBN 978-90-04-76567-2 (PDF)
DOI https://doi.org/10.1163/9789004765672

Library of Congress Control Number: 2026906815

Views expressed in this Yearbook are those of the authors and do not necessarily reflect views of, and should not be attributed to, any institution with which the authors or members of the editorial team are or have been affiliated.

Brill Nijhoff and Koninklijke Brill BV are part of De Gruyter Brill.
www.degruyterbrill.com

Questions about General Product Safety Regulation: productsafety@degruyterbrill.com

Contents

1 The Duty of Cooperation between Successful International Organizations and Supportive Member States 1
Essay: *Peter Quayle*

PART 1
Articles

2 Watchdogs or Paper Tigers? Tribunal Governance of Employment Frameworks at International Organizations 9
Joan Powers

3 Formal Constitutional Interpretation by the Bretton Woods Institutions 39
Edward Chukwuemeke Okeke

4 International Trust Funds at the World Bank and International Monetary Fund 68
Andrew Giddings, Gabriela Grinsteins and Hoang Pham

5 Sexual Misconduct and the United Nations: Organizational Tensions, Zero Tolerance and Unfinished Justice 97
Brenda Costecalde Orpineda and Mohamed Abdou

PART 2
Materials

6 A Proposal for 'Conditional Immunity': A New Approach for Resolving Private Claims against International Organizations 149
Position Paper: *David P. Stewart*

7 How to Be a Good Employer? The Duties of International Organizations Constituted by the ILO Administrative Tribunal 163
Manual: *Dražen Petrović and Bianca Carrer*

PART 3
YLPIO Interview

8 'There's a Liberian Expression: If You Mind the Noise of the Market You Will Not Buy Your Fish.' 235
Rhoda Weeks-Brown and Peter Quayle

ESSAY

The Duty of Cooperation between Successful International Organizations and Supportive Member States

*Peter Quayle**

Abstract This essay examines the legal and functional relationship between international organizations and their Member States, framed by an evolving mutual 'duty of cooperation' in international law. Drawing on Advisory Opinions of the International Court of Justice, *WHO and Egypt* (1980) and *Israel and United Nations* (2025), the essay contends that this duty affords a constructive framework for enhancing the effectiveness of – and mitigating the tensions inherent to – international organizations.

A fundamental of international law holds that, whilst constituted by, international organizations are legally autonomous from, their Member States.[1] Consequently, action is taken on behalf of the United Nations, for example, not in the name of the States that voted in the UN's Security Council or General Assembly for such an undertaking.[2] Yet this commonplace legal construction conceals the extent to which international organizations necessarily depend upon States to succeed. Certainly, international organizations can be led

* Editor-in-Chief, Yearbook of Legal Practices and International Organizations (Brill Nijhoff), peterquayle.ylpio@gmail.com. The views expressed in this editorial are solely those of the author. They do not necessarily reflect the views of, and should not be attributed to, any institution with which the author is, or has been, affiliated.

1 In its work on "Settlement of disputes to which international organizations are parties", the International Law Commission defines 'international organization' as "an entity possessing its own international legal personality, established by a treaty or other instrument governed by international law, that may include as members, in addition to States, other entities, and has at least one organ capable of expressing a will distinct from that of its members". Report of the International Law Commission on the Work on its Seventy-fourth Session (2023) UN Doc A/78/10, para 48.

2 Although this premise is the subject of considerable probing; see, for example, Dan Sarooshi, *International Organizations and their Exercise of Sovereign Powers* (Oxford University Press, 2007).

 | HTTPS://DOI.ORG/10.1163/9789004765672-002

well or poorly, by either a brilliant or an ineffectual executive head; yet in every case, this executive head is selected by Member States. International organizations may be staffed by intrepid and innovative international officials. However, Member State governance organs not infrequently intrude into the minutiae of staffing, often contributing inflexibility to the international civil service. Member States may demand frugality, but their delayed payment of obligatory funding and stop-start conditional financial contributions disrupt and distort the operations of international organizations. Prominently, without the laws and courts of Member States – especially host States – upholding the jurisdictional immunity of international organizations, institutionalized multilateralism becomes, at best impaired, and at worst impossible.

Construing the interrelationship between supportive Member States and successful international organizations through legal practices is challenging. In its Advisory Opinion, *WHO and Egypt* (1980),[3] the International Court of Justice (ICJ) struggles to develop a legal framework between an international organization and a host – also Member – State, outside specific treaty terms. The ICJ reformulates the question it is asked to answer as: "What are the legal principles and rules applicable to the question under what conditions and in accordance with what modalities a transfer of the [World Health Organization's] Regional Office from Egypt may be effected?"[4] It begins by noting that:

> [International organizations could not possess] some form of absolute power to determine and, if need be, change the location of the sites of their headquarters and regional offices [since] States for their part possess a sovereign power of decision with respect to their acceptance of the headquarters or a regional office of an organization within their territories.[5]

Or in other words, "an organization's power of decision is no more absolute in this respect than is that of a State".[6] The ICJ considers the terms of a bilateral agreement between the WHO and Egypt to be unhelpful to resolving the disputed relocation,[7] though "certain legal principles and rules are applicable in

3 *Interpretation of the Agreement of 25 March 1951 between the WHO and Egypt* (Advisory Opinion) [1980] ICJ Rep 73.
4 Ibid, para 35.
5 Ibid, para 37.
6 Ibid.
7 The Agreement does not specifically address the circumstances of the WHO closing its Regional Office, to then reopen it elsewhere; a review of the revision, termination and denunciation provisions of comparable agreements causes "the Court [to feel] bound to

the case of such a transfer".[8] The Court identifies mutual obligations of cooperation and consultation; nevertheless "the paramount consideration both for [an international organization] and the host State in every case must be their clear obligation to cooperate in good faith to promote the objectives and purposes of the [organization] as expressed in its [constituent instrument]".[9]

The significance of this 'duty of cooperation' between Member States and international organizations rearises in the ICJ Advisory Opinion, *Israel and United Nations* (2025).[10] The ICJ notes that two provisions of the UN Charter address cooperation between Member States and the United Nations. Article 2, paragraph 2 states: "All Members, in order to ensure to all of them the rights and benefits resulting from membership, shall fulfil in good faith the obligations assumed by them in accordance with the present Charter."[11] Further, Article 2, paragraph 5 adds: "All Members shall give the United Nations every assistance in any action it takes in accordance with the present Charter […]."[12] The Court reconfirms: "Compliance with this duty to render assistance is important for the effective functioning of the [United Nations], the fulfilment of its mandate, and the independence and efficacy of its personnel in the discharge of their duties."[13]

Importantly, in the discourse by the judges of the Court accompanying the Advisory Opinion, a 'duty of cooperation' is distinguished from simple adherence to the terms of the UN Charter. In the view of Judge Gómez Robledo:

> States' duty of cooperation is not confined to binding obligations in the strict sense. When the action required goes beyond this, that is, it requires States to take measures that do not necessarily derive from a specific obligation, then it is founded on a broader framework, specifically that which derives from the general duty to cooperate with the [UN]. Even though States enjoy a certain latitude in interpreting this obligation, the obligation to cooperate remains an

---

observe that in future closer attention might with advantage be given to their drafting" (*WHO and Egypt* (note 3), para 46).

8 *WHO and Egypt* (note 3), para 42.

9 Ibid, para 49.

10 *Obligations of Israel in Relation to the Presence and Activities of the United Nations, Other International Organizations and Third States in and in Relation to the Occupied Palestinian Territory* (Advisory Opinion) [2025] ICJ General List No 196.

11 Ibid, para 171.

12 Ibid, para 172.

13 Ibid, para 173.

> extensive one, since it is an integral part of the very object and purpose of the United Nations.[14]

The ICJ reaffirms *WHO and Egypt* and "the obligation to cooperate" between international organizations and Member States – even when some express treaty-based term is not engaged.[15] In the event of any differences arising between an international organization and a Member State, "the obligation to cooperate requires [them] to pursue consultation and negotiation [...]".[16] This duty of cooperation is inherent to the relationship between all international organizations and their Member States.

Separate from the obligation to adhere to the terms of the constituent instrument of an international organization, the duty of cooperation is the instrumentalization of 'good faith' interpretation of all treaties, in the functional context of international organizations.[17] It is also consistent with the "functionalist paradigm that underpins the law of international organizations – namely, that intergovernmental institutions are attributed functions by their Member States together with all necessary powers to fulfil such functions".[18] It could scarcely be credited that Member States attribute all the powers necessary to an international organization to achieve its mandate, whilst reserving to themselves permission to impede – not cooperate to fulfil – such ends.

In the duty of cooperation is also situated the coequality as international legal persons between international organizations and Member States. It has been noted that *WHO and Egypt* "was possibly the first time the [ICJ] addressed in clear terms the two-sided nature of the obligations resting on the organization and its host state, and the 'contractual' relationship as between

14 'Partially Dissenting Opinion of Judge Gómez Robledo' in *Israel and United Nations* (note 10), para 14.

15 *Israel and United Nations* (note 10), para 178.

16 Ibid.

17 'Good faith' pervades the authoritative interpretation of the constituent instruments of international organizations; see Peter Quayle, 'Treaties of a Particular Type: The ICJ's Interpretative Approach to the Constituent Instruments of International Organizations' (2016) 29 Leiden Journal of International Law 853.

18 Peter Quayle, 'The Modern Multilateral Bureaucracy: What is the Role of International Administrative Law at International Organizations?' in Peter Quayle (ed), *The Role of International Administrative Law at International Organizations* (Brill Nijhoff, 2020) <https://brill.com/display/book/9789004441033/BP000001.xml> accessed 6 January 2026, 2–3.

legal equals [...]. In that respect the Opinion may be taken as a marker".[19] *Israel and United Nations* consolidates this. Consistent with the duty of cooperation, albeit separately dealt with by the Court, are the several jurisdictional immunities of the United Nations, its property and personnel. For example: "In the view of the Court, the Secretary-General's determination of the scope of the official functions of the officials or experts in question creates a presumption that can only be set aside for the most compelling reasons and is to be given the greatest weight by States."[20] In this way, a duty to cooperate now traverses from obligating an earnest and engaged diplomatic interface between an international organization and its Member States, to a deference of Member States towards international organizations, redolent of the sovereign equality between States.[21]

However, litigating the relationship between international organizations and Member States is unlikely to lead to the success of the former and the support of the latter. More usefully, the timely recollection of the duty of cooperation may be constructive of revived mutual collaboration. So that the irreducible frustrations and flaws of institutionalized multilateralism are attributed, not to bad faith, but to the very improbability of what international organizations are established to attain – goals of worldwide betterment, no State alone can achieve.

---

19 Catherine Brölmann, 'The Significance of the 1980 ICJ Advisory Opinion Interpretation of the Agreement of 25 March 1951 between the WHO and Egypt' (2015) Amsterdam Center for International Law, University of Amsterdam, 4.

20 *Israel and United Nations* (note 10), para 204.

21 See Charter of the United Nations (adopted 26 June 1945, entered into force 25 October 1945), art 2, para 1.

PART 1

Articles

Watchdogs or Paper Tigers? Tribunal Governance of Employment Frameworks at International Organizations

*Joan Powers**

Abstract Under a typical appointment with an international organization, staff members must accept that the organization retains the authority to unilaterally amend the terms and conditions of their employment. But is this reservation of unilateral authority limitless, such that the organization could, at least from a legal standpoint, revise the employment terms and conditions of a staff member at will? This article identifies certain well-established principles of international administrative law – in particular, the doctrine of acquired rights and preservation of fundamental and essential terms of employment – which, even if not explicitly incorporated in the internal written law of the organization, constrain the ability of the governing organs to amend the rules and regulations that comprise the employment framework. Yet in practice, although the tribunals have invoked these concepts on numerous occasions, they rarely find that a change to the employment framework transgressed these principles. Does this suggest that the tribunals are essentially 'paper tigers', sounding forceful but actually ineffectual in practice? Or should the tribunals be regarded as 'watchdogs', ready to pounce and be aggressive in invalidating an impugned decision involving changes to the conditions of employment if the circumstances so warrant?

1 Introduction

It could be argued that international civil servants do *not* have a contractual relationship with the organization, and that the legal basis for their employment is an appointment rather than a contract. What is the difference? The critical distinction is that a contractual relationship requires mutual consent, namely, the terms of the contract may be amended only with the agreement of

* Joan Powers, formerly Assistant General Counsel of the International Monetary Fund, and currently Judge of the European Bank for Reconstruction and Development Administrative Tribunal and the GAVI Appeals Tribunal, joanpowers@yahoo.com. The views expressed herein are the personal views of the author. They do not necessarily reflect the views of the institutions that the author is, or was, associated with.

 HTTPS://DOI.ORG/10.1163/9789004765672-003

both parties. In contrast, under a typical appointment with an international organization, the staff member has accepted that the organization retains the authority to unilaterally amend the terms and conditions of employment.

However, this reservation of unilateral authority by the organization raises the fundamental question as to whether such power is limitless, such that the organization could theoretically, from a legal standpoint, invoke this authority to revise the employment framework of a staff member at any time. The answer lies in what are considered well-established principles of international administrative law, which – even if not explicitly incorporated in the internal law of the organization – constrain the ability of the governing organs to amend the rules and regulations that comprise the employment framework (which will herein be generically referred to as 'regulatory decisions').[1]

But this, in turn, raises the question of how, as both a legal and a practical matter, these general principles are to be applied to the exercise of rule-making authority by an international organization with respect to its employment framework which, by its very nature, is discretionary. Administrative tribunals have recognized their own lack of capacity to decide what type of employment conditions would best serve the interests of an organization, and they will accordingly defer to the judgment of the rule-making organs on such matters. At the same time, tribunals assert authority to protect staff against infringement of their acquired rights or fundamental and essential elements of employment. In the seminal *de Merode* case, the very first judgment of the World Bank Administrative Tribunal (WBAT), this balancing act was characterized as follows:

1 As succinctly stated by one tribunal, "[a]lthough some terms and conditions of employment can be prospectively altered, the principle that fundamental and essential terms and conditions of employment cannot unilaterally be amended is <u>now a recognized principle which can be regarded as part of the law common to international organizations.</u> That principle imposes a limitation on the powers of the governing bodies of every international organization, restraining the unilateral amendment of such terms and conditions". *Ferdinand P. Mesch and Robert Y. Siy v. Asian Development Bank (No. 3)*, ADBAT Decision No 18 (1996), para 22 (emphasis added). One observer suggests that "international administrative law acts to constrain a decision-maker, rather than to adjudicate a contractual bargain". Peter Quayle, 'The Modern Multilateral Bureaucracy: What is the Role of International Administrative Law at International Organizations?' in Peter Quayle (ed), *The Role of International Administrative Law at International Organizations* (AIIB Yearbook of International Law, Brill Nijhoff 2020) <https://brill.com/display/book/9789004441033/BP000001.xml> accessed 10 December 2025, 13.

> [I]t is not for this Tribunal to substitute its own judgment for that of the competent organs of the Bank in exercising that discretion [to amend the non-fundamental and non-essential elements of employment]. However, the Bank's power to amend non-essential terms may be exercised subject only to certain limitations. Discretionary power is not absolute power.[2]

A similar expression of this balancing act was ably summarized in reference to the ILOAT:

> Underlying the principle of acquired rights is the recognition that a delicate balance must be struck between two major competing needs: on the one hand, the possibility for the employer [international organization] to adapt its functioning and employment conditions to evolving circumstances, versus, on the other, the protection of the legitimate expectations of its personnel in being able to rely on the stability of their employment conditions and to be protected against arbitrary change and erosion of rights.[3]

This article examines how different administrative tribunals, through their jurisprudence, have articulated certain checks and balances on an organization's ability to revise its employment framework (for example, modifying its compensation system or its pension arrangements, or reducing the level of benefits), as well as an assessment as to whether, in practice, this has been effective as a limitation on such rule-making authority.

---

2 *Louis de Merode et al. v. The World Bank,* WBAT Decision No 1 (1981), para 45. The WBAT has also pronounced that in respect of policy-making "it is not for the Tribunal to override the Bank's considered judgment and to replace it with its own" (*Damian von Stauffenberg et al. v. The World Bank,* WBAT Decision No 38 (1987), para 123), nor to "consider which alternative would have been best or more effective to attain the desired objectives of the reform" (*H. Paul Crevier v. International Bank for Reconstruction and Development,* WBAT Decision No 205 (1999), para 17).

3 See Eva-Maria Gröniger-Voss, A. Kirsten Baxter and Arthur Nguyen Dao, 'The Principle of Acquired Rights With Particular Focus on the Jurisprudence of the Administrative Tribunal of the International Labour Organization' in Dražen Petrović (ed), *90 Years of Contribution of the Administrative Tribunal of the International Labour Organization to the Creation of International Civil Service Law* (International Labor Organization 2017) <https://www.ilo.org/sites/default/files/wcmsp5/groups/public/%40dgreports/%40trib/documents/meetingdocument/wcms_613944.pdf> accessed 10 December 2025 (90 Years of Contribution of the ILOAT), 109–128. This article observes that foremost among these general principles is that of acquired rights. Ibid, 110.

2 Applicable General Principles

If you ask a group of practitioners to identify the 'well-established' principles of international administrative law concerning an international organization's unilateral authority to revise the employment framework, they would probably mention such concepts as:

(i) non-retroactivity;
(ii) protection of acquired rights;
(iii) preservation of fundamental terms and conditions;
(iv) non-discrimination;
(v) proportionality;
(vi) properly motivated decisions in the exercise of discretion; and
(vii) adherence to rules unless and until they are duly amended (in Latin, *tu patere legem quam fecisti*).

It has been observed that these principles "have been developed and are continually applied by international administrative tribunals such as those of, inter alia, the International Labour Organization, the World Bank and the United Nations, and it is generally recognised that these principles must be respected by any intergovernmental organization [...] in the adoption and application of its employment law".[4] In this manner, general principles have implicitly become part of the terms of appointment of international civil servants. Indeed, there is widespread consensus as to the need to respect these general principles when the employment framework is reviewed and revised.[5]

But how have they been interpreted in practice? For example, when an organization decides to tighten the criteria for benefits eligibility, or reduce the financial value of a benefit (such as reducing the class of travel or frequency of entitlement for home leave), when is 'grandfathering' of existing staff (in other words, allowing existing staff to retain the entitlement they had as of the time of a decision altering the entitlement), or transitional arrangements required as a legal matter? In some instances, organizations may decide that it would be prudent to allow 'grandfathering' as a matter of maintaining harmonious employee relations, but that would be a matter of policy rather than legal obligation. Conversely, when are revisions to the employment framework considered not to infringe 'acquired rights' or affect 'fundamental' elements of employment, such that they may be adopted and

4 Ibid, 110.

5 As the UNAT held in *De Aguirre v. Secretary-General of the United Nations*, UNAT Judgment No 2016-UNAT-705, "in interpreting the terms of a staff member's appointment, we may draw upon general principles of law insofar as they apply to the international civil service" (footnote omitted).

applied prospectively to both current and future staff? Moreover, is the doctrine of acquired rights synonymous with the concepts of non-retroactivity or fundamental terms and conditions? If not, how do these terms differ in their interpretation and application by the various administrative tribunals?

3 Tribunal Review of Administrative Rule-Making Authority

As of today, there are numerous international administrative tribunals[6] serving either multiple or single international organizations.[7] The most longstanding of these, and the largest in terms of the affiliated organizations they serve, are the Administrative Tribunal of the International Labour Organization (ILOAT) and the UN Appeals Tribunal (UNAT). During the past 70 years, both the ILOAT and the UNAT (and its predecessor, the former UN Administrative Tribunal) have developed a considerable body of jurisprudence concerning the authority of organizations to unilaterally revise their employment frameworks, and the concomitant rights of staff to ensure that certain general principles are respected in that process. Other administrative tribunals that serve single organizations, including the World Bank Administrative Tribunal (WBAT), the Asian Development Bank Administrative Tribunal (ADBAT) and the International Monetary Fund Administrative Tribunal (IMFAT), have un-

6 The proliferation of international administrative tribunals is examined in detail in Chris de Cooker, 'Proliferation of International Administrative Tribunals' (2022) 12 Asian Journal of International Law 232.

7 The Administrative Tribunal of the International Labour Organization was created in 1947, replacing its predecessor body (the Administrative Tribunal of the League of Nations, founded in 1927). The United Nations Administrative Tribunal was created in 1949 but was replaced in 2009 by the UN Dispute Tribunal and the UN Appeals Tribunal (which did not necessarily adopt the jurisprudence of its predecessor as precedents). A non-exhaustive list of other tribunals that were subsequently established would include the Administrative Tribunal of the Council of Europe (1965); Administrative Tribunal of the Organization of American States (1971); World Bank Administrative Tribunal (1980); Administrative Tribunal of the Inter-American Development Bank (1981); Bank for International Settlements Administrative Tribunal (1987); Asian Development Bank Administrative Tribunal (1991); International Monetary Fund Administrative Tribunal (1992); the OECD Administrative Tribunal (1992); Commonwealth Secretariat Arbitral Tribunal (1995); African Development Bank Administrative Tribunal (1997); European Bank for Reconstruction and Development Administrative Tribunal (2002); NATO Administrative Tribunal (2013); European Stability Mechanism Administrative Tribunal (2013); GAVI Alliance Appeals Tribunal (2019); OPEC Fund Administrative Tribunal (2022).

dertaken their own analysis and application of this judicial authority in their respective jurisprudence.[8]

The following sections therefore examine, in the order in which these tribunals (or, in the case of the UNAT, its predecessor body, the former UN Administrative Tribunal) were established, the following aspects:

(i) the statutory basis on which the tribunal derives its authority to review changes to the organization's employment framework;
(ii) how general principles have been invoked and applied in the jurisprudence; and
(iii) summary observations as to the respective tribunal's approach.

3.1 ILOAT

3.1.1 ILOAT Statutory Basis

Article II (1) of the ILOAT Statute states:

> The Tribunal shall be competent to hear complaints alleging non-observance, in substance or in form, of the terms of appointment of officials of the [ILO and any other organization that has recognized the jurisdiction of the ILOAT], and of such provisions of the Staff Regulations as are applicable to the case.

3.1.2 ILOAT Jurisprudence

In *W. v. FAO,* the ILOAT drew extensively on its own experience in examining the doctrine of acquired rights.[9] Drawing on that earlier jurisprudence, the

8 For an overview of the factors to be considered by an organization in deciding whether to join an existing administrative tribunal or establish its own, see Katherine Meighan and Gabriel Rodríguez-Rico, 'To Join or Not to Join: A Comparative Analysis of Joining or Creating an International Administrative Tribunal' in Quayle (ed), *AIIB Yearbook of International Law* (note 1) <https://brill.com/display/book/9789004441033/BP000008.xml> accessed 10 December 2025, 119–140.

9 *W. v. FAO*, ILOAT Judgment No 4381 (2021), consids 13–15. The ILOAT acknowledged that the concept of breach of acquired rights had its genesis in *In re di Palma Castiglione v. International Labour Office*, an early decision given by its predecessor body in 1929. There, the League of Nations Administrative Tribunal had held: "The Administration is at liberty to establish for its staff such regulations as it may see fit, provided that it does not in any way infringe the acquired rights of any staff member." The ILOAT noted that "[o]ver the decades since, the basis for recognising and protecting acquired rights has evolved and, in particular, principles developed for demarking what are and are not such rights". Ibid, consid 13, citing Gröniger-Voss, Baxter and Dao (note 3).

ILOAT reiterated its prior summary of the applicable legal principles in terms of a three-part test:

> [T]he amendment of a rule to an official's detriment and without his consent amounts to breach of an acquired right when the structure of the contract of appointment is disturbed or there is impairment of any fundamental term of appointment in consideration of which the official accepted appointment [...]. [The] three-part test for determining whether the altered term is fundamental and essential [...] is as follows:
>
> (1) What is the nature of the altered term? "It may be in the contract or in the Staff Regulations or Staff Rules or in a decision, and whereas the contract or a decision may give rise to acquired rights the regulations and rules do not necessarily do so."
>
> (2) What is the reason for the change? "It is material that the terms of appointment may often have to be adapted to circumstances, and there will ordinarily be no acquired right when a rule or a clause depends on variables such as the cost-of-living index or the value of the currency. Nor can the finances of the body that applies the terms of appointment be discounted."
>
> (3) What is the consequence of allowing or disallowing an acquired right and the effect it will have on staff pay and benefits, and how do those who plead an acquired right fare as against others?[10]

Notwithstanding its embrace of the doctrine of acquired rights, the ILOAT has opined on numerous occasions and in a variety of contexts that the alteration of a benefit to the detriment of staff does not, in and of itself, breach an acquired right. Rather, an aggrieved staff member must demonstrate – and bears the burden of proving – that the structure of their employment contract was disturbed by the impugned change, and that the modifications impaired a fundamental term of appointment which they had taken into account in accepting employment.

Moreover, while recognizing that an organization may not abrogate the acquired rights of staff, the ILOAT has repeatedly stated that staff of international organizations are not entitled to have all the conditions of employment or retirement as provided in the staff rules and regulations in force at the time of their recruitment applied to them throughout their career and retirement. Most of those conditions may be altered, although, depending on the

10 ILOAT Judgment No 4381, consid 14, quoting Judgment 4195, consid 7.

nature and importance of the provision in question, staff may have an acquired right to their continued application.[11]

In fact, although the ILOAT has examined the issue of acquired rights in numerous cases, there have been relatively few instances in which the Tribunal found that the organization in question had exceeded its rule-making authority and improperly modified or breached an acquired right of staff. The ILOAT jurisprudence indeed confirms that changes made to the organization's employment framework are rarely (if ever) considered to infringe the acquired rights of staff, as shown in the following examples:

(i) ***F. (No. 14) v. EPO***: suppression of a lump sum payment for invalidity did not infringe an acquired right, as this feature cannot be considered an essential term of employment which induced staff to accept the appointment, given that an invalidity payment is a remote and contingent right that only arises upon the occurrence of permanent invalidity.[12]

(ii) ***K. (No. 3) and L. (No. 2) v. EPO***: amendment of provisions relating to grade promotion and replacing "quasi-automatic" promotion did not violate any acquired rights. Although the effect was to make career progression more dependent on performance, the opportunities for staff to be promoted "were not substantially affected" by the change.[13] The organization has always had the ability to amend these arrangements according to need.[14]

---

11 For example, see *H. v. Interpol*, ILOAT Judgment No 4662 (2023), consid 20 (staff do not necessarily have acquired rights with respect to the provisions in force at the time they were recruited, and have no right to continue with the same terms throughout their employment); *M. and P. v. BIPM*, ILOAT Judgment No 4580 (2023), consid 11; *B. v. IAEA*, ILOAT Judgment No 4465 (2022), consid 8; *G. v. CERN*, ILOAT Judgment No 3876 (2017), consid 7. See also *D.E. H. v. WMO*, ILOAT Judgment No 3074 (2012), consids 14–17.

12 *F. (No. 14) v. EPO*, ILOAT Judgment No 4898 (2024), consid 10. See also *R.-S. (No. 2) v. EPO*, ILOAT Judgment No 4398 (2021), consid 11.

13 *K. (No. 3) and L. (No. 2) v. EPO*, ILOAT Judgment No 4889 (2024), consid 7.

14 In *W. v. FAO*, ILOAT Judgment No 4381 (2021), the complainants argued that the reform of automatic step adjustments was not necessary, and the organization had not duly considered the wellbeing of staff and the financial impact this would have on them. However, the ILOAT rejected this argument, observing that "it is not for the Tribunal, in any event, to review the advisability or merits of the changes which an international organisation wishes to make to salary structures or to the arrangements for career progression, that form part of general staff management policy which an organisation is free to pursue in accordance with its interests". *K. (No. 3) and L. (No. 2) v. EPO*, ILOAT Judgment No 4889, consid 9. See also *F. (No. 15) v. EPO*, ILOAT Judgment No 4711 (2023), consid 8.

(iii) ***I. (No. 3) v. Eurocontrol***: in view of the relative amount involved, the pay reduction at issue cannot be regarded as disturbing the structure of the contract of appointment or impairing fundamental terms of appointment in consideration of which the complainant joined Eurocontrol.[15]

(iv) ***F. (No. 15) v. EPO***: abolition of automatic step advancement pursuant to the introduction of a new career system did not breach any acquired rights, as the former salary is preserved, and future step advancements are not precluded.[16]

(v) ***G., H. and D. S. G. (No. 2) v. CERN***: modifications to the subsistence allowance did not violate any acquired rights. The creation of a ceiling and its amount reducing the subsistence allowance, though substantial, is not demonstrably so significant to justify a conclusion that the "structure of the employment contract" was disturbed or that it impaired a fundamental term of appointment.[17]

(vi) ***R. v. Eurocontrol***: no violation of acquired right in abolition of supplemental day of annual leave for travelling time, as this did not affect the complainant's overall remuneration or reduce the entitlement to annual leave provided in the staff regulations.[18]

(vii) ***M. and P. v. BIPM***: the disputed increases in pension contributions, though significant, did not substantially alter the balance of the complainants' contractual obligations, and did not adversely affect a fundamental term of employment in consideration of which the complainants accepted their appointment or which subsequently induced them to stay on; increases to staff's required pension contri-

15 *I. (No. 3) v. Eurocontrol*, ILOAT Judgment No 4766 (2024), consid 4. But see *B. and others; A.-M. and others; A.-U. and others v. ILO*, ILOAT Judgment No 4134 (2019), consid 26 (invalidating revised post adjustment on the grounds that "[w]hile an international organization is free to choose a methodology, system or standard of reference for determining salary adjustments it must be a methodology which ensures that the results are stable, foreseeable and clearly understood or transparent" (citation omitted). In *D. L. M. v. WCO*, ILOAT Judgment No 3324 (2014), the ILOAT did not accept the organization's argument that the decision to not apply the salary adjustment recommended by the Co-ordinating Committee on Remuneration of the system of Co-ordinated Organisations for officials serving in Belgium was necessitated by budgetary constraints. It held that the departure from the recommendation violated the internal rules of the organization. It therefore remitted the matter to the organization to re-calculate the amount of the salary adjustment with respect to the complainant and approximately 70 other staff who had applied to intervene.

16 *F. (No. 15) v. EPO*, ILOAT Judgment No 4711 (2023), consid 8.

17 *G., H. and D. S. G. (No. 2) v. CERN*, ILOAT Judgment No 4707 (2023), consid 13.

18 *R. v. Eurocontrol*, ILOAT Judgment No 4593 (2023), consid 10.

butions did not violate any acquired rights, as pension contributions, by their very nature, are subject to variation.[19]

(viii) ***R. v. CERN***: no acquired right to a surviving spouse's pension in the event of marriage after retirement, given that the possibility for a spouse whom the official married after their retirement to benefit from a surviving spouse's pension does not qualify as a fundamental and essential term of employment.[20]

(ix) ***B. v. IAEA***: removal of financial assistance towards child's boarding costs at local schools as part of the education grant scheme "did not disturb the structure of the employment contract"; the changes were "rational, logical, and credible."[21]

(x) ***H. (No. 4) and others v. EPO***: introducing a requirement that staff pay medical insurance contributions with respect to coverage of gainfully employed spouses (which was previously free) did not violate any acquired rights; conditions under which health insurance for employees' spouses is provided do not give rise to an acquired right, and contribution rate may be adjusted if there are compelling reasons to do so (including budgetary reasons), within reasonable limits.[22]

(xi) ***L. v. WTO***: downward adjustment of pensions based on reduction in cost-of-living data did not transgress any acquired rights, as there is no principle that there can never be a downward adjustment of pensions.[23]

(xii) ***D. L. v. ESO***: changes in methodology for calculating pension contributions were justified by financial considerations; the mere fact that a pension contribution might change because of fluctuations in exchange rates would not engage the protection of the principle concerning acquired rights.[24]

---

19 *M. and P. v. BIPM*, ILOAT Judgment No 4580 (2023), consids 11–13.

20 *R. v. CERN*, ILOAT Judgment No 4498 (2022), consid 10. See also *G. v. CERN*, ILOAT Judgment No 3876 (2017), consid 7.

21 *B. v. IAEA*, ILOAT Judgment No 4465 (2022), consids 9–10.

22 H. *(No. 4) and others v. EPO*, ILOAT Judgment No 4195 (2019), consids 9–10. A similar conclusion was reached by the Administrative Tribunal of the BIS in Judgment No ATBIS 1/2006 in holding that, while staff had an acquired right to accident and health insurance, there was no entitlement to have such insurance fully funded by the organization.

23 *L. v. WTO*, ILOAT Judgment No 4057 (2019), consid 6.

24 *D. L. v. ESO*, ILOAT Judgment No 3676 (2016), consids 7–8. The ILOAT noted, moreover, that the fact that the organization was assuming a disproportionately greater obligation with respect to paying the total contributions in relation to the complainant and other staff was "a legitimate consideration and militates against a conclusion that the alteration of the methodology used involved an alteration of a fundamental term of employ-

(xiii) *D. E. H. v. WMO*: reduction in ceiling for payment of removal expenses upon separation did not implicate acquired rights, even though higher limits had been in place at the time of the staff member's recruitment.[25]

However, in a series of judgments culminating in *Ayoub (No. 2)*,[26] the ILOAT had concluded that the introduction of a new scale for pensionable remuneration meant that the complainants were "left worse off, to an extent indeed that goes beyond the bounds of the ILO's discretionary authority. The further reduction in the amounts that are one factor of the retirement pension is in breach of the essential terms of their employment".[27] The Tribunal further observed that, before the challenged measures took effect, the organization had not taken any decision that might have mitigated their harmful consequences.

With respect to relief, the Tribunal declared that, although it was competent to do so, it could not determine the organization's financial liability to each complainant, as this would depend on their age at the time of retirement and other factors that were not yet known. It therefore made a ruling in principle as to the complainants' claims to financial redress. The Tribunal provided a formula that, if the amount received by a complainant under the new scale dropped by a certain percentage as a result of the application of the new scale, compensation would be due. In this manner, the Tribunal

---

ment that would be protected by the principle concerning acquired rights. It also answers the complainant's argument that [the organization] failed to act on reasonable motives and failed to avoid causing unnecessary or undue injury". See also *Berthet (No. 3) et al. v. EMBL*, ILOAT Judgment No 2089 (2002), consids 14–16.

25 *D. E. H. v. WMO*, ILOAT Judgment No 3074 (2012), consids 14–17.

26 *Ayoub (No. 2) et al. v. ILO*, ILOAT Judgment No 986 (1989). This was the third case before the ILOAT involving modification of the scale of pensionable remuneration used by the ILO. The first case arose out of the introduction of a new scale in 1985, resulting in *Ayoub et al. v. ILO*, ILOAT Judgment No 832 (1987). There, the ILOAT held that, given the reasons for the amendment and notwithstanding the financial injury to the complainants, there was no breach of an acquired right. Nevertheless, the Tribunal kept open the possibility of further review if the financial injury to the complainants were to increase due to future decisions. In the second case, staff challenged the refusal to allow them to have an interim adjustment in pensionable remuneration, resulting in *Picard and Weder v. ILO*, ILOAT Judgment No 862 (1987), which dismissed the complaints. A new scale was introduced in 1987, and the organization's rules were amended accordingly. The application of the 1987 scale was at issue in *Ayoub (No. 2)*. Observers have commented that the *Ayoub* series of judgments resulted from the organization's so-called "salami" tactic, in which a series of measures incrementally sliced away the complainants' rights. See Gröniger-Voss, Baxter and Dao (note 3), 117.

27 Ibid, consid 23 (emphasis added).

kept open the possibility that the complainants could return to the Tribunal in due course to have their entitlements determined and their rights enforced.[28]

In *L. v. Eurocontrol*, the ILOAT reiterated its earlier pronouncements in *Lindsey* and *Ayoub (No. 2)* in considering the legality of the reduction of the basis for calculating the complainant's pension contributions upon the renewal of his contract. It held that, "on account of its magnitude, the alteration of the basis for calculating the complainant's contributions to the Eurocontrol Pension Scheme breached a fundamental and essential term of employment".[29]

3.1.3 Summary

The ILOAT initially considered that acquired rights resulted solely from contractual provisions, and not from those elements of employment that were statutory in nature, or in other words, set out in the staff employment rules.[30]

28 Ibid, consid 24.

29 ILOAT Judgment No 3571 (2016), consid 8 (emphasis added). As a remedy, the ILOAT set aside the impugned decision and ordered Eurocontrol to take all necessary steps to restore the complainant's rights in respect of the contributions to the Pension Scheme. It also prescribed that the same relief be provided to two similarly situated staff who had intervened in the case. The Tribunal had previously considered how the organization had dealt with the issue of transfer of previously accrued pension rights under the national pension system into the organization's pension scheme in its Judgment No 2986 (2011). In particular, over 100 complainants and intervenors claimed that the organization should have determined the pensionable years credited to them by reference to their basic salary and age and the exchange rate as of the date of their respective initial applications for the transfer, which had been submitted between 1991 (as a safeguard for such time as the transfers became possible) and 2007, when such transfers did go into effect. The ILOAT accepted the complainants' contention that the organization's receipt of such applications created an expectation that the applications were considered valid, and it referred the matter back to the organization so that the number of pensionable years could be determined accordingly.

30 The ILOAT has abandoned the distinction between 'contractual' and 'statutory' rights and recognizes either as a source of acquired rights. In *Gubin and Nemo v. Eurocontrol*, Judgment No 429 (1980), consideration 9, the ILOAT expressed the view that the protection of acquired rights does not depend on a specific provision in any staff rules. See also *Ayoub et al. v. ILO*, Judgment No 832 (1987), consid 12. The evolution in the ILOAT's approach to the determination of an acquired right is examined at length in Gröniger-Voss, Baxter and Dao (note 3), 114–115. However, in *Carlos Andres and Others v. ECB*, Case F-15/10 (2013), after reviewing changes to the ECB pension plan, the second chamber of the European Union Civil Service Tribunal (no longer in existence) held that, although the contractual terms of employment incorporated by reference statutory rules as well, because those rules made no mention of pension rights, it could not be concluded that the organization was legally precluded from changing the rules regulating the retirement

The ILOAT's approach evolved over time, and now incorporates by reference the organization's staff rules and regulations as a potential source of acquired rights. However, its approach has been somewhat tautological, defining an acquired right as "one the staff member may expect to survive any amendment of the rules. The meaning may be debatable, but the term is worth keeping […]. [I]t is a convenient enough way of describing a staff member's right to have some term of his appointment protected".[31] In this regard, the ILOAT has held that "an acquired right is breached only when the amendment of a rule to the official's detriment […] disturbs the structure of the contract or impairs fundamental terms of appointment in consideration of which the official accepted appointment".[32] Accordingly, the ILOAT, while repeatedly endorsing the need for protection of acquired rights, has been circumspect in finding such rights in the employment framework. As a result, it has largely deferred to the discretionary judgment of the respective rule-making authorities in revising the terms and conditions of staff employment except in very limited and unique factual circumstances.[33]

3.2 UNAT

3.2.1 UNAT Statutory Basis

The UNAT is competent to review appeals from judgments rendered by any of the UN Dispute Tribunal (UNDT) as well as directly from other organizations that have accepted its jurisdiction. The statutory subject matter jurisdiction (*ratione materiae*) of the UNDT in turn includes the following (Article 2):

---

plan (paras 374–375). Consequently, the complaint, which alleged that certain fundamental conditions of the applicants' employment contracts had been infringed, was rejected. Ibid, para 383. This judgment was upheld by the Appeals Chamber of the Court on 4 May 2016.

31 *Ayoub et al. v. ILO*, Judgment No 832 (1987), consid 12.

32 *V. A. (No. 4) v. Eurocontrol*, ILOAT Judgment No 4767 (2024), consid 4.

33 For example, in *Bhotlu and Mitroo v. WHO*, ILOAT Judgment No 1191 (1992), considerations 3–6, the ILOAT upheld a claim that an amendment imposing salary deductions aiming at clawing back a previous 9.2 per cent unconditional salary increase that had been announced to staff breached acquired rights, as "when the Organization has calculated a payment of salary and announced it, the officials entitled to it acquire a right which the Organization has no power to destroy" (citing *Connolly-Battisti (No. 5) v. FAO*, ILOAT Judgment No 323 (1977), consid 34). The relief ordered by the Tribunal was also applied to 15 intervenors, as they were considered to have the same rights as the complainants.

> 1. The Dispute Tribunal shall be competent to hear and pass judgement on an application filed by an individual, as provided for in [...] the present statute, against the Secretary-General as the Chief Administrative Officer of the United Nations:
>
> (a) To appeal an administrative decision that is alleged to be in non-compliance with the terms of appointment or the contract of employment. The terms "contract" and "terms of appointment" include all pertinent regulations and rules and all relevant administrative issuances in force at the time of alleged non[-]compliance; [...].

3.2.2 UNAT Jurisprudence

The case law of the UNAT – and its predecessor tribunal – has not been as prolific as that of the ILOAT with respect to whether an organization's exercise of rule-making authority has infringed staff's acquired rights or breached other general principles of international administrative law.[34]

In the *Mortished* case,[35] the now discontinued UN Administrative Tribunal examined whether changes to staff regulations infringed the acquired rights of staff members, particularly concerning repatriation grants. It concluded that the applicant had an acquired right to the grant based on prior regulations that did not require proof of resettlement to receive the grant, emphasizing that such rights must be respected despite subsequent amendments that introduced a requirement to provide such evidence.

However, later case law of the UNAT suggests that its approach to this question, and the criteria to be applied, has narrowed the concept of acquired rights. In particular, the UNAT has essentially held that the concept of 'acquired rights' is tantamount to the principle of non-retroactivity:

> An "acquired" right should be purposively interpreted to mean a vested right; and employees only acquire a vested right to their salary for services already

34 According to a 2017 UNDT judgment, the Office of Legal Affairs had found that although the UNAT had substantively discussed the concept of acquired rights in some 60 cases, only in approximately 12 of those did the Tribunal find a breach of an acquired right. See *Mirella et al. v. Secretary-General of the United Nations*, UNDT Judgment No UNDT/2017/099, para 146, which was later vacated by the UNAT in Judgment No 2018-UNAT-842.

35 Former UN Administrative Tribunal Judgment No 273 (1981). This judgment was reviewed by the International Court of Justice at the behest of the US Government. In its Advisory Opinion of 20 July 1982, the ICJ found that the Tribunal had not exceeded its jurisdiction or erred on a question of law relating to the provisions of the UN Charter. See *Application for Review of Judgement No. 273 of the United Nations Administrative Tribunal* (Advisory Opinion) [1982] ICJ Rep 325.

> rendered. Promises to pay prospective benefits, including future salaries, may constitute contractual promises, but they are not *acquired* rights until such time as the *quid pro quo* for the promise has been performed or earned. Moreover, the fact that increases have been granted in the past does not create an acquired right to future increases or pose a legal bar to a reduction in salary.[36]

In the view of the UNAT:

> The protection of acquired rights therefore goes no further than guaranteeing that no amendment to the Staff Regulations may affect the benefits that have accrued to, or have been earned by, a staff member for services rendered before the entry into force of the amendment. Amendments may not retrospectively reduce benefits already earned. [...] [T]he doctrinal protection of acquired rights is essentially an aspect of the principle of non-retroactivity. The aim is to protect individuals from harm to their vested entitlements caused by retrospective statutory instruments.[37]

The following decisions by the UNAT offer guidance on how the doctrine of acquired rights has been interpreted in practice:

(i) ***Lloret-Alcañiz et al.***: The UNAT concluded that the contested decisions did not violate the staff members' acquired rights, as the General Assembly resolutions altered only their future salaries. It further held that staff members only acquire a vested right to their salary for services already rendered, and that amendments affecting future salaries did not violate acquired rights.[38]

(ii) ***Quijano-Evans et al.***: Similar to the *Lloret-Alcañiz* case, this judgment addressed the reduction of salaries due to the Unified Salary Scale. The UNAT determined that staff members do not have an acquired right to the continued application of salary computation methods in force at the time of their appointment.[39]

---

36 *Lloret-Alcañiz et al. v. Secretary-General of the United Nations*, UNAT Judgment No 2018-UNAT-840, para 90 (emphases in original).

37 Ibid, para 91 (emphasis added). The UNAT observed that "the fact that the [staff members'] letters of appointment state that their initial salary 'may rise' [did] not constitute an express promise by the Organization to continue to increase their rate of pay and never to reduce it. [...] The salary entitlements of staff members [...] may be unilaterally amended by the General Assembly". Ibid, paras 93–94.

38 *Lloret-Alcañiz et al. v. Secretary-General of the United Nations,* UNAT Judgment No 2018-UNAT-840, para 90.

39 *Quijano-Evans et al. v. Secretary-General of the United Nations,* UNAT Judgment No 2018-UNAT-841, para. 52.

(iii) ***Nicholas***: The UNAT upheld the decision of the UNDT that the discontinuation of a right to boarding assistance at the tertiary level (university), as per a General Assembly resolution, did not abrogate any acquired right or fundamental term of the appellant's employment, notwithstanding the abolition of a benefit she had been receiving before implementation of the resolution.[40]

By conflating the doctrine of acquired rights with non-retroactivity, the UNAT approach has been criticized by one scholar as undermining the core meaning of the doctrine. In this observer's view:

> The acquired rights doctrine limits the ability of an international organisation [...] to unilaterally amend a staff member's conditions of employment to his or her detriment. The leading international administrative tribunals, especially the [ILOAT] refined and developed the doctrine's meaning and scope over decades. There has been a general consensus that the acquired rights doctrine protects a staff member's essential terms of employment both retrospectively and prospectively. However, in its recent jurisprudence, the [UNAT] has rendered the acquired rights doctrine with little work to do by reducing it to the principle of non-retroactivity. As a result, the consensus as to the doctrine's core meaning is now undermined. International civil servants having access to the ILOAT are much better protected from unilateral adverse amendments to their conditions of employment when compared to those international public officials whose organisations have subscribed to the jurisdiction of the UNAT. This is an unwelcome development for the content of substantive protections is now more dependent on the tribunal approach, as opposed to a coherent development of the law.[41]

This criticism seems justified in light of the fact that the prohibition on retroactivity is so well-established that the UNAT's conflation of acquired rights

---

40 *Caroline Wendy Nicholas v. Secretary-General of the United Nations*, UNAT Judgment No 2020-UNAT-1045. The UNAT noted that "[d]isputed issues of acquired rights stem from Staff Regulation 12 which itself emanated from UN Resolution 13(I) adopted as long ago as 1946. Staff Regulation 12.1 purports to allow the General Assembly to amend or supplement those Regulations where it does so 'without prejudice to the acquired rights of staff members'" (para 48). Citing *Lloret-Alcañiz et al*, the UNAT held that "an acquired right must be a right that has vested [...]. While promises to pay prospective benefits may constitute contractual promises, they do not become acquired rights until such time as the *quid pro quo* for the promise has been performed or earned" (para 54).

41 See Rishi Gulati, 'Acquired Rights in International Administrative Law' (2021) 24 Max Planck Yearbook of United Nations Law 82 <https://doi.org/10.1163/18757413_02401004> accessed 10 December 2025.

with non-retroactivity renders the former concept superfluous and eviscerates the protections it is intended to confer.

Moreover, in reviewing various types of challenges involving decisions of general application, the UNAT has examined the exact nature of the challenge in order to assess, on a case by case basis, whether staff members were effectively challenging the legality of a decision taken by a regulatory body such as the General Assembly or the International Civil Service Commission,[42] or whether the staff members' cause of action was based on the implementation of a regulatory measure in their individual cases.[43] In this regard, the UNAT has also ruled that staff may only challenge a regulatory decision (namely, the legality of the rule itself) in the context of its implementation in their individual case.[44]

The distinction between regulatory decisions and their implementation is perhaps best illustrated in *Tintukasiri*. There, the UNAT found that the Secretary-General's decisions to adopt revised salary scales for the General Service and National Officer categories of staff in Bangkok, based on the results of a salary survey, were not reviewable administrative decisions, as they did not involve an individual application. However, the UNAT opened the possibility for the staff members concerned to challenge these decisions when implemented in their individual cases through their payslips. In this respect, the UNAT endorsed the following conclusion of the UNDT:

---

42 See, for example, *Tintukasiri et al. v. Secretary-General of the United Nations*, UNAT Judgment No 2015-UNAT-526; *Kagizi et al. v. Secretary-General of the United Nations*, UNAT Judgment No 2017-UNAT-750; and *Reid v. Secretary-General of the United Nations*, UNAT Judgment No 2015-UNAT-563.

43 See, for example, *Ovcharenko et al. v. Secretary-General of the United Nations*, UNAT Judgment No 2105-UNAT-530 and *Pedicelli v. Secretary-General of the United Nations*, UNAT Judgment No 2015-UNAT-555.

44 In this respect, the distinction drawn by the UNAT for purposes of receivability between challenges to a rule of general applicability and its implementation through individual decisions is applied by other tribunals such as the ILOAT, the WBAT and the ADBAT, which have pronounced that staff may not challenge a general rule unless if it directly affects them and has been applied to them individually and in a prejudicial manner. See, for example, *F. (No. 14) v. EPO*, ILOAT Judgment No 4898 (2024), consid 2; *Briscoe v. IBRD*, WBAT Decision No 118 (1992), paras 30–31 (dismissing for lack of jurisdiction insofar as the application was in effect directed against a general rule regarding employment benefits, rather than an individualized application of that rule to the applicant himself); *Perrin et al. v. ADB*, ADBAT Decision No 109 (2017), paras 50, 55–56 (dismissing as irreceivable a challenge to changes in the education assistance policy, in absence of evidence as to how the new rule had adversely affected each applicant).

> It is only at the occasion of individual applications against the monthly salary/payslip of a staff member that the latter may sustain the illegality of the decision by the Secretary-General to fix and apply a specific salary scale to him/her, in which case the Tribunal could examine the legality of that salary scale without rescinding it. As such, the Tribunal confirms its usual jurisprudence according to which, while it can incidentally examine the legality of decisions with regulatory power, it does not have the authority to rescind such decisions.[45]

Similarly, in *Abu Ayyash*, the UNAT held that there was no error in the UNDT's conclusion that the appellant had not challenged a discretionary administrative decision that breached the terms of his appointment; rather, he was challenging the underlying rule providing for the calculation of separation benefits, including the applicable interest rate. It pointed out that:

> The Appeals Tribunal has through its jurisprudence consistently defined an "administrative decision" as:
>
>> [...] a unilateral decision taken by the administration in a precise individual case (individual administrative act), which produces direct legal consequences to the legal order. This type of decision is distinguished from other administrative acts, such as those having regulatory power (which are usually referred to as rules or regulations), as well as from those not having direct legal consequences.
>
> We agree that the Appellant does not challenge "an appealable administrative decision" in that he does not contest "a unilateral decision taken by the administration in a precise individual case".[46]

On this basis, the UNAT concluded that the appeal did not concern "an administrative decision" that produced direct legal consequences, and concluded that the appeal was therefore irreceivable (as well as time-barred).

---

45 *Tintukasiri et al.*, UNAT Judgment No 2015-UNAT-526, para 38 (footnote omitted; emphasis added).

46 *Abu Ayyash v. Commissioner-General of the United Nations Relief and Works Agency for Palestine Refugees in the Near East*, UNAT Judgment No 2015-UNAT-543, paras 16–17.

3.2.3 Summary

The approach of the UNAT has been that the concept of acquired rights is essentially synonymous with that of non-retroactivity, in that an 'acquired right' refers to a vested right arising from services already rendered, but not as to future services.

3.3 WBAT

3.3.1 WBAT Statutory Basis

Article II (1) of the WBAT Statute states:

> The Tribunal shall hear and pass judgment upon any application by which a member of the staff of the Bank Group alleges non-observance of the contract of employment or terms of appointment of such staff member. The words "contract of employment" and "terms of appointment" include all pertinent regulations and rules in force at the time of alleged non-observance including the provisions of the Staff Retirement Plan.

3.3.2 WBAT Jurisprudence

The landmark ruling in *de Merode* continues to serve as a reference for the WBAT and other tribunals in assessing the scope and permissibility of unilateral revisions to the terms and conditions of employment of staff.[47] There, the WBAT – albeit somewhat tautologically – characterized fundamental conditions of employment as those that are fundamental and essential in the balance of rights and duties of the staff member. Specifically:

> The Tribunal considers that in examining the numerous and varied elements of the conditions of employment, a major distinction must be drawn. Certain elements are fundamental and essential in the balance of rights and duties of

---

47 In *de Merode* (note 2), the applicants challenged decisions taken by the World Bank regarding tax reimbursement and salary adjustment, contending that the decisions amounted to non-observance of their contracts of employment or terms of appointment. The Tribunal distinguished between, on the one hand, the principles of reimbursement and, on the other hand, the method of implementation. It concluded that, while the Bank could not unilaterally abolish the tax reimbursement system, it could alter the method of its implementation as a non-essential element of the conditions of employment. Ibid, para 82.

> the staff member; they are not open to any change without the consent of the staff member affected. Others are less fundamental and less essential in this balance; they may be unilaterally changed by the Bank in the exercise of its power, subject to the limits and conditions which will be examined later.[48]

There are various pronouncements in the *de Merode* judgment that may be cited in support of arguments both for and against whether a particular element of employment is 'fundamental and essential'. The WBAT offered limited guidance in this regard:

(i) No retroactive effect: "The Bank cannot deprive staff members of accrued rights for services already rendered."[49]

(ii) No abuse of discretion: "Changes must be based on a proper consideration of relevant facts" and "reasonably related to the objective which they are intended to achieve."[50]

(iii) No discrimination: "[Changes] must not discriminate in an unjustifiable manner between individuals or groups within the staff."[51]

(iv) Avoidance of harm: "Amendments must be made in a reasonable manner seeking to avoid excessive and unnecessary harm to the staff."[52]

While recognizing that the legal test does not depend on staff's subjective expectations or on the motivating factors that might have induced them to accept or remain in employment with the organization,[53] the WBAT acknowledged that the distinction between what is essential and nonessential, or reasonable and unreasonable, depends on the nature and context of the particular term of employment. Unfortunately, such a vague and open-ended standard provides scant guidance to either staff or the organization, as it provides little predictability if the issues can only be assessed on a case-by-case basis.[54]

---

48 Ibid, para 42.

49 Ibid, para 46.

50 Ibid, para 47.

51 Ibid.

52 Ibid.

53 Ibid, para 41.

54 Ibid, paras 36 and 43. Nevertheless, the WBAT recognized that "this difficulty has not prevented distinctions of this kind playing a central role in the application of the law generally and the Tribunal sees no reason for rejecting the relevance of such a distinction in the internal law of the Bank". The WBAT added that "[s]ometimes it will be the principle itself of a condition of employment which possesses an essential and fundamental character, while its implementation will possess a less fundamental and less essential character. In other cases, one or another element in the legal status of a staff member will belong entirely – both principle and implementation – to one or another of

The WBAT has had occasion to consider and apply the 'balancing act' reflected in *de Merode* in several subsequent cases. In *Pinto*, the Tribunal examined a decision taken in the context of a job grading exercise, in which the grade of the applicant's position had been reduced. Although the applicant's salary was maintained at its current level, their salary was to be frozen, and they would not be eligible for any further salary adjustments, including periodic adjustments due to cost-of-living increases. The Tribunal held that this violated the principles enunciated in *de Merode*, in which it had found "that a consistent practice of periodic adjustment has been established, and that the Bank makes these adjustments out of the conviction that it is legally obliged to do so".[55] The Tribunal considered that this established practice had created a legal obligation on the Bank to make periodic adjustments reflecting changes in the cost of living and other factors, and that this obligation was a fundamental element in the applicant's conditions of employment.[56]

The Tribunal thus concluded that the freezing of the applicant's salary unjustifiably deprived her of the right to benefit from periodic adjustments reflecting changes in the cost of living and other factors, which – a fundamental element of Bank employment – could not be changed unilaterally. However, the WBAT's ruling by its terms applied only to the applicant and not to all similarly situated staff, such that another such staff member had to bring her own challenge, citing the *Pinto* decision, in order to obtain the same relief.[57]

---

these categories. In some cases the distinction will rest upon a quantitative criterion; in others, it will rest on qualitative considerations. Sometimes it is the inclusion of a specific and well-defined undertaking in the letters of appointment and acceptance that may endow such an undertaking with the quality of being essential". Ibid, para 43.

55 *Lyra Pinto v. IBRD*, WBAT Decision No 56 (1988), para 40, citing *de Merode* (note 2), para 111.

56 Ibid.

57 *Elena Gavidia v. IFC*, WBAT Decision No 66 (1988). However, in other cases raising the issue of infringement of a fundamental or essential element of employment, the WBAT concluded that the regulatory change in question did not infringe any fundamental condition of employment and was within the discretionary authority of the Bank. For example, see *Rafael P. Rofman v. IBRD*, WBAT Decision No 669 (2022) (changes to the definition of net salary for pension purposes were not improper); *BL v. IBRD*, WBAT Decision No 446 (2010), para 40 (changes in coordination of expatriate benefits for Bank/Fund couples "were reasonable and justified by the legitimate objectives of the policies of the two Organizations"); *Anu Oinas v. IBRD*, WBAT Decision No 391 (2009), para 41 (upholding reduction in mandatory retirement age, as differences of treatment on grounds of age are not discriminatory when objectively and reasonably justified by a legitimate aim); *Ramesh Bhatia v. IBRD*, WBAT Decision No 473 (2013), para 43 (introduction of requirement to participate in national health insurance scheme did not violate any guaranteed rights of staff).

3.3.3 Summary

The WBAT continues to invoke the broad principles articulated in the *de Merode* case as to whether a change in the employment rules infringes a 'fundamental and essential' element of employment or involves alteration of a non-fundamental element. However, the WBAT considers that this distinction cannot be defined in the abstract and will depend on the nature and context of the particular term of employment.

3.4 ADBAT

3.4.1 ADBAT Statutory Basis

Article II (1) of the ADBAT Statute states:

> The Tribunal shall hear and pass judgment upon any application by which an individual member of the staff of the Bank alleges nonobservance of the contract of employment or terms of appointment of such staff member. The expressions "contract of employment" and "terms of appointment" include all pertinent regulations and rules in force at the time of alleged nonobservance including the provisions of the Staff Retirement Plan and the benefit plans provided by the Bank to the staff.

3.4.2 ADBAT Jurisprudence

In practice, the ADBAT has invoked the principles enunciated in its own prior jurisprudence,[58] as well as *de Merode,* in reviewing the Asian Development Bank's power to make unilateral changes to the terms and conditions of staff employment. In *Perrin et al. (No. 3)*, the Tribunal considered whether changes made to the education assistance policy violated the doctrine of acquired

58 In *Carl Gene Lindsey v. ADB*, ADBAT Decision No 1 (1992), para 4, the Tribunal identified the sources of law to be considered: "In addition to the constituent instruments of the Bank and of the Tribunal, as well as general principles of law, these rules are to be derived from the contract between the Bank and the staff member, the Staff Rules and Regulations of the Bank, the *Personnel Handbooks* for professional and support staff, and Administrative Orders and Circulars, as promulgated and applied from time to time, subject to the recognition of any acquired right of the staff, and, by analogy, from the staff practices of international organizations generally, including the decisions of international administrative tribunals dealing with comparable situations. There is, in this sphere, a large measure of 'common' law of international organizations to which, according to the circumstances, the Tribunal will give due weight" (emphasis added).

rights.[59] It reviewed a number of relevant factors in reaching the conclusion that the changes did not affect a fundamental or essential element of employment. In doing so, the Tribunal observed that the concept of "acquired rights" was "a notion that has evolved over time",[60] recognizing that the term was "simply a handy expression of this unchangeable character, of which the cause and the justification are to be found in the fundamental and essential character of the relevant conditions of employment".[61]

The Tribunal then applied an analytical framework involving the following factors, which it considered relevant to the assessment of the impugned change at issue:

(i) Scope of review with regard to managerial decisions in general;
(ii) Whether the changes were rational, legitimate and reasonably related to the underlying objectives of the changes;
(iii) Whether the changes were based on proper consideration of the relevant facts;
(iv) Whether the changes were proposed in good faith and not prompted by improper motives;
(v) Did the changes have retroactive effect;
(vi) Whether there was different treatment of various groups of staff or did the changes discriminate in an unjustifiable manner;
(vii) Whether the changes were proportionate to the objectives of the changes and reasonable, and did they avoid excessive and unnecessary harm;
(viii) Should affected staff have been 'grandfathered' or eligible for transitional rules; and
(ix) Did the changes upset the economic balance of the contract?

On the basis of this assessment, the Tribunal considered that the notion of "upsetting the balance of the contract" would involve a much more significant realignment of the employment relationship than had occurred with respect to the changes at issue.[62] In the ADBAT's view, the decrease in education assistance "cannot reasonably be considered as upsetting the economic balance of the relationship that Applicants had and still have with the Bank", and although the decisions impugned may have an impact in the future, "that is of itself not enough to establish breach of an acquired right".[63] Accordingly, it

59 *Perrin et al. (No. 3) v. ADB*, ADBAT Decision No 113 (2018).
60 Ibid, para 59.
61 Ibid, paras 38, citing *Lindsey*, ADBAT Decision No 1 (1991), para 44.
62 Ibid, para 92.
63 Ibid, paras 92 and 93.

ruled that the Bank had not violated any essential or acquired rights of the applicants or acted in breach of its obligations towards its staff.[64]

3.4.3 Summary

Expanding on the principles enunciated by the WBAT in *de Merode*, the ADBAT has developed its own multi-faceted analytical framework for assessing the 'fundamental and essential' character of the relevant conditions of employment, including whether the changes at issue upset the economic balance of the employment contract. Although the ADBAT has recognized the need to protect fundamental and essential conditions of employment, in practice (not unlike other administrative tribunals), it has been loath to conclude that changes made to the employment framework are of this character, and it has deferred to the organization's discretionary judgment concerning the need to revise the employment framework. Nevertheless, its multi-faceted framework provides a useful basis for assessing the extent to which the economic balance in the employment relationship between the applicant(s) and the Bank has been upset by the change in question.

64 Ibid, para 101. See also the *Mesch and Siy* cases, where applicants Mesch and Siy brought a series of appeals before the ADBAT invoking the principle of equal pay for equal work to challenge the lack of tax reimbursement for US and Filipino staff who were subject to national income tax on their salaries. The Tribunal initially concluded that, even in the absence of any previous program of tax reimbursement or ADB statements confirming such a program in any way, tax reimbursement was a condition of employment. The Tribunal therefore ordered appropriate compensation for the years in dispute. *Ferdinand P. Mesch and Robert Y. Siy v. ADB,* ADBAT Decision No 2 (1994). However, there was no precise holding that tax reimbursement was fundamental and unchangeable. The ADB's Board of Directors thereupon abolished the reimbursement, which was appealed by the same applicants. The Tribunal held that, given the absence of any past practice or confirming statements by the ADB with respect to tax reimbursement, such reimbursement was a non-fundamental and nonessential condition of employment, and could therefore be abolished by the Bank. The majority concluded that although there was indeed a fundamental principle of equal pay for equal work, the equality requirement could be satisfied by equal compensation before the imposition of national income taxes, which was a circumstance over which the Bank had no control. *Mesch and Siy (No. 4)*, ADBAT Decision No 35 (1997). For a fuller overview of the *Mesch and Siy* cases, see Christine Griffiths, 'History of the ADB Administrative Tribunal's 20 Years of Operation' in *The Administrative Tribunal of ADB – 20 Years of Operation* (ADB 2012) <https://www.adb.org/sites/default/files/publication/29906/adb-administrative-tribunal.pdf> accessed 10 December 2025, 86–87.

3.5 IMFAT

3.5.1 IMFAT Statutory Basis

Article II of the IMFAT Statute states:

> 1. The Tribunal shall be competent to pass judgment upon any application:
>   a. by a member of the staff challenging the legality of an administrative act adversely affecting him; or
>   b. by an enrollee in, or beneficiary under, any retirement or other benefit plan maintained by the Fund as employer challenging the legality of an administrative act concerning or arising under any such plan which adversely affects the applicant.
> 2. For purposes of this Statute:
>   a. the expression "administrative act" shall mean any individual or regulatory decision taken in the administration of the staff of the Fund;
>   b. the expression "regulatory decision" shall mean any rule concerning the terms and conditions of staff employment, including the General Administrative Orders and the Staff Retirement Plan, but excluding any resolutions adopted by the Board of Governors of the Fund; [...].

The IMFAT Statute is unique in several key respects. The first distinct characteristic of the IMFAT Statute is that it explicitly defines the subject matter jurisdiction of the Tribunal in terms of two types of decisions:

(i) *Individual* decisions applying or interpreting the rules of the employment framework with respect to an individual case; and
(ii) *Regulatory* decisions adopting or modifying rules of general applicability.[65]

The second distinct characteristic concerns the timing of such challenges. In drafting the IMFAT Statute, it was considered advantageous to allow for direct review of the legality of a regulatory decision within three months after its announcement or effective date, which would enable the question to be resolved promptly, even before the decision was applied to staff in individual decisions.[66] This could occur, for example, if the modification of the method-

65 Article III of the IMFAT Statute explicitly envisages that regulatory decisions, although discretionary in nature (as they involve the exercise of rule-making authority), are reviewable on grounds of "generally recognized principles of international administrative law concerning judicial review of administrative acts".

66 See Commentary on the Statute of the IMFAT <https://www.imf.org/external/imfat/report.htm> accessed 10 December 2025.

ology for adjusting the salary system could be challenged even before the revised methodology had been applied in a given adjustment of salaries. If the change were considered to infringe on a fundamental element of employment, this would invalidate the decision adopting the modification, which would thereupon be null and void.

The third distinct characteristic is that, if a direct review of a regulatory decision results in a holding that the decision is invalid, such ruling annuls the decision. As a result, the regulatory decision may no longer be applied, and any individual decision taken on the basis of that regulatory decision, whether before or after the annulment, that adversely affects a staff member is null and void. Thus, the invalidation of a change to the employment framework through a direct challenge automatically applies to all similarly affected staff; there is no need for a *de facto* 'class action' with multiple applicants in order to achieve this result.[67]

The IMFAT Statute also anticipates the possibility that the legality of an individual decision (for example, with respect to entitlement to or eligibility for benefits and allowances) may depend on the legality of the underlying rule or policy on which the decision is based.[68] The IMFAT Statute thus authorizes the review of a regulatory decision at any time (no statute of limitations) in the context of reviewing a timely challenge to an individual decision.[69]

Moreover, the IMFAT's Rules of Procedure provide that all staff are to be notified when the Tribunal receives an application and the issues involved; as a result, any staff member who has a right that may be affected by the judgment has an opportunity to apply to intervene in the matter and participate in the proceedings as a party.[70]

---

67 IMFAT Statute, Article XIV, Section 3 provides as follows: "If the Tribunal concludes that an application challenging the legality of a regulatory decision is well-founded, it shall annul such decision. Any individual decision adversely affecting a staff member taken before or after the annulment and on the basis of such regulatory decision shall be null and void."

68 As an example, see *Ms. G (Applicant) and Mr. H (Intervenor) v. IMF*, IMFAT Judgment No 2002-3 (upholding changes to the policy governing eligibility for expatriate benefits).

69 The only exception to this jurisdictional authority is with respect to regulatory decisions that were approved before 15 October 1992, the date on which the proposal to establish the Tribunal was approved by the Executive Board for transmittal to the Board of Governors; such decisions are not subject to legal challenge.

70 Rule IV(f) of the Rules of Procedure provides that the Registrar shall: "upon the transmittal of an application to the Fund, unless the President decides otherwise, circulate within the Fund a notice summarizing the issues raised in the application, without disclosing the name of the Applicant, in order to inform the Fund community of proceedings pending before the Tribunal". The IMFAT may also, as remedy, order the Fund to notify all staff that may be affected by the illegality of a regulatory decision of meas-

3.5.2 IMFAT Jurisprudence

These statutory provisions have enabled the IMFAT to take a flexible approach in cases involving the legality of particular rules or policies, either directly or as applied in individual cases.

An example of direct review of a regulatory decision is *Elkjaer et al.* (*No. 3*),[71] where the issue before the IMFAT was whether a decision to modify a particular element of the compensation system infringed a fundamental and essential condition of employment. In this regard, the Tribunal noted the distinction between general principles and their implementation. In relation to the Fund's staff compensation system, the Tribunal has recognized two principles as "fundamental and essential" to that system: that it is "rules based" and that it is "comparator-based".[72] The Tribunal observed that "[h]ow these principles are implemented through particular rules is, by contrast, a matter for the Fund's discretionary authority, reviewable by this Tribunal for abuse of discretion".[73] With respect to the impugned decision to modify an element of the compensation system, the Tribunal considered whether the decision was: (i) properly motivated; (ii) reasonably related to the objective that it was intended to achieve; and (iii) based on an appropriate consideration of relevant facts. It found that all of these criteria were met and accordingly denied the applications.

An example of review of the legality of an employment policy promulgated by management is found in *Mr. B. Tosko Bello*.[74] The case arose out of a downsizing exercise in which financial benefits were offered to staff members who volunteered to separate from the organization. After the voluntary phase of the exercise concluded, it was announced that anyone who had volunteered to separate would no longer be eligible for any future contractual relationship with the IMF, which was contrary to the existing provisions allowing staff to take up contractual appointments after the period equivalent to the recipi-

ures taken to rectify the flaws found. For example, in *Elkjaer et al.* (*No. 2*) *v. IMF*, IMFAT Judgment No 2023-1, the IMFAT ordered the organization to correct a flaw in the methodology for the annual compensation review and further directed the IMF, in the interests of transparency, to "notify all staff members that it has taken the above steps and the results thereof, along with the essential elements of the underlying analysis [...]".

71 *Elkjaer et al.* (*No. 3*) *v. IMF*, IMFAT Judgment No 2023-5. In *Daseking-Frank et al. v. IMF*, IMFAT Judgment 2007-1, the IMFAT upheld the legality of various changes to the methodology for the annual compensation review as involving non-fundamental terms of employment.

72 *Elkjaer et al.* (*No. 3*), IMFAT Judgment No 2023-5, para 70.

73 Ibid.

74 *Mr. B. Tosko Bello v. IMF*, IMFAT Judgment No 2013-2.

ent's discretionary separation payments had ended. A staff member who had voluntarily resigned in the downsizing exercise challenged this new lifetime prohibition on his re-employment, as he had expected to be able to return to the IMF as a consultant after the period of his separation package had concluded. In this regard, he was able to point to the response to a question about eligibility for future employment provided by the organization in FAQs issued during the downsizing, which had restated the existing rule.

The IMFAT acknowledged that the applicant's complaint against the 'individual decision' as to ineligibility for employment rested entirely on his challenge to the underlying policy. It concluded that the 'regulatory decision' challenged in this case was invalid because it was inconsistent with an undertaking expressly made to those staff members who had volunteered for separation under the downsizing exercise. Accordingly, it annulled the impugned decision and ordered the IMF to individually notify each former staff member who separated voluntarily under the 2008 Fund-wide downsizing program that the ban on re-hiring of those volunteers has been nullified.[75]

3.5.3 Summary

The IMFAT Statute is distinctive among international administrative tribunals in that it explicitly permits challenges to regulatory decisions, including unilateral amendment to the terms and conditions of employment by the organization. As the application of the IMFAT's invalidation of the prohibition on re-employment on staff who had volunteered to separate not only to the individual applicant, but also to all similarly situated staff, demonstrates, there is no need under the statutory basis of the IMFAT for separate legal actions by other staff – and each received individual notification of this result.

4 Conclusion

Administrative tribunals have recognized their own lack of capacity to decide what type of employment terms and conditions would best serve the interests of an international organization, and they will accordingly defer to the judgment of the rule-making organs on such discretionary matters. Yet, at the same time, tribunals recognize the duty to protect the rights of staff and their legitimate expectations as to the preservation of fundamental terms and conditions.

75 Ibid, paras 83–84.

Legal challenges before administrative tribunals to changes in the employment framework have rarely been successful, as the administrative tribunals have rarely invalidated the discretionary rule-making authority of the organization based on general principles of international administrative law. This raises the question whether these general principles provide sufficient 'guardrails' on the regulatory authority of international organizations; in other words: Does the doctrine of acquired rights have any meaningful impact? Are the pronouncements by various tribunals concerning the need to protect acquired rights and fundamental and essential terms of employment merely a 'paper tiger', namely, sounding strong on paper but weak in practice? Or do such pronouncements have an inherent prophylactic effect, acting as a constraint in the organization's internal decision-making process?

This article contends that it is the latter. There is admittedly no empirical evidence as to whether the very existence of general principles of international administrative law has reined in the exercise of the unilateral authority of international organizations to alter the terms of employment. However, the fact that such principles are considered to be 'well established' undoubtedly affects the internal decision-making process within international organizations, which are typically risk-averse with respect to litigation of any type and seek to maintain harmonious relations with staff, recognizing that it is preferable to handle changes to personnel policies and the conditions of service through engagement and consultation with staff rather than through litigation. In this manner, these unwritten principles – and the willingness of the tribunals to consider their applicability to a given set of facts – have arguably helped to 'level the playing field' in employment relations and constrain the exercise of discretionary authority within international organizations.

The above overview confirms that each administrative tribunal has articulated and applied its own interpretation of these principles in assessing legal challenges arising from changes to the employment framework. Although the tribunals have articulated these principles in somewhat different ways, there has been a broad convergence (with the possible exception of the UNAT) as to how the concepts of 'acquired rights' and 'fundamental and essential terms of employment' should be interpreted and applied, thereby creating what has been referred to by at least one tribunal as the "'common' law of international organizations to which, according to the circumstances, the Tribunal will give due weight".[76]

76 *Lindsey*, ADBAT Decision No 1 (1992), para 4.

In this manner, the tribunals have undertaken the 'balancing act' envisaged in such decisions as *de Merode* and *Perrin (No. 3)*, by acknowledging the discretionary authority of each international organization to determine what type of employment framework best serves its interests, while at the same time being prepared to invalidate what they consider to be a transgression of generally accepted principles regarding the exercise of that authority.

Formal Constitutional Interpretation by the Bretton Woods Institutions

*Edward Chukwuemeke Okeke**

Abstract The constituent instruments of international organizations are living documents in that they can adapt or evolve over time through interpretations that allow them to respond to changing circumstances, without the necessity of formal amendments, and always remain relevant. They not only create international organizations but also delineate their functions and competences, the allocation of powers of their organs, and the procedures for decision-making within the organs. The effectiveness of international organizations depends on their ability to carry out their missions. To be fit for purpose, international organizations should have the ability to evolve and adapt themselves to a constantly and rapidly changing world. The evolution of international organizations is about their ability to adapt to change and bring about change. To evolve, international organizations may resort to the interpretation or amendment of their constituent instruments to address changing circumstances or new developments, anticipated or unforeseen by their drafters. This article examines how the Bretton Woods institutions, namely the International Bank for Reconstruction and Development, and the International Monetary Fund, have interpreted their respective Articles of Agreement. With the benefit of these interpretations, these organizations have managed to evolve and avoid a recourse to amendments to address some problematic issues presented in the application of the constituent instruments. It also discusses the mandates and missions, the institutional design and governance structure of these institutions, as well as the nature and scope of the power of interpretation. The choice of these institutions is informed by the novelty of the provisions in their Articles of Agreement which vest with the internal organs, not international courts or tribunals, the power of the formal interpretation of their constituent instrument. This is an up-to-date synthesized compilation of the law and practice of these institutions.

*Former Lead Counsel, Global Knowledge and Research, Legal Vice Presidency, World Bank, meke.okeke@yahoo.com.

 | HTTPS://DOI.ORG/10.1163/9789004765672-004

1 Introduction

The Bretton Woods institutions were born out of the wartime initiative to create an international system for economic and financial cooperation and development. In July 1944, with World War II still raging, 730 delegates from 44 countries met at the United Nations Monetary and Financial Conference in Bretton Woods, New Hampshire, United States, and agreed to create the International Monetary Fund (IMF or Fund) and the International Bank for Reconstruction and Development (IBRD or Bank or World Bank).[1] The IMF would address issues with exchange rates and lend its reserve currencies to nations with balance of payments deficits while the World Bank would provide financial assistance for reconstruction after the war and the economic development of developing countries. Membership of the World Bank is restricted to members of the IMF while membership of the latter is currently open to virtually all sovereign states.[2] The World Bank and the IMF have distinctive and specific, but related, mandates under their respective constituent instruments.

The constituent instruments of the IMF and the World Bank were adopted on 22 July 1944.[3] These constituent instruments are multilateral treaties that not only create the international organizations but also delineate the functions and competences of the organizations, the allocation of powers of their organs, and the procedures for decision-making within the organs, amongst other provisions. The constituent instruments of international organizations are also living documents because they may be amended or interpreted to account for changing circumstances or new developments, either anticipated or unforeseen by their drafters.[4] To be and remain effective, international organizations should have the ability to evolve and adapt themselves to a

1 Sometimes, the term World Bank is used to refer to International Bank for Reconstruction and Development (IBRD) and International Development Association (IDA) jointly.

2 Article II, Section 1: "(a) The original members of the Bank shall be those members of the International Monetary Fund which accept membership in the Bank before the date specified in Article XI, Section 2(e)"; and "(b) Membership shall be open to other members of the Fund, at such times and in accordance with such terms as may be prescribed by the Bank."

3 Articles of Agreement of the International Monetary Fund (adopted 22 July 1944, entered into force 27 December 1945), 2 UNTS 39 (IMF Articles), amended seven times, with the latest amendment adopted on 15 December 2010 and effective 26 January 2016; Articles of Agreement of the International Bank for Reconstruction and Development (adopted 22 July 1944, entered into force on 27 December 1945), 2 UNTS 134 (IBRD Articles), amended three times: 17 December 1965, 16 February 1989 and 27 June 2012.

4 Constituent instruments are variously termed as Charter, Constitution, Convention, or Articles of Agreement.

constantly and rapidly changing world. The transformation can happen through either the interpretation or amendment of the constituent instruments.

Amendment, which is a change in the constituent instrument, is a different process from interpretation, with a different procedure. However, amendment is an arduous process and is rarely resorted to as a result. It can only be made by the competent organ within the organization. In addition, an amendment may require (political) action by member States for it to become effective. In other words, the acceptance of a proposed amendment may require members to follow whatever the procedure is under their respective national law and practice. For example, in the case of the United States, the Bretton Woods Agreements Act provides: "Unless Congress by law authorizes such action, neither the President nor any person or agency shall on behalf of the United States […] accept any amendment under article XXVIII of the Articles of Agreement of the Fund or article VIII of the Articles of Agreement of the Bank."[5] This requirement of Congressional authorization does not extend to a vote by the Governor appointed by the United States on a resolution of the Board of Governors of the IMF or the World Bank to approve a proposed amendment. Because of the super-majority vote required for amendments and the weighted voting power of the United States, its action alone is determinative of whether an amendment is accepted and becomes effective. For example, an amendment of the Articles of Agreement of the IMF requires the acceptance of "three-fifths of the members, having eighty-five percent of the total voting power" and the voting power of the United States is 16.49%.[6]

5 Bretton Woods Agreements Act 1945, P.L. No 79-171, 59 Stat 512 (USA) (amended through P.L. No 118-47, enacted 27 March 2024), Section 5. Upon entry into force on 1 April 1978 of the amendments to the Articles of Agreement of the IMF, the first sentence of Section 5, as provided for in Section 3 of Public Law 94-564, was amended and restated. It formerly read as follows: "Unless Congress by law authorizes such action, neither the President nor any person or agency shall on behalf of the United States (a) request or consent to any change in the quota of the United States under article III, section 2, of the Articles of Agreement of the Fund; (b) propose or agree to any change in the par value of the United States dollar under article IV, section 5, or article XX, section 4, of the Articles of Agreement of the Fund, or approve any general change in par values under article IV, section 7; (c) subscribe to additional shares of stock under article II, section 3, of the Articles of Agreement of the Bank; (d) accept any amendment under article XVII of the Articles of Agreement of the Fund or article VIII of the Articles of Agreement of the Bank; (e) make any loan to the Fund or the Bank."

6 International Monetary Fund, 'IMF Members' Quotas and Voting Power, and IMF Board of Governors' (Last Updated: 21 May 2025) <https://www.imf.org/en/About/executive-board/members-quotas> accessed 10 December 2025. See also IMF Articles of Agreement, Article XXVIII.

The same goes for the amendment of the Articles of Agreement of the World Bank where the voting power of the United States is 15.98%.[7] This super-majoritarian vote requirement is however non-egalitarian in the sense that a single member has the power to block an amendment.[8] The provision for the amendment of the Articles of Agreement of the World Bank under Article VIII is substantially the same as that of the IMF under Article XXVIII. No organ of these Bretton Woods institutions has the authority to amend their Articles of Agreement, without the acceptance of the requisite percentage of members.[9]

Amendment of constituent instruments, therefore, occurs through the super-majoritarian consent and express decision of member States in accordance with established procedure: "Formal amendment is surely the most obvious (and uncontroversially legitimate) mechanism through which the constitutions of international organizations evolve over time."[10] Informal or unauthorized amendments in the guise of interpretations are controversial because they short-circuit the amendment process. Interpretations of the Articles of Agreement of the Bretton Woods institutions are by simple majority vote as opposed to the super-majority required for amendments. An informal or unauthorized amendment under the guise of an interpretation would deprive some members of the protection of their interests under the charter as guaranteed by the super-majority vote required for amendments under the charter. Such an unauthorized amendment can impose upon some members obligations that are different from those that they accepted when they joined the organization or even subvert their legitimate expectation that the activities of the organization would be constrained by the constituent instrument until amended through the proper procedures. Amendments are, therefore, more legitimate than interpretations in the evolution of international organizations.

7 World Bank, 'Voting Powers' <https://www.worldbank.org/en/about/leadership/votingpowers> accessed 1 May 2026. See IBRD Articles, Article VIII.

8 Similarly, any of the five permanent members of the Security Council of the United Nations has a veto power over the entry into force of an amendment under Articles 108 and 109 of the Charter of the United Nations.

9 This requirement is different from Article VII(a) of the Articles of Agreement of the International Finance Corporation (open for signature 25 May 1955, entered into force 20 July 1956) 264 UNTS 117, which provides for the amendment by a decision of the Board of Governors with stipulated majority votes, without the (additional) requirement of acceptance by members.

10 Julian Arato, 'Treaty Interpretation and Constitutional Transformation: Informal Change in International Organizations' (2013) 38 Yale Journal of International Law 289, 306 (citation omitted).

Considering the burdensome nature of the amendment procedure, international organizations operate and evolve mainly through the interpretation of their constituent instruments: "Any policy, action, deliberate non-action, decision, or practice of an international organization involves an interpretation of its basic instrument."[11] The mere application of a treaty provision entails an effective interpretation or sometimes a formal interpretation of that provision in the process of performing the functions of an international organization. A formal interpretation may affect the activities of the organization acting in its capacity as an international organization or those of the member State(s) vis-à-vis the organization, in other words, the relations between the organization and its members. Interpretation can, therefore, take two forms: informal and formal. Informal interpretation, which is prevalent, occurs through decisions taken by either the Executive Board or Management in the ordinary conduct of the business of the institutions.[12] Formal interpretation, on the other hand, which is the subject of this article, is when it is done pursuant to a specific provision in the constituent instrument as is the case with the Bretton Woods institutions and other international financial institutions where the power of interpretation is vested in their internal organs.[13] To be sure, the Bretton Woods institutions, like any other specialized agencies of the United Nations, can seek advisory opinions by the International Court of Justice (ICJ) with the authorization of the General Assembly of the United Nations under Article 96(2) of the Charter of the United Nations.[14] However, the advisory opinions exclude the interpretation of the constituent instruments.[15] The idea of formal interpretation by internal organs, as opposed to

11 Ervin P. Hexner, 'Teleological Interpretation of Basic Instruments of Public International Organizations' 123, *reprinted* from Salo Engel (ed), *Law, State, and International Legal Order: Essays in Honor of Hans Kelsen* (University of Tennessee Press 1964).

12 Interpretations undertaken outside of the interpretative powers under the Articles of Agreement are not the focus of this article.

13 See Article X(a) of the Articles of Agreement of the International Development Association (IDA); Article VIII(a) of the Articles of Agreement of the International Finance Corporation (IFC); Article 56(a) of the Convention of the Multilateral Investment Guarantee Agency (MIGA), and Article 11(i)(a) of the Agreement Establishing the International Fund for Agricultural Development (IFAD). MIGA is a member of the World Bank Group (WBG) but not a specialized agency of the UN.

14 See Agreement between the United Nations and the International Bank for Reconstruction and Development (approved by the Board of Governors of the Bank, 16 September 1947, and by the United Nations General Assembly, 15 November 1947), Article VIII.

15 See Convention on the Privileges and Immunities of the Specialized Agencies (adopted 21 November 1947, entered into force 2 December 1948) 33 UNTS 261, Article IX, Section 32. Annexes V and VI pertaining to the IMF and World Bank respectively make it explicit that the request for advisory opinion from the ICJ is limited to controversies

judicial bodies, was conceived and negotiated during the Bretton Woods conference to account for the economic and financial nature of the institutions being created:

> They also wished to create a framework within which the principal policies of the institutions could be evolved with due consideration to the balance of interests indicated by the different quotas. Furthermore, they aimed at the creation of a constitutional framework which would not preclude the adjustment of policies to changing political and economic circumstances.[16]

Evolution of international organizations is not only about adapting to changes but also about bringing about changes: "The self-generated evolution of the Bank's policies and operations has been supported, and in some cases initiated, through this internal interpretative process."[17] The effectiveness of the Bretton Woods institutions is best measured against their ability to carry out their mandates, as well as against their adaptability to accomplish their missions through their activities, operations, policies, and processes: "As the effectiveness and continuity of international organizations depend to no small extent on their ability to adapt themselves constantly to a rapidly evolving world, the necessary flexibility must be ensured by provisions included in the constitutions of the organizations."[18]

Article IX of the Articles of Agreement of the World Bank, which is similar to Article XXIX of the IMF Articles, provides the Executive Directors with the authority to interpret the Articles of Agreement:

> (a) Any question of interpretation of the provisions of this Agreement arising between any member and the Bank or between any members of the Bank shall be submitted to the Executive Directors for their decision. If the question particularly affects any member not entitled to appoint an Executive Director, it shall be entitled to representation in accordance with Article V, Section 4(h).

---

arising out of the interpretation and application of the Convention, not to the privileges and immunities derived from the Articles of Agreement.

16 Ervin P. Hexner, 'Interpretation by Public International Organizations of their Basic Instruments' (1959) 53 American Journal of International Law 341, 344.

17 Ibrahim F.I. Shihata, *The World Bank Legal Papers* (Martinus Nijhoff 2000), Introductory Chapter, LX.

18 Ralph Zacklin, *The Amendment of the Constitutive Instruments of the United Nations and Specialized Agencies* (Martinus Nijhoff 2005).

> (b) In any case where the Executive Directors have given a decision under (a) above, any member may require that the question be referred to the Board of Governors, whose decision shall be final. Pending the result of the reference to the Board, the Bank may, so far as it deems necessary, act on the basis of the decision of the Executive Directors.

Similarly, Article XXIX of the Articles of Agreement of the IMF provides:

> (a) Any question of interpretation of the provisions of this Agreement arising between any member and the Fund or between any members of the Fund shall be submitted to the Executive Board for its decision. If the question particularly affects any member, it shall be entitled to representation in accordance with Article XII, Section 3(j).
>
> (b) In any case where the Executive Board has given a decision under (a) above, any member may require, within three months from the date of the decision, that the question be referred to the Board of Governors, whose decision shall be final. Any question referred to the Board of Governors shall be considered by a Committee on Interpretation of the Board of Governors. Each Committee member shall have one vote. The Board of Governors shall establish the membership, procedures, and voting majorities of the Committee. A decision of the Committee shall be the decision of the Board of Governors unless the Board of Governors, by an eighty-five percent majority of the total voting power, decides otherwise. Pending the result of the reference to the Board of Governors the Fund may, so far as it deems necessary, act on the basis of the decision of the Executive Board.[19]

The interpretation is final and binding on the member States of the organization, and not subject to any external judicial review. Appeal of the interpretation by the Executive Directors can only be to the Board of Governors. So far, at the IMF, the appellate process for challenging or reviewing an interpretation by the Executive Directors has been utilized only once.[20] At the World Bank, it has never been resorted to. Any member or organ of the organization can initiate the interpretation procedure which can be employed not only for

---

19 The provision on interpretation was originally under Article XVIII before the Articles of Agreement were amended and renumbered.

20 See the sixth interpretation of the IMF Articles of Agreement, as outlined in Section 5.

the settlement of disputes but also resolution of differences or doubts regarding other provisions of the Articles of Agreement.[21]

The binding nature of the interpretations on member States was articulated in the proceedings before the United States Federal Communications Commission (FCC) regarding the privileges of communication of the World Bank and the IMF under their Articles of Agreement.[22] The FCC stated:

> We believe that the question as to the application of the term "treatment" in the Bank and Fund Articles to rates has been conclusively determined by the Bank and Fund Executive Directors' interpretation, by unanimous vote, that the language in question applies to rates charged for official communications of the Bank and the Fund. Under the terms of the Bank and Fund Articles of Agreement, this interpretation, in effect, is final. This procedure for issuing interpretations binding member governments does indeed appear novel; but it also appears to point the way toward speedy, uniform and final interpretations. This procedure is not only an integral part of the Bank and Fund Articles, which have been accepted by the United States, but its use was specifically invoked with respect to questions of interpretation by Sections 12 and 13 of the Bretton Woods Agreements Act; and the United States Congress, by directing that an amendment of the Articles be sought if the requested interpretations were not satisfactory, appears to have recognized in these two sections that the United States is bound by the results of the interpretations. The United States Government is therefore bound by the Executive Directors' interpretation of the term "treatment" and is under an international obligation to act in conformity therewith.[23]

---

21 For a comprehensive analysis of the IMF's interpretation of its constituent instrument, see Joseph Gold, 'The Interpretation by the International Monetary Fund of Its Articles of Agreement' (1954) 3 International and Comparative Law Quarterly 256; Joseph Gold, 'Interpretation by the International Monetary Fund of Its Articles of Agreement – II' (1967) 16 International and Comparative Law Quarterly 289; Hexner, 'Interpretation by Public International Organizations of their Basic Instruments' (note 16 above).

22 See *International Bank for Reconstruction and Development and International Monetary Fund v. All America Cables and Radio, The Commercial Cable Company, Mackay Radio & Telegraph Company, Inc., R.C.A. Communications, Inc., The Western Union Telegraph Company*, FCC Docket No 9362, 53–303.

23 FCC Decision, para 3 of Conclusions, *reproduced* in Hexner, 'Interpretation by Public International Organizations of their Basic Instruments' (note 16 above).

2 Mandates and Missions

Like most international organizations, the World Bank and the IMF have specific mandates under their constituent instruments which delineate their authority. In the case of the World Bank, Article I of its Articles of Agreement stipulates the purposes of the organization which delimit the nature and scope of its activities, actions and decisions and concludes by stating that the "Bank shall be guided in all its decisions by the purposes set forth" in the Article. Additional delimitations are set out in Article IV, Section 10, which prohibits the Bank and its officers from interfering in the political affairs of its member States and from being influenced in their decision by the political character of the member States. It consequently enjoins that "[o]nly economic considerations shall be relevant to their decisions". Over the course of its existence, the missions of the World Bank have evolved.[24] Presently, the "mission is to end extreme poverty and boost shared prosperity in a livable planet".[25] Even though the missions have changed or evolved, the mandates have remained the same, thanks to both the informal and formal interpretations of its Articles of Agreement to allow an extension or expansion of its activities without any specific amendment of the Articles of Agreement to that effect. This evolution has resulted in what has been characterized by some as mission creep.[26] Recently, the United States Treasury Secretary had stated that the "IMF and World Bank have enduring values. But mission creep has knocked these institutions off course" and called on them to "refocus on their core missions of macroeconomic stability and development".[27]

As is the case with the World Bank, the purposes of the IMF are stipulated in Article I of its Articles of Agreement which also enjoins that the "Fund shall be guided in all its policies and decisions by the purposes set forth in this Article". Principally, the IMF advises member countries on economic and financial policies that promote stability, reduce vulnerability to crises, and

24 See Katherine Marshall, *The World Bank: From Reconstruction to Development to Equity* (Routledge 2008).

25 World Bank Group Annual Report 2024, 3.

26 See Jessica Einhorn, 'The World Bank's Mission Creep' (2001) 80 *Foreign Affairs* 22 <https://www.foreignaffairs.com/world/world-banks-mission-creep> accessed 10 December 2025.

27 US Department of The Treasury, 'Treasury Secretary Scott Bessent Remarks Before the Institute of International Finance' (23 April 2025) <https://home.treasury.gov/news/press-releases/sb0094> accessed 10 December 2025. See David J. Lynch, 'Trump administration says IMF, World Bank "falling short" of missions' (Washington Post, 23 April 2025) <https://www.washingtonpost.com/business/2025/04/23/bessent-world-bank-imf-treasury/> accessed 10 December 2025.

encourage sustained growth and high living standards. In addition, it provides technical assistance to help strengthen members' institutional capacity and makes resources available to them to facilitate adjustment in the event of a balance of payments crisis. The IMF has evolved throughout its history to retain a central role within the international financial architecture.

3 Institutional Design and Governance Structure

As constituted under its Articles of Agreement, the IMF has a Board of Governors, an Executive Board, and a Managing Director.[28] The Board of Governors is the plenary organ of the IMF and consists of one governor and one alternate governor appointed by each member country.[29] It is the highest decision-making organ of the IMF: "All powers under this Agreement not conferred directly on the Board of Governors, the Executive Directors, or the Managing Director shall be vested in the Board of Governors."[30] Except for powers conferred directly on the Board of Governors, it may delegate to the Executive Board the authority to exercise any of its powers under the Articles of Agreement.[31] The Board of Governors has delegated most of its powers to the Executive Board, with the exception of those powers conferred directly by the Articles on the Board of Governors to approve quota increases, allocate or cancel special drawing rights (SDR), admit new members, decide on the compulsory withdrawal of members, and approve and accept proposed amendments to the Articles of Agreement and the By-Laws. The Board of Governors also hears appeals of the interpretations of the Articles of Agreement by the Executive Board.

The Executive Board is composed of 25 Executive Directors who are elected by member countries or groups of member countries. It represents the 191 member countries and is primarily "responsible for conducting the business of the Fund, and for this purpose shall exercise all powers delegated to it by the Board of Governors".[32] When the Executive Board makes a decision by voting, the votes of each member equal the sum of its basic votes (equally distributed among all members) and quota-based votes. Therefore, a member's quota determines its voting power in the weighted voting system. The

28 IMF Articles of Agreement, art XII, sec 1.
29 IMF Articles of Agreement, art XII, sec 2.
30 IMF Articles of Agreement, art XII, sec 2(a).
31 IMF Articles of Agreement, art XII, sec 2(b).
32 IMF Articles of Agreement, art XII, sec 3(a).

Executive Board selects the Managing Director who serves as its chairman but has no vote, except a deciding vote in case of an equal division.[33] The Managing Director is the head of the staff and management of the Fund.[34]

The World Bank has a Board of Governors, Executive Directors and a President.[35] All the powers of the World Bank are vested in the Board of Governors which is the plenary organ in the organization where each member country is represented by one governor and one alternate.[36] The Board of Governors delegates most powers to the Executive Directors who comprise the Board of Directors. However, the Board of Governors retains the power to decide appeals from interpretations of the Articles of Agreement by the Executive Directors. The Executive Directors represent the World Bank's 189 member countries and are responsible for the conduct of the general operations of the Bank.[37] The Executive Directors oversee the Bank's strategic direction and represent member countries' viewpoints on the Bank's role. They decide on proposals made by the President for loans and guarantees; policies; the administrative budget; and other operational and financial matters. The Executive Directors select a President, who serves as Chair of the Board of Executive Directors where the President has no vote but to break a deadlock in case of an equal division of votes.[38] The President of the World Bank is head of the staff and management of the organization.[39]

4 Nature and Scope of the Power of Interpretation

The constituent instruments of international organizations "can raise specific problems of interpretation owing, *inter alia*, to their character which is conventional and at the same time institutional; the very nature of the organization created, the objectives which have been assigned to it by its founders, the imperatives associated with the effective performance of its functions, as well as its own practice, are all elements which deserve special attention when the time comes to interpret these constituent treaties".[40] Formal interpretations

33 IMF Articles of Agreement, art XII, sec 4 (a).

34 IMF Articles of Agreement, art XII, sec 4 (b).

35 IBRD Articles of Agreement, art V, sec 1.

36 IBRD Articles of Agreement, art V, sec 2.

37 IBRD Articles of Agreement, art V, sec 4.

38 IBRD Articles of Agreement, art V, sec 5(a).

39 IBRD Articles of Agreement, art V, sec 5(b).

40 *Legality of the Use by a State of Nuclear Weapons in Armed Conflict* (Advisory Opinion) [1996] ICJ Rep 66, para 19.

are deemed necessary to enable the organizations to fulfill their functions and achieve their mandates. They serve to clarify the meaning of the text of the constituent instruments which are binding *intra vires* on the member States. They also serve as gap fillers in the constituent instruments which allow for adaptation to changing realities.

In addition, as noted by the Institute of International Law (IIL), "interpretation is necessary when the constituent instrument of an international organization is ambiguous or silent of a specific issue".[41] Furthermore, evolutive interpretation may also be necessary "in the absence of any relevant text addressing the issue at hand".[42] The IIL also noted that "organs of international organizations routinely interpret their constituent instruments in the course of their operations and should be able to adjust quickly to the new challenges in their changing environment in order to remain relevant and perform their assigned functions".[43] It then adopted the following resolution: "Evolutive interpretation by international organizations of the constituent instruments shall be consistent with those instruments and in particular with their object and purpose."[44] The teleological approach is prevalent in the interpretation of the constituent instruments of international organizations.[45] This interpretative approach focuses on giving effect to the purpose of the international organization. It seeks a solution that serves best the objectives of the institution. This is so because of the common understanding that international organizations are created for a purpose.[46] This teleological approach has informed the interpretation of the constituent instruments of the Bretton Woods institutions by their plenary organs.

The power of interpretation of the Bretton Woods institutions is distinguishable from that of other international organizations:

---

41 Institute of International Law, 'Are there Limits to the Dynamic Interpretation of the Constitution and Statutes of International Organizations by the Internal Organs of such Organizations (with Particular Reference to the UN System)?' (7th Commission, 4 September 2021) 7 RES EN.

42 Ibid.

43 Ibid.

44 Ibid. The "Resolution employs the term 'evolutive interpretation' to refer to the interpretation of constituent instruments in order to achieve perceived needs of an international organization that are consistent with its object, purpose and functions".

45 For a discussion of the approach of the International Court of Justice to the interpretation of constituent instruments of international organizations, see Peter Quayle, 'Treaties of a Particular Type: The ICJ's Interpretation Approach to the Constituent Instruments of International Organizations' (2016) 29 Leiden Journal of International Law 853.

46 See Tim Clark, 'The Teleological Turn in the Law of International Organizations' (2021) 70 International and Comparative Law Quarterly 533.

> [F]irst, because the function of authoritative interpretation rests with the ordinary executive organs of these institutions and not with any tribunal external to them; second, because the exercise of the interpretative function is not limited to decisions on actual disagreements, but is used also to resolve doubts in interpretation and thus to prevent controversies and to assure the uniform application of operative arrangements; third, because the executive organs have exclusive jurisdiction to decide on questions of interpretation of the instrument that may arise between the organization and its members or between members themselves; and fourth, because the persons exercising the interpretative function represent interested parties and their votes are weighted according to certain defined criteria.[47]

The rationale for this power of interpretation was articulated in the brief for the IMF and the World Bank in the proceedings before the FCC regarding the interpretation of Article VII, Section 7, and Article IX, Section 7, of the Articles of Agreement of the World Bank and the IMF respectively:

> The basic purpose of these provisions is to assure an expeditious, uniform interpretation of complicated financial agreements, which will enable the Bank and Fund to operate as effective institutions. It is apparent that one of the greatest difficulties in the operation of international organisations in the past has been that no mechanism was established for a speedy settlement of questions of interpretation arising under their basic charters, a settlement which would be binding on all their members.[48]

The power of interpretation has been characterized as quasi-judicial and quasi-legislative.[49] However, the power is not limitless. In this regard, Ibrahim Shihata, General Counsel of the World Bank from 1983 to 1998, stated:

> Their power of interpretation clearly involves a much wider discretion than that of a judicial authority. It cannot, nevertheless, be so wide as to ignore the

---

47 Hexner, 'Interpretation by Public International Organizations of their Basic Instruments' (note 16 above).

48 Brief for the Complainants (Fund and International Bank) in the proceeding before the US Federal Communications Commission *reproduced* in Joseph Gold, 'The Interpretation by the International Monetary Fund of Its Articles of Agreement' (note 21 above).

49 See Ervin P. Hexner, 'The Executive Board of the International Monetary Fund: A Decision-Making Instrument' (1964) 18 International Organization 74, 82; Aron Broches, 'International Legal Aspects of the Operation of the World Bank' (1959) 98 Recueil des cours, Collected Course of The Hague Academy of International Law, 313.

> explicit language of the interpreted text (unless such language leads in a certain situation to manifestly absurd or unreasonable results), run counter to the other provisions of the Articles or undermine the purposes of the text and the overall objectives of the institution as stated in its Articles. In other words, although the interpretation given by the Executive Directors could admittedly include such elements of ingenuity and creativity as may be required for the successful pursuit of the Bank's objectives, it should not amount in fact to an amendment of the Articles. This latter process is entrusted to the Board of Governors acting according to a certain procedure and subject to acceptance by a special majority of the Bank's members and, in the case of certain provisions, by all members. Amending the Articles under the guise of interpreting them would evidently constitute an excessive exercise of the power of interpretation, a typical *excès de pouvoir* tantamount to an abuse of power, which cannot be condoned under the Articles.[50]

The interpretations are always a collaborative process between the Executive Directors and the Management.[51] Some of the interpretations are at the initiative of the Management. The legal principles applicable to treaty interpretation have been applied to the interpretation of constituent instruments.[52] Even though the power of interpretation is vested in the Executive Directors, they do consider the views or legal opinions of the General Counsel before deciding. The legal opinions, as legally sound as they may be, are not binding on the Executive Directors but, so far, have never been discounted. They are not the authoritative interpretation of the constituent instruments even though they may be relied upon by the Executive Board in their interpretations. The legal opinions of the General Counsel and the interpretations by the Executive Board are informed by the purposes and interests of the organization and its members with the ultimate objective of finding solutions engendered by provisions of the constituent instruments. The legal opinions of

---

50 Shihata, *The World Bank Legal Papers* (note 17 above), 8. Shihata noted that this understanding about the power of interpretation had been shared by previous General Counsels of the institution.

51 For example, in a 4 June 1947 Memorandum with Regard to Organization and Loan Procedure, the Board of Executive Directors and the President of the World Bank reached an understanding on their working relationship and agreed: "Whenever, in connection with the operations of the Bank, decision of a question of policy becomes necessary, the President will submit such question to the Executive Directors with recommendations of the management as the action to be taken." World Bank Document R-106/7 (on file with the author).

52 See Ibrahim Shihata, 'Valuation of IBRD Capital, Opinion of the Senior Vice President and General Counsel' (15 December 1993), paras 15, 18–23 (on file with the author).

the General Counsel do consider the rules applicable to treaty interpretation as embodied in customary international law, including as codified in the 1969 Vienna Convention on the Law of Treaties (VCLT), as well as other relevant sources.[53]

Article 5 of VCLT provides that the Convention "applies to any treaty which is the constituent instrument of an international organization and to any treaty adopted within an international organization without prejudice to any relevant rules of the organization". However, the constituent instruments of the Bretton Woods institutions do not stipulate any rules applicable to their interpretations, except to the extent they provide that the organizations shall be guided in all their decisions by the purposes set forth in their respective Article I. The IMF Articles, though, have an Explanation of Terms to guide in the interpretation of their provisions.[54] The interpretations by the Executive Board may be appealed to the Board of Governors whose decision is final and not subject to judicial review by any court or tribunal. There is no recourse to the International Court of Justice to interpret the constituent instruments.[55] Consequently, only these internal organs of the organizations have the jurisdiction to decide on the correctness or consistency of their own interpretations, with the Articles of Agreement. At any rate, these institutions have developed principles, policies, practices, and precedents that constitute a body of law to draw upon in their interpretation of the constituent instruments.

5 Interpretation of IMF Articles

The Articles of Agreement of the IMF have been formally interpreted nine times so far.[56] India requested the first interpretation, regarding Article XII, Section 3(b)(i) and 3(f), on the appointment and election of Executive Direct-

53 See Vienna Convention on the Law of Treaties (adopted 23 May 1969 and entered into force 27 January 1980) 1155 UNTS 331, arts 5 and 31–33; Richard Gardiner, *Treaty Interpretation* (Oxford University Press 2008); Mark Villiger, *Commentary on the 1969 Vienna Convention on the Law of Treaties* (Martinus Nijhoff 2009) 444–449.

54 IMF Articles of Agreement, art XXX.

55 As specialized agencies of the United Nations, pursuant to Article 57 of the United Nations Charter, the Bretton Woods institutions can seek advisory opinion from the International Court of Justice under Article 96 of the same Charter, but not in connection with the interpretation of their constituent instruments.

56 Since after the first amendment of the Articles of Agreement, effective 28 July 1969, IMF has not made any formal interpretations of its Articles.

ors and their term of office.[57] The interpretation, on 8 May 1946, was that any member with one of the five largest quotas at the date of a regular election or at any other date between regular elections was entitled to appoint an Executive Director who will hold office until the next general election without prejudice to the right of another member to appoint an Executive Director if it ends up having one of the five largest quotas.[58]

The second interpretation, on 12 September 1946, was made at the request of the United States where the Board of Governors adopted a resolution inviting the Executive Directors:

> [T]o interpret the Articles of Agreement, pursuant to Article XVIII (a), as to whether the authority of the Fund to use its resources extends beyond current monetary stabilization operations to afford temporary assistance to members in connection with seasonal, cyclical, and emergency fluctuations in the balance of payments of any member for current transactions, and whether the Fund has authority to use its resources to provide facilities for relief, reconstruction, or armaments, or to meet a large or sustained outflow of capital on the part of any member.[59]

The Executive Directors interpreted the Articles of Agreement "to mean that authority to use the resources of the Fund is limited to use in accordance with its purposes to give temporary assistance in financing balance of payments

---

57 Executive Board Decision No 2-1 (8 May 1946) in *First Annual Meeting of the Board of Governors, Report of the Executive Directors and Summary Proceedings* (Executive Directors Report 1946), 107.

58 Ibid.

59 The request was made pursuant to Section 13 of the Bretton Woods Agreements Act 1945 (note 5 above) which provides:

"(a) The governor and executive director of the Fund appointed by the United States are hereby directed to obtain promptly an official interpretation by the Fund as to whether its authority to use its resources extends beyond current monetary stabilization operations to afford temporary assistance to members in connection with seasonal, cyclical, and emergency fluctuations in the balance of payments of any member for current transactions, and whether it has authority to use its resources to provide facilities for relief, reconstruction, or armaments, or to meet a large or sustained outflow of capital on the part of any member. (b) If the interpretation by the Fund answers in the affirmative any of the questions stated in subsection (a), the governor of the Fund representing the United States is hereby directed to propose promptly and support an amendment to the Articles of Agreement for the purpose of expressly negativing such interpretation. The President is hereby authorized and directed to accept an amendment to that effect on behalf of the United States".

deficits on current account for monetary stabilization operations".[60] Although neither the question by the United States nor the interpretation by the Executive Directors specified which provisions of the Articles of Agreement were being interpreted, it can be extrapolated that the question and interpretation were in respect of Article V, Section 3, and Article XIV, Section 1, which dealt with the use of the resources of the IMF limited to temporary assistance.[61]

The third interpretation related to Article IV, Section 5(f), and was requested by the United Kingdom seeking clarification on whether, considering the terms of Article I(ii) and (v) of the Articles of Agreement, "steps necessary to protect a member from unemployment of a chronic or persistent character, arising from pressure on its balance of payments, shall be measures necessary to correct a fundamental disequilibrium".[62] On 26 September 1946, the Executive Directors' interpretation was that these steps "are among the measures necessary to correct a fundamental disequilibrium; and that in each instance in which a member proposes a change in the par value of its currency to correct a fundamental disequilibrium the Fund will be required to determine, in the light of all relevant circumstances, whether in its opinion the proposed change is necessary to correct the fundamental disequilibrium".[63]

The fourth interpretation, on 10 June 1949, pertained to the enforceability of certain exchange contracts pursuant to Article VIII, Section 2(b), the first sentence of which provided: "Exchange contracts which involve the currency of any member and which are contrary to the exchange control regulations of that member maintained or imposed consistently with this Agreement shall be unenforceable in the territories of any member."[64] This provision requires members of the Fund to assist each other in their currency exchange regulations by giving certain exchange contracts territorial effect. The interpretation was that the exchange contracts which involve the currency of any member and which are contrary to the exchange control regulations of that member

60 Executive Board Decision No 71-2 (26 September 1946), Executive Directors Report 1946 (note 57 above), 106. The interpretation was subsequently clarified by the Executive Directors on 26 July 1961 that it "does not preclude the use of the Fund's resources for capital transfers in accordance with the provisions of the Articles, including Article VI." Executive Board Decision No 1238-(61/43) (28 July 1961) in IMF Annual Report 1962, 232.

61 Ibid.

62 Executive Board Decision No 71-2 (26 September 1946), Executive Directors Report 1946 (note 57 above), 105–106.

63 Ibid.

64 Executive Board Decision No 446-4 (10 June 1949), IMF Annual Report 1949, Appendix XIV, 82–83.

maintained or imposed consistently with this Agreement shall be unenforceable in the territories of any member.[65]

The fifth interpretation, on 20 February 1950, related to the privileges of communications under Article IX, Section 7, and was at the request of the Executive Director for the United States.[66] The interpretation was provided by a joint committee of the Executive Directors of the World Bank and the IMF Executive Board. The interpretation was occasioned by the revision of tariffs by cable companies operating in the United States which took away the preferential rates accorded to international organizations, except for the United Nations, and established the same rates as those accorded to private commercial users. The joint committee concluded that the obligation of a member State under the applicable provisions of the constituent instruments is to accord to the official communications of the IMF and World Bank the same rates that it accords to the official communications of other member States, not the one that it accords to its own official communications.

The sixth interpretation, on 11 August 1954, dealt with the conditions for compulsory withdrawal of a member of the Fund.[67] Czechoslovakia had requested an interpretation of Article XV, Section 2, following complaints that it had failed to fulfil its obligations under the Articles by not providing the

65 Ibid.

66 Executive Board Decision No 534-3 (20 February 1950), IMF Annual Report 1950, 118–119. See also *International Bank for Reconstruction and Development and International Monetary Fund v. All America Cables and Radio*, The *Commercial Cable Company, Mackay Radio & Telegraph Company, Inc., R.C.A. Communications, Inc., The Western Union Telegraph Company*, FCC Docket No 9362 (note 22 above). The Executive Director for the United States at the World Bank sought a similar interpretation from the Executive Directors of the World Bank (eighth interpretation of the Articles of Agreement of the World Bank). A major significance of the interpretation is that it underscored the significance of its binding nature on member States. During the proceedings before the FCC, Jack Tate, Deputy Legal Adviser of the United States Department of States (more famously known for the 1952 Tate Letter in connection with the restrictive doctrine of foreign sovereign immunity), had written a letter dated 2 June 1950 regarding the position of the United States on the matter. It stated: "By virtue of its membership in the Fund and Bank, the United States is obliged to conform to the provisions of the respective Articles of Agreement, including the provisions of the respective Articles relating to the interpretation of the Articles [...]. United States is under an international obligation to act in conformity with the interpretations issued by the respective Executive Directors of the Fund and Bank." Hexner, 'Interpretation by Public International Organizations of their Basic Instruments' (note 16 above), 356.

67 Executive Board Decision No 344 (54/47) (11 August 1954) and confirmed by Resolution of Board of Governors Res. No 9-7 (28 September 1954), published in *International Monetary Fund Summary Proceedings of the Ninth Annual Meetings of the Board of Governors 1954*, 112–113.

IMF with the information necessary for the organization to discharge its duties under Article VIII, Section 4. Czechoslovakia had argued that national security considerations were legal justification for withholding the information. The Executive Board decided:

> In response to the request of the Government of Czechoslovakia, and after having considered the arguments put forward by that Government, the Executive Directors, acting pursuant to Article XVIII (a) of the Fund Agreement, interpret Article XV, Section 2 as follows:
>
> Action may be taken by the Fund to require a member to withdraw when the following conditions have been met:
>
> 1. The member has been declared ineligible to use the resources of the Fund pursuant to Article XV, Section 2(a);
> 2. A reasonable time has passed since the member was declared ineligible to use the resources of the Fund pursuant to Article XV, Section 2(a), whether or not a fixed period of time had been prescribed in connection with such action, and the member persists in failing to fulfill its obligations;
> 3. The member has been informed in reasonable time of the complaint against it and given an adequate opportunity to state, both orally and in writing, any fact or legal argument relevant to the issue before the Fund.[68]

Czechoslovakia appealed to the Board of Governors which, on 28 September 1954, confirmed the interpretation and adopted the recommended resolution of the Executive Board requiring Czechoslovakia to withdraw from the IMF.[69] This was a contentious case dealing with the conditions for the compulsory withdrawal of a member of the Fund.

The seventh interpretation, on 24 August 1955, dealt with Article V, Section 3 (a)(iii), on the extent of drawing rights of members.[70] The Article specifies the conditions under which a member may purchase foreign currency from the IMF in exchange for its own currency, one of which is that the purchase should not cause the Fund's holding of that member's currency to increase by more than 25% of its quota within the twelve months period ending on the date of purchase. The Executive Board interpreted the quantitative limit of 25% of quota in relation to drawing rights and decided that in any twelve-month

68 Ibid.

69 See *International Monetary Fund Summary Proceedings of the Ninth Annual Meeting of the Board of Governors 1954* (note 67 above), 97–101, 112–114, 121–122, 135–180.

70 Executive Board Decision No 451 (55/52) (24 August 1955), IMF Annual Report 1956, 135.

period a member can purchase equal to a basic amount of 25% of its quota, which accords with the idea that the use of the resources of the IMF is temporary and revolving.[71] The interpretation clarified an ambiguous provision on the determination of member's drawing rights.

The eighth interpretation was on 25 January 1956 and dealt with investment of the assets of the Fund in regard of Article IV, Section 8(a).[72] At issue is if and under what conditions, the Fund can raise income by investing part of its gold assets. The Executive Board noted:

> [The IMF] has had and may continue to have an excess of expenditure over income and that the greater part of the Fund's administrative expenditure has been and will continue to be in United States dollars [...]. [I]n the interest of good administration and conservation of the Fund's resources it would be appropriate to raise income towards meeting the deficit by the investment of a portion of the Fund's gold in a manner which will enable the Fund to reacquire gold at any time and will maintain the gold value of the investment.[73]

It interpreted the provisions to permit the IMF to sell portions of its gold for United States dollars and invest the proceeds in United States Treasury bills, and that they require the United States to maintain the gold value of these assets, notwithstanding changes in the par or foreign exchange value of the currency of the United States. It must be noted that the provisions of the Articles do not prescribe or proscribe such investment of the assets of the Fund.

The ninth interpretation, on 25 July 1956, was of Article VI, Section 3, which dealt with Controls on Capital Transfers.[74] The Executive Board decided:

> Subject to the provisions of Article VI, Section 3, concerning payments for current transactions and undue delay in transfers of funds in settlement of commitments:
>
> (a) Members are free to adopt a policy of regulating capital movements for any reason, due regard being paid to the general purposes of the Fund and without prejudice to the provisions of Article VI, Section 1.

71 Ibid.

72 Executive Board Decision No 488(56/5) (25 January 1956), IMF Annual Report 1956, 147–148.

73 Ibid.

74 Executive Board Decision No 541 (56/39) (25 July 1956), IMF Annual Report 1957, 162.

(b) They may, for that purpose, exercise such controls as are necessary, including making such arrangements as may be reasonably needed with other countries, without approval of the Fund.[75]

6 Interpretation of IBRD Articles

So far, the Articles of Agreement of the World Bank have been formally interpreted 15 times.[76] In 1946 alone, the first year of operation, there were three interpretations. The first interpretation, on 9 May 1946, related to Article V, Sections 4(b)(i) and 4(d), and dealt with the right of the five largest shareholders to appoint an Executive Director without prejudice to the right of a subsequently admitted member to appoint an Executive Director if it has one of the five largest subscriptions.[77] The Executive Directors interpreted the provision to mean that any member having one of the five largest subscriptions at the date of a regular election or at any date between regular elections shall be entitled to appoint an Executive Director who shall hold office until the next regular election without prejudice to the right of a subsequently admitted member to appoint an Executive Director if it has one of the five largest subscriptions. The interpretation was at the behest of India which sought the clarification in case the Soviet Union became a member before the next election to the Executive Board.[78] The interpretation permitted the appointment of six Executive Directors on a temporary basis to deal with the situation that would have arisen if the Soviet Union had then joined the World Bank, which would have resulted in the Soviet Union displacing India as the fifth largest shareholder at the time. Thus, Article V, Section 4(b)(i), was con-

---

75 Ibid. The interpretation resolved any doubts on the kind of measures that members may exercise for capital controls without the approval of the Fund.

76 The third, fourth, fifth, seventh, and eighth interpretations were requested by the Executive Director for the United States while the twelfth interpretation was requested by the Executive Director representing the United Kingdom. Interpretations 1 through 13 are compiled in Bank Document: Decisions of Executive Directors under Article IX of the Articles of Agreement on Questions of Interpretation of the Articles of Agreement, on file with the author.

77 Executive Directors' Resolution No 3 (9 May 1946). The IMF's first interpretation of 8 May 1946 dealt with a similar subject.

78 The Soviet Union ended up not joining the World Bank until 1991, and there was no need to apply this interpretation until 1971 when Japan became the fifth largest shareholder and appointed an Executive Director, but India became the sixth largest shareholder and was permitted to maintain its appointed Executive Director until the election in 1972.

strued to permit six appointed Executive Directors as temporary solution to a situation not explicitly addressed by the constituent instrument.

The second interpretation, on 20 June 1946, pertained to Article IV, Section 2(a), as to whether the United States had the power to control the use of United States dollars paid to the World Bank in lieu of gold pursuant Article II, Section 7(i).[79] The Executive Directors decided that "the United States does not have the power under Article IV, Section 2(a) of the Articles of Agreement to control the use of United States dollars paid to the Bank in lieu of gold pursuant to Article II, Section 7 (i)".[80]

The third interpretation, on 20 September 1946, was necessitated by Section 12 of the Bretton Woods Agreements Act.[81] The Board of Governors, at the request of the Governor for the United States, invited the Executive Directors to interpret the Articles of Agreement regarding "the authority of the World Bank to make or guarantee loans for programs of economic reconstruction and the reconstruction of the monetary systems, including long-term stabilization loans".[82] The Executive Directors decided that the World Bank has the authority to make or guarantee such loans. It had determined that under Article III, Section 4(vii), the World Bank could "make or guarantee loans for programs of economic reconstruction and the reconstruction of monetary systems, including long-term stabilization loans, even if such loans are not for specific projects of reconstruction of development within the meaning of such Section".[83] Normally, loans and guarantees are for financing specific projects with productive purposes but based on this interpretation, the World Bank has also made loans for programs.

After the first three interpretations in 1946, there were nine subsequent interpretations from 1947 to 1964. The fourth interpretation, on 2 April 1947, dealt with the right of the World Bank to call on the 80% of its capital subscription which is subject to call to meet its obligations created under Article IV, Section 1(a)(ii) and (iii), which deals with the methods of making or facilitating loans.[84] The Executive Directors decided that the Bank has the right to make the calls and that the 80% is part of the assets of the Bank of which it is bound to avail itself, as and when necessary, to meet such obligations which it creates under the provisions of the Article.

79 Board of Executive Directors (Committee on Interpretation) Report R-14 (20 June 1946).

80 Report of the Committee on Interpretation, approved on 20 June 1946.

81 Bretton Woods Agreements Act (note 5 above).

82 First Annual Report by the Executive Directors (27 September 1946), Annex E; Executive Directors' Report R-28 (20 September 1946).

83 Ibid.

84 Executive Directors' Report R-91 (2 April 1947).

The fifth interpretation, on 18 June 1947, was of Article IV, Section 2(c), on the use of currencies received by the World Bank on account of principal of loans made out of borrowed funds.[85] The Executive Directors interpreted that the Article does not limit the use of those currencies and that the provisions "are intended to make it clear that currencies so received can be used by the Bank, without restrictions by its members, for the purpose of making amortization payments on, or of anticipating payment of, or re-purchasing, all or part of the obligations of the Bank".[86] They also interpreted that the provisions "do not prohibit the Bank from using any currencies so received for any purpose for which the funds so borrowed by it could have been used, including the making of loans".[87]

The sixth interpretation, on 28 April 1948, was of Article II, Section 9(a), which deals with the maintenance of value of certain currency holding of the World Bank.[88] What happens where the Bank determines that there is a significant depreciation in the foreign exchange value of the currency of a member within its territories after it lends to a borrower in that member's own currency from its paid-in capital in accordance with Article II, Section 7(i), and prior to the repayment of such loan?[89] The interpretation was that where there is such depreciation, the "member is obligated to pay to the Bank [...] an additional amount of its own currency sufficient to maintain the value, as of the time of initial subscription, of the amount of such member which is held by the Bank [...] at the time when the Bank makes a determination that such depreciation has occurred".[90]

The seventh interpretation rendered on 8 July 1948 was of Article IV, Section 5(c) and was requested by the Alternate Executive Director for the United States before the member State shall be asked to approve the sale of securities in its country as provided in Section 8 of the Article.[91] The question was whether the provisions of the Article apply to guarantees by the World Bank of securities in which it has invested and which it so guaranteed for the purpose of facilitating their sale in accordance with Article IV, Section 8(ii). The

85 Executive Directors' Resolution No 53, and Report R-113 (23 July 1947).

86 Ibid.

87 Ibid.

88 Executive Directors' Report R-163 (28 April 1948).

89 Article II, Section 7, provides for the method of payment of subscription for shares which shall be made in gold or United States dollars and in the currency of the member. Two percent of the price of each share shall be payable in gold or United States dollars, and when calls are made, the remaining 18% shall be paid in the currency of the member.

90 Ibid.

91 Executive Directors' Report R-183 (8 July 1948).

Executive Directors decided that Section 5(c) "applies only to guarantees by the Bank of loans placed through the usual investment channels as provided in said Section 5 and does not apply to guarantees of securities in which the Bank has invested and which it so guarantees for the purpose of facilitating their sale as provided in Section 8(ii)".[92]

The eighth interpretation, on 17 February 1950, was of Article VII, Section 7, on the privilege for communications.[93] It was requested by the Alternate Executive Director for the United States regarding the treatment to be accorded by a member of the World Bank to the official communications of the organization.[94] The Executive Directors decided that Section 7 applies to rates charged for the official communications of the World Bank and that a member which exercises regulatory powers over such communications is not relieved of its obligation under the Section because the facilities for transmitting such communications are privately owned or operated or both. It also decided that that obligation is not satisfied if the official communications of the Bank may be sent only at rates which exceeded the rates accorded the official communications of other members in comparable situations.

The ninth interpretation, rendered on 23 May 1950, was of Article II, Section 9(a) and (b), on the maintenance of value of 18% currencies loaned by the World Bank.[95] At issue is the allocation of currency exchange risk between the Bank and a borrower where the Bank lends to a borrower part of the currency of a member and there is a reduction in the par value of the currency of the member or the Bank determines that there is a significant depreciation in the foreign exchange value of such currency within the territories of the member. The Executive Directors interpreted Section 9(a):

> [I]f (a) the Bank advances to a borrower, pursuant to a loan agreement, part of the currency of a member to which said Section is applicable; and (b) after the date of the advance and prior to the date on which repayment of the principal of such advance is made, the par value of a currency of such member is reduced or the Bank determines that the foreign exchange value of such currency has depreciated to a significant extent within such member's territories; and (c) such reduction or depreciation continues in effect on the date on which such

---

92 Ibid.

93 Executive Directors' Report R-260 (17 February 1950).

94 The Executive Director for the United States at the IMF sought a similar interpretation from the Executive Board of the IMF (fifth interpretation of the Articles of Agreement of the IMF), and the interpretation was provided by a joint committee of the Executive Directors of the World Bank and the IMF Executive Board.

95 Executive Directors' Report R-324 (23 May 1950).

> repayment is made; such member is obligated to pay to the Bank, in respect of the amount to be repaid, an additional amount of such currency sufficient to maintain the value, as of the time of initial subscription, of the currency so repaid.[96]

They interpreted Section 9(b) conversely to mean that "if the par value of such currency is increased (rather than reduced) in the circumstances described [regarding Section 9(a) above] and such increase continues in effect on the date of such repayment, the Bank is obligated to return to such member an amount of the currency so repaid equal to the increase in value of such currency".[97]

The tenth interpretation, on 14 June 1951, was of Article II, Section 9, and Article IV, Section 2(b), on portfolio sales.[98] The Executive Directors interpreted Article II, Section 9:

> If the Bank, pursuant to a loan agreement, advances to a borrower currency of a member paid to the Bank under Article II, Section 7(i) [Method of payment of subscriptions for shares] and receives obligations of the borrower representing such advances and payable in the currency of that member, and if the Bank sells such obligations, the proceeds of the sale received by the Bank are subject to the provisions of Article IV, Section 2(b) [Availability and transferability of currencies].[99]

They also interpreted that in the circumstances described above, "the proceeds of the sale received by the Bank are currency to which the provisions of Article II, Section 9 [Maintenance of value of certain currency holdings of the Bank] are applicable and such proceeds are to be treated as a repayment of the principal of the loan for the purposes of Article II, Section 9, as interpreted by the decision of the Executive Directors of May 23, 1950".[100]

The eleventh interpretation, rendered on 24 May 1960, was of Article IV, Section 1(a)(ii) and (iii), on calls on the 2% and 18% portions of increases in capital subscriptions of members as authorized, subject to call only to meet

96 Ibid.

97 Ibid. Compare with the sixth interpretation which dealt with the maintenance of value of certain currency holdings of the World Bank, that is, the foreign exchange value of the currency of the member, when the loan by the Bank to the borrower is part of the 18% of the capital paid in by the member in its own currency pursuant to Article II, Section 7(i).

98 Executive Directors' Resolution No 192 (14 June 1951).

99 Ibid.

100 Ibid.

obligations of the World Bank.[101] The Executive Directors recalled their fourth interpretation on 2 April 1947 on the right of the Bank to make calls on the 80% of the subscriptions to its capital stock which is subject to call only when required to meet obligations of the Bank under this Section of the Article. They also recalled whether that decision applies correspondingly to such 2% and 18% of portions of the same subscriptions and decided that the earlier decision "applies *mutatis mutandis* to any portion of the subscriptions to the capital stocks of the Bank which, by virtue of its Articles of Agreement or by the Resolution of the Board of Governors, is from time to time subject to call only when required to meet obligations of the Bank created under Section 1(a) (ii) and (iii) of Article IV".[102]

The twelfth interpretation, on 30 July 1964, was of Article V, Section 14(a), on allocation of net income.[103] The Executive Directors opined "that the purposes of the Bank and the interests of the members would best be served by the transfer of [a portion of the Bank's net income for the fiscal year ended 30 June 1964] to the International Development Association by way of grant".[104] The Executive Director for the United Kingdom had requested the interpretation before action was taken on the proposal to transfer $50 million from the Bank's net income to the International Development Association. The Executive Directors decided that if the Board of Governors shares their opinion on the question of interpretation, it may, consistent with the Articles of Agreement, make the proposed transfer to the International Development Association.

The thirteenth interpretation, on 14 October 1986, was of Article II, Section 2(a) and Section 9(a), and addressed the valuation of the capital of the World Bank and other issues, including the demise of the Gold Dollar.[105] Article II, Section 2(a), defines the authorized capital stock of the Bank "in terms of the United States dollars of the weight and fineness in effect on July 1, 1944". However, because of the Second Amendment of the IMF Articles of Agreement which came into effect on 1 April 1978 and abrogated the par value system that had been established under the Articles, this pre-existing basis for valuation of the capital of the Bank was effectively abolished. The Articles could have been amended to deal with this issue where the text of the provisions is devoid of meaning because of the abolition of the dollar's par value. In fact,

---

101 Executive Directors' Resolution No. 60-23 (24 May 1960).
102 Ibid.
103 Executive Directors' Resolution No. 64-29 (30 July 1964).
104 Ibid.
105 Executive Directors' Report R-86-203; R86-203/1 (14 October 1986).

"the Executive Directors regard[ed] the existence of a common standard of value as inherent in the Articles of Agreement which cannot be abolished without amending the Articles of Agreement".[106] Notwithstanding, they decided that, until when the relevant provisions of the Articles were amended, Section 2(a) meant that the value of the capital stock of the World Bank was the SDR introduced by the IMF as it was valued in terms of the United States dollar immediately before the introduction of the basket method of valuing the SDR in 1974. They also decided that maintenance of the value of payments to the Bank pursuant to Section 9 will be based on the interpretation of Section 9(a) of the same Article.

The fourteenth interpretation, rendered on 6 July 2010, was of Article V, Section 4(b)(i), on the right of the five largest shareholders to appoint Executive Directors.[107] The interpretation was requested by the Executive Directors for France and the United Kingdom to address the situation where they both would become the fifth largest shareholders, each with equal shares, following the subscription to the shares allocated in the Selective Increase in Authorized Capital Stock. This situation of two fifth largest shareholders potentially claiming the right to appoint an Executive Director is not addressed by the Articles of Agreement. The Executive Directors interpreted the Article to permit, on an exceptional basis and as a temporary measure, that France and the United Kingdom may each appoint an Executive Director to address this extraordinary situation until the first Board elections after 2015.

The fifteenth interpretation, on 30 July 2015, was of Article VII, Sections 5 and 8, and dealt with the privileges and immunities of the World Bank.[108] The interpretation was sought by Management in connection with a litigation in Canada implicating the privileges and immunities of the World Bank and its staff. The provisions were interpreted to mean that each privilege and immunity under the Article is separate and distinct, and that a waiver of a particular one does not constitute a waiver of all of them. They were also interpreted to

---

106 Ibid.

107 Executive Directors' Resolution No 2010-0003 (6 July 2010). The same provision in the Articles was interpreted in 1946 to permit six appointed Executive Directors on a temporary basis to deal with the unusual situation and possibility that the Soviet Union would join the Bank and become one of the five largest shareholders and bump India to the sixth position. However, the Soviet Union ended up not joining the Bank then, obviating the need for application of the interpretation.

108 Executive Directors' Resolution No 2015-0145/2 (30 July 2015).

mean that the archival immunity applies to all Bank information held in paper, electronic and all other formats.[109]

7 Conclusion

It is not within the scope of this article to discuss these formal interpretations in detail. Nevertheless, it is safe to say that every interpretation has been purposive, but it would be a stretch to state that each has resulted in a fundamental change in the character and activities of these international financial institutions. Some interpretations were mere clarifications or confirmations of common understanding or certain principles of the Articles of Agreement. The main purpose of the interpretations was to find workable solutions to legal or economic problems under the auspices of the Articles of Agreement. For example, the thirteenth interpretation of the Bank's Articles addressed the changed circumstances engendered by the introduction of the SDR by the IMF. The Articles of Agreement of the IMF had to be amended, effective on 28 July 1969, to essentially augment the purposes of the IMF under Article I. The amendment created the SDR for purposes of meeting the need for a supplement to the existing reserve assets of members by allocating to them SDR as new reserve assets. The thirteenth interpretation was a policy decision and to characterize it as an amendment in the guise of interpretation would not be too farfetched. The Executive Directors, themselves, even contemplated the possibility of amending the Bank's Articles to address the problem caused by the introduction of the SDR by the IMF vis-à-vis the measure of the capital valuation of the World Bank. After an initial flurry of interpretations, the IMF has not made a formal interpretation of its Articles of Agreement since the first amendment in 1969.

There is no denying that today's world is different from when the Bretton Woods institutions were created about 80 years ago. There have been significant strides in economic and social development in the member States of the World Bank, but development challenges still abound. To meet these challenges, the World Bank has evolved and expanded its activities. Without evolution, the World Bank would run the risk of becoming dysfunctional, ineffective or irrelevant. The same goes for the IMF as it must seek to meet the

109 Although the interpretation was sought in connection with a litigation, it was never introduced as evidence. For a discussion of the issues in the case, see *World Bank Group v. Wallace*, 2016 SCC 15, [2016] 1 SCR 207 (Supreme Court of Canada).

evolving needs of its global membership and deliver on its principal objectives of economic policy advice, lending, and capacity development. Through the interpretations of their Articles of Agreement, the Bretton Woods institutions are evolving to remain relevant and meet the needs of their shareholders and stakeholders.

International Trust Funds at the World Bank and International Monetary Fund

Andrew Giddings, Gabriela Grinsteins and Hoang Pham *

Abstract This article focuses on a less well-documented part of the global financial and development architecture: international trust funds, as operationalized at the International Monetary Fund and the World Bank. It discusses how these two institutions have established and developed trust funds and financial intermediary funds, as important parts of their organizational mandate. The article assesses the historical, legal, and operational context to examine how these funds have filled a gap in the international order to provide resources to help address a wide range of emerging challenges and crises, ranging from broad balance of payments support to specific development objectives such as climate change and global health, while providing global public goods. The article then discusses how they are designed to provide flexibility but stay consistent with each institution's mandate and therefore how they differ between the institutions, how they provide financing, and how many are essentially a form of partnership to bring together different actors – all in an effort to maximize impact. The article also discusses how the World Bank's financial intermediary fund model has served as a launching pad for, and has sustained, many key global initiatives, as well as, at times, has helped create important new international financing vehicles.

* Andrew was Senior Counsel, Legal Vice Presidency, World Bank. Before that, he was the former Senior Director, Head of Ethics & Business Conduct of the Consultative Group on International Agricultural Research (CGIAR) as well as a former Senior Counsel and Counsel with the International Monetary Fund (IMF). Andrew is also on the Board of Directors of the Northern Virginia Conservation Trust; Gabriela is Senior Counsel, Legal Vice Presidency, World Bank; Hoang is Assistant General Counsel, Legal Department, IMF. The views expressed in this article are those of the authors and do not necessarily represent the views of the IMF and the World Bank, or each institution' respective Executive Board or management.

HTTPS://DOI.ORG/10.1163/9789004765672-005

1 Introduction

Trusts or trust funds, as adopted or recognized across different legal systems, have their origins traced back to the Roman law and were later developed under the English common law and embraced in continental Europe. There is no uniform definition of trust funds under various national jurisdictions and many countries have not developed any legal frameworks for trusts at all.[1] Notwithstanding these variations, trust funds are commonly understood as an arrangement between a provider of assets or funds (typically known as settlors, donors or grantors) and a trustee under which the latter would manage and distribute these assets or funds to advance a specific purpose or for the benefit of specific beneficiaries as intended by the former.[2] For example, Article 2 of the 1985 Hague Convention on the Law Applicable to Trusts and on Their Recognition defines the term 'trust' to mean "the legal relationships created – *inter vivos* or on death – by a person, the settlor, when assets have been placed under the control of a trustee for the benefit of a beneficiary or for a specified purpose". Under the state laws in the United States, "[a] trust [...] is a fiduciary relationship with respect to property [...] subjecting the [trustee] to duties to deal with it for the benefit of charity or for one or more persons".[3]

International organizations have borrowed the concept and legal features of 'trusts', as developed under national laws, to establish international trust funds through a varied set of arrangements under their own legal frameworks. In practice, in line with their relevant mandate, international organizations have used international trust funds to fill in gaps and find new ways to provide financing, in many cases as partnerships, to achieve specific objectives and address the emerging challenges of the times. While international trust funds

---

1 The Hague Convention on the Law Applicable to Trusts and on Their Recognition (adopted 1 July 1985, entered into force 1 January 1992, 1664 UNTS 311) is a multilateral treaty intended to establish a standardized framework for recognizing and applying a common framework to govern trusts across different jurisdictions.

2 See John H Langbein, 'The Contractarian Basis of the Law of Trust' (1995) 105 Yale Law Journal 625. The law of trusts has been subject to debate as to whether it is closer to property law (granting or conveying to claimants rights to obtain certain property or assets, or 'in rem' rights), or to contract law (granting claims rights against other persons to require performance, actions or non-action, or 'in personam' rights). It seems to be settled that trust law is a blend, and also serves as organizational law, which means an organizational and legal tool to 'split' the trustee into two persons, one for itself and one for the beneficiary (as trustee), and thus shielding trust assets from the claims of the trustee's personal creditors against the trustee. See Robert Sitko, 'An Agency Costs Theory of Trust Law' (2004) 89 Cornell Law Review 621.

3 Restatement (Third) of Trusts § 2 (American Law Institute, 2003).

have been broadly employed, public knowledge of these funds is still limited. This has prompted the World Bank, which maintains a large number of international trust funds, to 'demystify' its trust funds, through public statements, its Annual Reports, and more, to highlight them as tools that provide flexibility.[4] But given their importance, they remain underexamined in terms of their history and role in international economic law, governance and policy.

For both the IMF and the World Bank, their trust funds are a key financing pillar – external to financing from their general resources. To illustrate this: the total disbursements by IMF trust funds in 2024 topped over $10 billion, and the World Bank made average annual trust funds disbursements of $9 billion during the fiscal years running from 2020 to 2024. By comparison, annual disbursements financed by the general resources of the IMF stood at about $22 billion,[5] and average International Bank for Reconstruction and Development (IBRD) and the International Development Association (IDA) financing for the fiscal years running from 2020 to 2024 stood at $50.6 billion.[6]

Notwithstanding their prominent roles, the IMF and the World Bank have not developed a legal definition of 'trust funds'. However, this approach is standard among international organizations, allowing them to maintain flexibility in employing and adjusting the trust fund modality in response to the need of their memberships. In this regard, Bantekas pointedly observed that neither international development banks nor the United Nations had pro-

4 As Maitreyi Bordia Das, Director for Trust Funds and Partner Relations in the Development Finance Vice Presidency at the World Bank notes, "Someone recently said that World Bank trust funds were difficult to understand. So we're demystifying them. (Spoiler alert: they are mostly grant resources intended for specific issues or geographical areas. The majority are country targeted and implemented by recipient governments)." Maitreyi Bordia Das, 'What are we talking about when we talk about trust funds?' (LinkedIn, 7 January 2025) <https://www.linkedin.com/in/maitreyi-das/recent-activity/all/>, referring to Srimathi Sridhar, 'Why does the World Bank have trust funds' (Instagram, 13 December 2024) <https://www.instagram.com/reel/DDh8levPoV5/?igsh=MWE3ZTFtdTJzZjRsMQ%3D%3D> both accessed 11 December 2025.

5 For data on the IMF's annual disbursements, see IMF, 'Past IMF Disbursements and Repayments for all members from May 01, 1984 to November 30, 2025' <https://www.imf.org/external/np/fin/tad/extrep1.aspx> accessed 11 December 2025; and for the IMF's total outstanding credit amounts, see IMF, 'Total IMF Credit Outstanding for all members from 1984–2025' <https://www.imf.org/external/np/fin/tad/extcred1.aspx> accessed 11 December 2025.

6 World Bank Group, '2024 Trust Fund Annual Report, Partnerships in Action', 2, Figure 1 <https://tfar.worldbank.org/assets/images/tf_report/pdf/WBG-Trust-Fund-report.pdf> accessed 11 December 2025.

vided any overarching definition of trust funds through their institutional law, as such a definition could potentially limit their future uses.[7]

For the IMF, its power to establish trust funds was codified in the second amendment to its Articles of Agreements, effective 1 April 1978. Under Article V, Section 2(b) of the IMF's Articles of Agreement, adopted as part of the second amendment, the IMF "may decide to perform financial and technical services, including the administration of resources contributed by members, that are consistent with the purposes of the Fund".[8] Paragraph 5(c) of Schedule M of the IMF's Articles of Agreement also recognizes a potential role of the IMF as a trustee. Prior to the second amendment, the IMF's authority to establish trust funds was not expressly provided in the Articles of Agreement, but instead originated from the IMF's implied power based on its general purposes under Article I and its capacity to contract under Article IX, Section 2.[9]

The IMF currently maintains two categories of trust funds, known as 'IMF trusts' and 'IMF administered accounts', with their differences derived mainly from their purposes and governance structures. Both IMF trusts and administered accounts could be financed by external contributors (including IMF members, other international organizations, or private entities) and are designed to support IMF member countries. Their assets would be under the legal ownership of the IMF and protected by the IMF's privileges and immunities. While IMF trusts have been used only for providing financing to eligible IMF member countries (either providing loans or grants), IMF administered accounts have served various purposes, including to provide financing to IMF members, pay for the IMF's technical services, and temporarily hold IMF members' resources. Their differences are also derived from the relationship with the beneficiaries and the discretionary role of the IMF. An IMF trust would have a direct creditor relationship (in the case of a lending trust) or

7 Ilias Bantekas, *Trust Funds under International Law: Trustee Obligations of the United Nations and International Development Banks* (T.M.C. Asser Press 2009) 8.

8 The IMF Executive Board's 1976 report to the IMF Board of Governors on the proposed second amendment explicitly referred to the IMF's power to establish trust funds to provide financial and technical services. See IMF, 'Proposed Second Amendment to the Articles of Agreement of the International Monetary Fund - A Report by the Executive Directors to the Board of Governors' in IMF, *Summary Proceedings Annual Meeting 1976 - Supplement* (IMF 1976).

9 See Joseph Gold, *The Second Amendment of the Fund's Articles of Agreement* (IMF, 1978). Under the doctrine of implied powers, these powers have been recognized for an international agency where the powers were (a) incidental to the exercise of expressly granted powers; (b) necessary or appropriate for the performance of the functions of the international agency; and (c) not in conflict, directly or indirectly, with the provisions of the treaty establishing the agency.

the grantor relationship (in the case of a debt relief trust) with the beneficiary member countries, with the IMF (through its Executive Board) acting as trustee – normally taking discretionary decisions on key issues (such as qualification, disbursements, and amount of financing) when providing financing to specific IMF members. In an IMF administered account, the account's contributors can have a direct, bilateral relationship with the beneficiary or beneficiaries, and would determine the qualification, amounts, repayment and interest rates, among other things, as applicable. The IMF would only receive and hold resources, and conduct payments to facilitate such bilateral arrangements.[10]

The World Bank has a long history of establishing trust funds, based on the doctrine of implied powers[11] and in alignment with the purposes set forth in IBRD's and IDA's Articles of Agreement.[12] The first trust fund of the World Bank was the Indus Basin Development Fund, established on 19 September 1960.[13] Whereas now, the requirement of maintaining consistency with the purposes of IBRD and IDA's Articles of Agreement is clearly expressed in the Bank's Policy on Trust Funds,[14] issued by the Boards of Executive Directors, as follows:

10 For example, the IMF established in April 2022 an administered account for Ukraine to channel donor resources in the form of grants and loans aimed at assisting Ukraine to meet its balance of payments and budgetary needs and help stabilize its economy.

11 See Ibrahim FI Shihata, *The World Bank Legal Papers* (Kluwer Law International 2000) 852. For more views on the legal personality of international organizations and implied powers, see Manuel Rama-Montaldo, 'International Legal Personality and Implied Powers of International Organizations' (1970) 44 British Yearbook of International Law 111; and Viljam Engström, 'Implied Powers of International Organizations: On the Character of a Legal Doctrine' (2003) 14 Finnish Yearbook of International Law 129.

12 Articles of Agreement of the International Bank for Reconstruction and Development (adopted 22 July 1944, entered into force on 27 December 1945), 2 UNTS 134 <https://thedocs.worldbank.org/en/doc/722361541184234501-0330022018/original/IBRDArticlesOfAgreementEnglish.pdf>; and Articles of Agreement of the International Development Association (adopted 26 January 1960, entered into force 24 September 1960), 439 UNTS 249 <https://thedocs.worldbank.org/en/doc/2a209939e876fdcd0d957036daebff6e-0410011960/original/IDA-Articles-of-Agreement-English.pdf> both accessed 11 December 2025.

13 Indus Basin Development Fund Agreement (signed 19 September 1960, entered into force 1 April 1960) 444 UNTS 259 <https://documents1.worldbank.org/curated/en/239781468100481033/pdf/Loan-0266-Pakistan-Indus-Basin-Project-Development-Fund-Agreement.pdf> accessed 11 December 2025.

14 Bank Policy contains rules approved by the Board of Executive Directors of IBRD, IDA or both, as applicable and as set forth in the Bank Policy on Policy and Procedure Framework, Section II(1)(a) <https://ppfdocuments.azureedge.net/2865.pdf> accessed 11 December 2025.

> Consistent with the overall purposes of IDA and IBRD set out in the Articles of Agreement, the Bank establishes and administers Trust Funds as a complement to IDA and IBRD financing to promote development and aid effectiveness by leveraging its capacity and development knowledge. In administering a Trust Fund and holding the Trust Fund resources, the Bank acts in a fiduciary capacity in accordance only with the provisions of the agreement concerning the Trust Fund.[15]

More concretely, the concept of World Bank trust funds is defined through its policy, in referring to its most basic elements, as a “financing arrangement established by the Bank with contributions from one or more donors, and in some cases from a World Bank Group Institution”.[16] Also through policy, the World Bank differentiates World Bank Trust Funds and Financial Intermediary Funds (FIFs) as two distinct categories of trust funds determined by the potential use of funds or the potential financial services provided.[17] These tools – World Bank Trust Funds and FIFs – achieve many different objectives, ranging from reducing the borrowing costs of member countries to providing financing for projects benefiting communities in territories where the World Bank cannot provide financing to the member country.[18] These additional aspects help advance the argument that the concept of trust funds is inherently functionalist in nature. In particular, trust funds ultimately exist only with the support of member States and because they do what member States want them to do “for the greater good”.[19] Hence, international trust funds are

15 World Bank Policy on Trust Funds (effective 21 January 2021), sec III(2) <https://ppfdocuments.azureedge.net/1e51451c-cf3b-4fde-8c79-286565dbbcd9.pdf> accessed 11 December 2025.

16 Ibid, sec III(1).

17 Ibid, secs III(7)-(8).

18 World Bank Group, ‘Understanding Trust Funds’ (October 2024) <https://thedocs.worldbank.org/en/doc/e54485341ed618b0b1529af70e47c638-0060072024/related/Brochure-Trust-Funds-11-1-2024.pdf> accessed 11 December 2025.

19 Jan Klabbers, ‘The EJIL Foreword: The Transformation of International Organizations Law’ (2015) 26 European Journal of International Law 9, 11. Sometimes trust funds would advance the objectives supported by non-sovereign donors, but they would always have to be consistent with the overall mandate of a member-based international organization and endorsed by member States. For a recent discussion on the overall functionalism debate, see, for example, Andreas Kotsakis, ‘Beyond the Machinery Metaphors: Towards a Theory of International Organizations as Machines’ (2024) 37 Leiden Journal of International Law 608.

examples of David Kennedy's description of international organizations law as a "discipline of deeds" and not words.[20]

The International Finance Corporation (IFC) and the Multilateral Investment Guarantee Agency (MIGA) have also established trust funds as a financing mechanism aligned with their mandates, without providing a limiting definition.[21] For example, IFC uses trust funds to support its upstream and advisory work as well as its blended finance products.[22] MIGA has also set up trust funds under its MIGA Strategic Priorities Program with contributions from one or more development partners[23] and it combines trust fund financing with its own resources to issue guarantees.[24]

Given these basic definitional descriptions of international trust funds, this article: examines a brief history of international trust funds; then focuses upon IMF trust funds; followed by World Bank trust funds; before contextually considering the innovative contribution of international trust funds to partnership and institution-building; before offering a conclusion, reflecting overall how international trust funds match the mandates of their respective institutions and address the challenges of our time.

2 Brief History of International Trust Funds

The origin of trusts under national and sub-national laws goes far back in history. There had long been notions of trusts as originated in England in medieval times, with Roman law antecedents in the *fideicommissum*.[25] Later, when trusts were embraced in continental Europe, the *fiducia* under Roman law has been presented as having similarities to the concept of trust under civil law.[26]

The origin of international trust funds was more recent, and unlike trust funds governed under national or sub-national laws, international trust funds are self-regulated and subject to policies of the international organizations

20 David Kennedy, 'The Move to Institutions' (1986) 8 Cardozo Law Review 841, as cited in Kotsakis (note 19), 2.

21 IFC and MIGA, together with IBRD, IDA and the International Center for the Settlement of Investment Disputes (ICSID), are considered the World Bank Group Institutions.

22 World Bank Group, '2024 Trust Fund Annual Report' (note 6), 19.

23 MIGA, 'Trust Funds and Blended Finance' <https://www.miga.org/trust-funds> accessed 11 December 2025.

24 World Bank Group, '2024 Trust Fund Annual Report' (note 6), 19.

25 Joseph Gold, 'Trust Funds in International Law: The Contribution of the International Monetary Fund to a Code of Principles' (1978) 72 American Journal of International Law 856, 858.

26 Bantekas (note 7) 14–16.

that administer, host or provide financial services for them. The history of international trust funds goes back to the early 20th century, at least to the founding of the Bank for International Settlements (BIS) in 1930, "the oldest international organization in the field of international monetary cooperation".[27] As noted by Jenks, in the Statutes of the BIS there is an express authorization for the BIS to "act as trustee or agent in regard to international financial settlements entrusted to it under agreements with the parties concerned".[28] Indeed, one of the BIS's first and key roles in May 1930 was to act as trustee to receive and distribute World War I reparations payments from Germany to creditor governments (as part of the Young Plan, a revision of prior reparations deals).[29] The BIS also acted as agent in connection with the issue of the German Government International 5 1/2% Loan 1930 (Young Loan), "for the service of which it had agreed to perform the functions of trustee".[30] Importantly as well, the role of the BIS was not limited to "mere collection and distribution", but also included what could be considered broader trustee functions.[31] The BIS was also named trustee for the Austrian International Loan of 1930.[32]

---

27 Mario Giavanoli, 'The Role of the BIS in International Monetary Cooperation and Its Tasks Relating to the ECU' in Robert C Effros (ed), *Current Legal Issues Affecting Central Banks* (Vol 1, IMF 1992), 39.

28 C Wilfred Jenks, *The Proper Law of International Organisations* (Stevens & Sons Ltd. 1962) 187, referring to the Statutes of the Bank for International Settlements, art 3.

29 Ibid, referring to the Trust Agreement concerning Annuities Payable by Germany between the Creditor Governments and the Bank for International Settlements of 17 May 1930, see Manley O Hudson (ed), *International Legislation* (Carnegie Endowment for International Peace 1936) 200–214. See also Roger Auboin, 'The Bank for International Settlements, 1930–1955' (1955) 22 Princeton Essays in International Finance, 3–4.

30 Auboin (note 29), 7. As Auboin notes: "Under the Hague Agreements, one-third of this amount was received by the German Government and the remaining two-thirds went to six countries, creditors of Germany, which thus mobilized part of their reparations claims."

31 Ibid, 8: "The duties of the BIS as trustee for the governments concerned were not confined, however, to the mere collection and distribution, in accordance with the Hague Agreements, of the payments made by Germany. Its function was much wider, for it was also to play an essential part in the execution of the Young Plan by setting up 'machinery which will provide an elastic element between the payments to be made by Germany and their realization.' It was, in particular, the task of the [BIS] to help to prevent a suspension of the transfers by granting direct aid to the Reichsbank in the form of foreign currency credits or by giving indirect aid through the investment in Reichsmarks of part of the annuity receipts on the German market in agreement with the Reichsbank. Thus, in order to ensure the regular flow of the transfers, the BIS was to influence the exchange markets by the purchase of Reichsmarks in periods of strain and by a reduction of its investments in Reichsmarks when conditions for transfer were more favorable. It was left to the Bank itself to decide when and to what extent it ought to intervene."

32 Ibid, 9.

Notwithstanding later concerns with how reparations issues ultimately played out,[33] it is noteworthy that this international trust concept – covering both reparations payments and loans – predated the Bretton Woods institutions. It may go further back than the BIS, since Jenks cites the BIS essentially as an *example* of an "international body corporate as trustee of loans", but it is unclear if they found earlier example.[34]

As Jenks notes, a key concept of the BIS as a trustee was that it was subject only to its "proper law and to any provision for international arbitration contained in its statutes or in the trust agreement" – an idea that persists today for international trust funds.[35] One of the advantages is that it makes it "unnecessary to have a trust agreement subject to any particular system of municipal law".[36] As Jenks notes, this allows a degree of freedom in how to use the trust resources to address a particular issue. Again, this is something that continues to be relevant today, as international organizations ensure that trust funds are administered pursuant to their policies and procedures, and notwithstanding the requirements of the contributors' or the recipients' particular municipal laws. Dating to at least the BIS, there is a good argument that international trust funds were always contemplated to *not* be subject to these requirements (of course, with the caveat that unless this is otherwise agreed in the agreement). The role of the BIS then, in these trustee arrangements, was to "perform certain technical duties determined in advance and considered necessary for the execution of a particular agreement".[37] And it continued these duties in other capacities, such as in duties in connection with the European Payments Union and the European Coal and Steel Community.[38]

There is another antecedent of international trust funds: voluntary donations to international organizations. As described by Schermers (and later Schermers and Blokker), "[a]lready during the life of the League of Nations,

33 Further discussed by Liaquat Ahamed, *Lords of Finance: The Bankers Who Broke the World* (Penguin Press 2009).

34 Jenks (note 28) 187. This could be the subject of further inquiry, since even a recent article specifically on war reparations used post-WWII as the starting point. See Oona A Hathaway, Maggie M Mills and Thomas M Poston, 'War Reparations: The Case for Countermeasures' (2024) 76 Stanaford Law Review 971 <https://review.law.stanford.edu/wp-content/uploads/sites/3/2024/05/Hathaway-et-al.-76-Stan.-L.-Rev.-971.pdf> accessed 11 December 2025.

35 Jenks (note 28) 187.

36 Ibid.

37 Ibid, referring to Auboin (note 29) 2.

38 Auboin (note 29) 4.

international organizations suffered from a lack of funds".[39] So "[t]he High Commissioner for Refugees, the Health Organization and the Committee on Intellectual Cooperation of the League made appeals for voluntary contributions and gifts from governmental and non-governmental sources".[40] This history helps inform the ultimate development of trust funds from voluntary contribution – as opposed to a conduit for reparations. Schermers and Blokker note, "[f]or all practical purposes, the creation of a new trust fund means the same as the creation of a new voluntary program".[41] The examples of UN trust funds provided by Schermers and Blokker are all dated *after* the World Bank's Indus Basin Development Fund Agreement of 1960, even if they use the UN as the main example and the IMF and the World Bank as "outside the UN" creators of trust funds. Regarding the creation of trust funds, Schermers and Blokker observe that the "competence to create trust funds appears to be inherent in any international organization. Many trust funds have been created in the absence of any constitutional provision".[42]

As aforementioned, the Indus Basin Development Fund is considered as the first precedent for modern trust funds at the World Bank. However, it was not called a 'trust fund' at the time even if it fits the general definition under the current World Bank trust fund policy. Later, the World Bank's General Counsel from 1983 to 1998, Shihata, clarified that that Bank started using the "Common Law term 'trust fund'".[43] Based on the IMF's establishment of the International Monetary Fund Trust Fund in 1976 for the use of gold sale proceeds, Shihata credits the General Counsel of the IMF, Gold, with not only the trust fund terminology, but essentially with the overall concept of the *international trust fund* – beyond the regional Indus fund and going to a broader concept with certain principles. Shihata writes:

> I first met Joseph Gold in the mid-seventies. He was then General Counsel of the IMF; I was Director-General of the OPEC Fund for International Development. A controversy erupted at the time about the use of the proceeds of gold to

39 Henry G Schermers and Niels M Blokker, *International Institutional Law: Unity within Diversity* (4th rev edn, Martinus Nijhoff Publishers 2003) §1022, 655, 1302.

40 Ibid.

41 Ibid, §1028, 660.

42 Ibid, §1031, 661. They cite the Inter-American Development Bank as an example, with the receipt of funds from the United States into a trust fund, without any specific mention of such funds in its constitutive documents.

43 Ibrahim FI Shihata, 'Techniques to Avoid Proliferation of International Organizations – The Experience of the World Bank', in Niels M Blokker and Henry G Schermers (eds), *Proliferation of International Organizations* (Kluwer Law International 2001), 125.

> be sold by the IMF. Industrial countries were to donate their share of these proceeds to a trust fund established by the IMF to help countries in need. They insisted that OPEC countries did the same. The latter were against the principle of being treated as industrial countries in that context, even though most of them did not mind the donation of the proceeds after they received them. With the help of the Iranian Executive Director in the IMF at the time, Mr. Amouzegar, I proposed that the money be given by the IMF to the OPEC Fund which in turn would donate it on behalf of its members to the IMF trust fund through a series of paper transactions. It took no time for Joseph Gold to recognize the practicality of the solution and to support it. On that occasion, by the way, he was the one to initiate the practice of establishing "international trust funds", of which there are hundreds at present, and he devised the principles that govern them to this day.[44]

These trust fund principles are set out in a short pamphlet by Gold.[45] It should be noted that – notwithstanding the recognition by Shihata of Gold initiating the practice – what was understood to be an 'international trust fund' started to then diverge between the IMF and the Bank, in line with their respective mandates and functions. However, while acknowledging the "many examples" of trusts in the practice of international organizations and among states and identifying the key principles recognized by the IMF, Gold also noted that there was nothing "resembling an established code of principles relating to trusts at the international level".[46]

44 Ibrahim FI Shihata, 'In Memoriam – Sir Joseph Gold' (2000) 94 American Society of International Law Proceedings of the Annual Meeting 344.

45 The principles are: (i) the rights of ownership of property subject to a trust are divided between the trustee and the beneficiary or beneficiaries; (ii) a trustee must keep trust property separate from his own property and from the property of other trusts, and must earmark trust property as such, unless relieved of this obligation by law or the terms of the trust; (iii) a trust is not a legal entity in the sense that it is the bearer of rights or the subject of duties; (iv) a trustee may not engage in 'self-dealing' in administering the trust; (v) a trustee must administer the trust solely in the interest of the beneficiary; and (vi) in administering a trust, the trustee must use reasonable care and skill and avoid unreasonable risk. With respect to (iii), Gold notes that "[t]o give legal personality to a trust it is necessary to take action in accordance with applicable law *beyond the creation of the trust itself*". This issue of legal personality of a trust (and its Board) has come up in a number of FIFs in particular, as they seek in some instances to become 'more' independent. See Gold, 'Trust Funds in International Law' (note 25) 870–874.

46 See Gold, 'Trust Funds in International Law' (note 25) 858.

3 IMF Trust Funds

This section examining international trust funds administered by the IMF is organized under the following headings: firstly, 'Initial IMF Trust Funds'; and second, 'Current IMF Trust Funds'.

3.1 Initial IMF Trust Funds

The IMF established its first trust funds in the mid-1970s in response to the increasing demand for new financial support to its developing member countries, which faced serious economic challenges during the oil crisis. From its foundation in December 1945 until the late 1960s, the IMF largely provided its financing to more developed member countries. Following decolonization in the 1960s and 1970s, the IMF membership grew rapidly with the admission of many low-income and developing countries, which faced different types of economic challenges. In response, the IMF added new lending facilities, funded by the IMF's general resources, including the Compensatory Financing Facility in 1963, the Buffer Stock Financing Facility in 1969, and the Extended Fund Facility in 1974.[47] These facilities were designed to help members address 'special' balance of payments (BoP) problems that tended to arise more often with low-income countries (LICs), even though they would be available to any IMF member facing the same BoP problems. However, these facilities did not provide concessional financing and thus proved insufficient to help LICs in dealing with severe economic havoc wrought by the mid-1970s oil crisis. Intensifying pressure and increasing international support led to the establishment of the IMF's initial trust funds, the Subsidy Account in 1975 and the Trust Fund in 1976.

Funded with donors' resources, the Subsidy Account and the Trust Fund allowed the IMF to provide tailored support to LICs. Prior to the second amendment of the IMF's Articles of Agreement (effective 1 April 1978), the IMF's only financial resources were its general resources in its General Resources Account (GRA). Since the establishment of the IMF, its general resources have always been subject to strict restrictions under the Articles of Agreement. Specifically, the use of these resources must be available to all IMF members only temporarily (so only for 'lending', not grant funding), on a uniformity basis (in other words, no preferential financial treatment can be granted to any subset of IMF membership) and subject to IMF lending condi-

47 See James M Boughton, *Tearing Down Walls* (IMF 2012) 632 <https://www.imf.org/external/pubs/ft/history/2012/> accessed 11 December 2025.

tions and charges.[48] As financing sources for both the Subsidy Account and the Trust Fund came from donors, they were not subject to the same restrictions and their use could be much more flexible.

For the Subsidy Account, its resources consisted of donations by major oil exporting, industrial and other developed countries, and were used as grant funding to subsidize charges that LICs paid on their borrowings from the IMF's Oil Facility for up to 5 percent per annum.[49] Financing of the Trust Fund came from the sale of IMF gold through a set of complex transactions that reflected constraints under the IMF's Articles of Agreement on the use of IMF gold at that time. Specifically, prior to the amendment in 1978, the IMF and its members might only sell and purchase gold at a regulated price at par value of Special Drawing Right (SDR) 35 per ounce, plus a small margin prescribed by the IMF.[50] Arrangements were therefore made for the IMF to sell some of its gold holdings to certain members which in turn sold this gold to the Trust Fund at the same regulated price. The Trust Fund, not subject to that regulation, was then able to sell this gold amount at the market price, generating the total profit of US$3,350 million. With this profit amount as its resource, the Trust Fund was able to lend to LICs at the very concessional interest rate of only 0.5 percent per annum.[51]

Structuring the Subsidy Account and the Trust Fund as 'trusts' leveraged the IMF's advantages in the management and the accomplishment of the in-

---

48 Under the framework only in effect after the second amendment and currently in place, the IMF may use its resources in the Special Disbursement Account (SDA), which originated from the IMF's past gold sale and is separate from the GRA, to provide BoP assistance to developing members on special terms. These SDA resources, together with donors' resources, have been financing the IMF's concessional lending and debt relief trust funds since 1986.

49 See Margaret Garritsen de Vries, *IMF History (1972–1978)* (Vol 1, IMF 1985), chap 18: A Second Oil Facility <https://www.elibrary.imf.org/display/book/9781451922684/ch018.xml> accessed 11 December 2025. With the total SDR 165 million, the Subsidy Account effectively helped 39 members to reduce their annual charge rate from about 7.7 percent to 2.7 percent.

50 Special Drawing Right, or SDR, is an interest-bearing international reserve asset created by the IMF in 1969 and allocated to IMF members to supplement other reserve assets of member countries. The SDR is based on a basket of international currencies comprising the US dollar, Japanese yen, euro, pound sterling and Chinese Renminbi. It is not a currency, nor a claim on the IMF, but is potentially a claim on freely usable currencies of IMF members. The value of the SDR is set daily by the IMF on the basis of fixed currency amounts of the currencies included in the SDR basket and the daily market exchange rates between the currencies included in the SDR basket.

51 See Margaret Garritsen de Vries, *IMF History (1972–1978)* (Vol 2, IMF 1996), chap 34: A Trust Fund Established <https://www.elibrary.imf.org/display/book/9781451931068/ch034.xml> accessed 11 December 2025.

tended objectives of the new entities. During the initial discussion, two other alternative structures were also considered: depository account(s) where the IMF would only serve as agent in administering resources deposited by contributors, and a separate international organization. For the former, the assets in the account would not be legally owned by the IMF and thus might not benefit from the IMF's then-existing network of depositories, which were typically the IMF members' central banks designated to hold the IMF's legally owned assets. Accordingly, new and costly depository relationships would be needed. For the latter, the legal and operational process of establishing a new international organization would be even more complicated and time-consuming, and unresponsive to the need to quickly launch new entities with very limited purposes. In contrast, establishing a trust fund would be less challenging procedurally. Furthermore, the transfer of the legal ownership of trust assets to the IMF, as trustee, would allow these assets to benefit from various immunities applicable to assets under the IMF's ownership and to be held by the IMF's depositories under its existing depository arrangements.[52] In addition, this modality would better utilize the IMF's existing expertise, operational experience, and organizational structure for its role as trustee in the management of the new entities.[53]

While both the Subsidy Account and the Trust Fund were structured and considered as 'trusts', their special features distinguished them from regular trusts under national laws and many other international trust funds. Firstly, eligible LIC members of the IMF were the beneficiaries of the trust funds but they did not have any beneficial ownership interest or any direct recognizable rights, making these trust funds similar to charitable or purpose trusts.[54] Second, the IMF's Executive Board 'created' the trust funds, adopted their instruments granting itself with broad discretion to amend the terms of trust fund instruments, managed the trust funds and unilaterally terminated them. Meanwhile, contributors played a minor role and had limited options in shap-

---

52 See IMF, 'Proposed Second Amendment' (note 8). The IMF and its assets enjoy very extensive immunities under its Articles of Agreement, which is an international treaty respected by all of its 191 member countries. Under Article IX, Sections 3 and 4, the IMF and its assets are immune from judicial process, and its assets are also immune from all executive and legislative actions.

53 See Gold, 'Trust Funds in International Law' (note 25) 864. There was also some discussion as to whether the IBRD, instead of the IMF, might serve as the trustee to the Trust Fund. However, the IMF was selected since the Trust Fund's purpose of providing BoP support is more similar to the IMF's mandate. See de Vries, chap 34: A Trust Fund Established (note 51).

54 These features were also observed in World Bank trusts and many other international law trusts. See Bantekas (note 7), 190–192.

ing the IMF trust funds beyond exercising their influence through financial contributions and through their representatives serving as the IMF's Executive Directors. For example, trust fund instruments only provided contributors with the right to request the return of the remaining amounts of their contributions in limited scenarios when the IMF modified the list of beneficiaries or extended the operational periods of the trust fund.[55] Another example was the liquidation provision in the instrument of the Trust Fund, which prescribed that all remaining assets after the liquidation be transferred to the IMF, and none to be returned to contributors. Finally, there was no specific body of law that would govern the management and operations of trust funds, but the IMF's own legal framework, and the IMF itself would have broad flexibility in determining whether the fundamental principles of trust law would be observed. For the establishment and management of these initial trust funds, the IMF built into the trust fund instruments key features consistent with the fiduciary principles of separation of assets and restriction against self-dealing.[56]

3.2 Current IMF Trust Funds

With the overall success of the Subsidy Account and the Trust Fund, the trust fund modality has become a key tool for the IMF in a wide range of its financing activities. The IMF's current trust funds, as well as its past trust funds (now dissolved), fall into two categories, being referred to under the Fund's legal framework as 'IMF trusts' and 'IMF administered accounts'. The first category includes the lending and debt relief trusts. Currently, the IMF has two lending trusts, the Poverty Reduction and Growth Trust (PRGT) which provides concessional financing to 70 eligible LIC members to help address their BoP problems,[57] and the Resilience and Sustainability Trust (RST) which provides financing to 143 eligible LICs and middle-income members to help strengthen their prospective (future) BoP stability.[58] The IMF also maintains

55 See, for example, Section IV, paragraph 1 of the Instrument to Establish the Trust Fund, or paragraph 7 of the IMF Executive Board's Decision on the Subsidy Account (Decision No 4773-(75/136), 1 August 1975), in IMF, *Selected Decisions of the International Monetary Fund and Selected Documents* (8th issue, IMF 1976), 193 and 83, respectively.

56 See Gold, 'Trust Funds in International Law' (note 25) 863–865.

57 The IMF determines the eligibility for LIC members based on two criteria: (i) a member country's per capita income levels, and (ii) its ability to borrow from international financial markets.

58 Resources in the IMF's lending trusts, the PRGT and RST, consist of three types: the loan, subsidy and reserve resources. Loan resources are borrowed from creditor members and on-lent to eligible members. The subsidy resources are used to cover all or part of the

two debt relief trusts at present, the Trust for Special Poverty Reduction and Growth Operations for the Heavily Indebted Poor Countries (PRG-HIPC Trust) and the Catastrophe Containment and Relief Trust (CCRT), which provide debt relief grants to eligible LICs to help reduce their external debt burden to sustainable levels.[59]

The second category currently includes nine administered accounts, which serve the purposes of either temporarily holding donors' resources, or channeling these resources to pay for the cost of the IMF's technical assistance or facilitate BoP financing assistance (loans or grants or both) to specified IMF member countries. While the IMF's role in managing these accounts is mostly administrative, somewhat similar to the role of an agent and custodian, the IMF also acts as a trustee when investing and managing the account resources and holding the legal ownership of these assets.[60]

As noted, Article V, Section 2(b) of the IMF's Articles of Agreement provides the legal basis and lays out the key requirements for the establishment of IMF trust funds. Under this Article, the IMF may provide financial services if the services are consistent with its purposes, do not impose obligations on members without their consent, and do not subject the IMF's GRA to any risk of loss. The IMF's purposes are listed in Article I of its Articles of Agreement, all of which are of an economic nature and centered on the promotion of the macroeconomic and financial stability of member countries and ensuring the effective operation of the international monetary system. They include promoting international monetary cooperation, facilitating the expansion and balanced growth of international trade, promoting exchange stability, assisting the establishment of a multilateral system of payments, and providing financing to assist members in correcting their BoP maladjustments.

---

interest payments to creditor members, while the reserve resources are used to protect creditor members against potential credit loss. Subsidy and reserve resources include donations from member countries (and in the case of the PRGT, those resources also come from the IMF's own donations of gold sale profit) and loan resources that the IMF, as Trustee, would invest to generate investment income for the use as subsidy or reserve resources.

59 The IMF's PRG-HIPC Trust was established in 1996, in a joint multilateral initiative with the World Bank and other international financial organizations to help reduce the high-level external debt of LICs. There are 39 LICs eligible for grants from this trust, among which 37 countries have received full benefits from this trust. The debt relief process for Sudan is currently held off due to its civil war. Eritrea is the only remaining eligible country. The IMF's CCRT was established in 2010 to provide debt relief to eligible LICs affected by natural or public health disasters.

60 For the list of the current administered accounts of the IMF, see the IMF Financial Statements 2024 (26 June 2025) <https://www.imf.org/en/Data/IMF-Finances/Quarterly-Financial-Statements?page=1> accessed 11 December 2025.

All of the IMF's lending or debt relief trust funds have been linked to one or more purposes of the IMF through their support of members' BoP position. Lending under the PRGT and debt relief under the PRGT-HIPC Trust or the CCRT are designed to assist members to address their BoP problems, following closely the IMF's BoP financing purpose under Article I(v) of the IMF Articles of Agreement. The RST, which was established in 2022, is the first lending trust designed to advance another IMF purpose. Specifically, the RST may lend to members even when they do not face any BoP issue, provided that this arrangement helps members reduce macro-critical risks to their prospective (future) BoP stability. This would be consistent with the IMF's purpose to promote members' external (BoP) stability under Article I(iii) of the IMF's Articles of Agreement.[61] While the RST currently focuses on longer-term challenges relating to climate change and pandemic preparedness, it may later be expanded to cover other challenges if supported by contributors to the RST.

The IMF has so far limited its trusts and administered accounts, which are designed to channel contributors' resources to facilitate financing assistance to members, to supporting members' BoP position, either to address current BoP issues or to strengthen future BoP stability. This approach helps maintain the coherence of IMF financing and its consistency with the IMF's monetary character. Furthermore, it keeps the IMF from getting into financing development and thus overlapping with financing provided by the World Bank and other development banks.[62]

In addition to its broad authority, the IMF also maintains the relatively simple establishment process and a lean governance structure for its trust funds, which gives the IMF significant flexibility to use the trust fund modality in response to a broad range of membership needs. The IMF's trust funds were established by the IMF's Executive Board through its adoption of the trust funds' instruments that set out the rights of contributors, the authority and responsibility of the IMF as trustee, and the eligibility and the terms and con-

61 IMF, 'Proposal To Establish a Resilience and Sustainability Trust' (18 April 2022) <https://www.imf.org/en/Publications/Policy-Papers/Issues/2022/04/15/Proposal-To-Establish-A-Resilience-and-Sustainability-Trust-516692> accessed 11 December 2025. The RST may also provide financing to address members' BoP gaps which arise from members' implementation of reforms established under an RST lending arrangement.

62 See François Gianviti, 'Evolving Role and Challenges for the International Monetary Fund' (2001) 35 The International Lawyer 1371 (The IMF's purposes "clearly demonstrated the monetary character of the Fund", in contrast to the World Bank which "was established as a development agency"). The IMF has not established any lending trust that is not linked to supporting members' BoP or that provides financing to non-members.

ditions for the use of the trust funds' assets. While contributors' political and financial support was critical for the setting of the IMF's trust funds, it has always been the IMF in the driving seat for the design of its trust funds.

The IMF may decide to apply conditions on the use of its trust fund resources similar to or different from those applicable to lending funded by its GRA, depending on the purposes of the relevant trust funds. For example, both the PRGT's current lending facilities and the equivalent GRA lending facilities are subject to the same types of conditionality which are designed to help borrowing members to address their BoP difficulties. Meanwhile, the RST lending, which is designed to help strengthen members' prospective BoP stability, would be subject to different conditions. In addition, the instruments of some administered accounts do not specify any lending conditions as they are left to the bilateral arrangements between contributors and beneficiaries, while the IMF would only facilitate disbursements and repayments upon receiving the contributors' notifications.

The IMF has secured significant support and resources for its trust funds over the years. This result is largely attributable to the IMF's unique role in the global financing structure, which comes with its global economic coverage through its near universal membership, its broad data access to and close consultation with its 191 member countries, as well as its macroeconomic expertise and financial capacity. This distinctive position tends to place the IMF at the center of political discourse for dealing with any major global economic issues, and makes it easier for the IMF to generate funding for its trust funds to tackle those issues. The IMF's lending objectives and conditionality designed to assist member countries to restore their macroeconomic stability and implement structural reforms, and its strong record for getting repaid also appear to be well aligned with the broad interest, and to mitigate credit risk concerns, of official lenders and grant contributors. In addition, IMF members incur relatively low costs on their loans to the IMF's lending trusts as they may continue counting these loans as their reserve assets. This feature is possible thanks to the IMF's ability to borrow from a broad set of its members and to arrange for prompt and early repayment to any lending member that faces a BoP crisis.[63]

63 The IMF and its lending trusts also have the fund-raising advantage over other international organizations since they may borrow from national central banks in the European Union (EU). Specifically, Article 123 of the Treaty on the Functioning of the EU (TFEU) prohibits overdraft facilities or any other type of credit facility by the European Central Bank (ECB) or national central banks in the EU in favor of EU institutions, bodies, offices or agencies, central governments, regional, local or other public author-

4 World Bank Trust Funds

This section examining international trust funds administered by the World Bank is organized under the following headings: firstly, 'Origins of World Bank Trust Funds'; and second, 'Current Policy Framework for World Bank Trust Funds'.

4.1 Origins of World Bank Trust Funds

Since the origination of the World Bank trust funds, a large number of trust funds and financial intermediary funds have been established to this date. By their nature they have been designed to address problems of their times. In more recent years, their role has evolved not only to address certain specific development needs, but also to address global public goods.[64]

The current focus on "global and regional issues that transcend national boundaries" is also relevant to the establishment of the Indus Basin Development Fund, as the first trust fund at the World Bank, and simultaneously a mechanism to finance development within a transboundary waterway.[65] The Indus Basin Development Fund was cited by Shihata as "an early important example" of a World Bank fund – rather than the 'first' – but it is uncertain whether this was just a term of art.[66] This is the first example of a legal arrangement where the World Bank not only provided financing for a specific regional project, but also accepted contributions from specific sovereign donors for purposes of financing that specific regional project.

---

ities, other bodies governed by public law, or public undertakings of member States. However, Article 7 of EU Council Regulation 3603/93 includes a specific exemption from Article 123 of the TFEU, under which the financing of national central banks of obligations falling upon the public sector vis-à-vis the IMF is not regarded as prohibited central credit to the government. The ECB has interpreted this regulation to exempt not only lending to the IMF, but also to its two lending trusts (the PRGT and the RST) since the central banks' claims against these two trust funds have the reserve asset quality (meaning that a central bank of an EU member may encash its claims against the trusts at any time when the EU member has BoP need). No other trust fund or international organization currently enjoys a similar exemption.

64 For a general look at the focus on global public goods, see Development Committee, 'Global Public Goods: A Framework for the Role of the World Bank' (28 September 2007) <https://www.cbd.int/financial/interdevinno/wb-globalpublicgoods2007.pdf> accessed 11 December 2025.

65 World Bank Group, '2024 Trust Fund Annual Report' (note 6), 23.

66 Shihata, 'Techniques to Avoid Proliferation of International Organizations' (note 43), at 124.

There is a history of international trust funds and their impact from 1960 to the more recent present – covering everything from trust funds designed to finance development programs and projects, to financial intermediary funds including the Global Environment Facility (GEF) aimed at meeting international environmental goals,[67] the Heavily Indebted Poor Country (HIPC) initiative aimed at reducing the debt burden of eligible countries,[68] the Global Fund to Fight AIDS, Tuberculosis and Malaria,[69] the Consultative Group on International Agricultural Research (CGIAR) to address agriculture research and coordination,[70] and others. For any particular issue of concern or emerging challenge in international affairs, trust funds and partnerships were almost always part of the proposed solutions.

4.2 Current Policy Framework for World Bank Trust Funds

The current hierarchy of World Bank specific rules on Trust Funds is headed by the World Bank Policy on Trust Funds effective 21 January 2021[71] which builds on the prior Operational Policy (OP) 14.40 regulating trust funds.[72] Key aspects of the 2021 policy include: the receipt of contributions from single or multiple donors, as well as World Bank Group Institutions;[73] not extending benefits or unfair advantages to the donor;[74] and the categorization of trust funds into World Bank Trust Funds and FIFs, with a clarification that for FIFs the World Bank may serve as a limited trustee, secretariat or implementing entity.[75]

67 Additional information about GEF is available at its website <https://www.thegef.org/who-we-are> accessed 11 December 2025.

68 Additional information about the HIPC initiative is available in the HIPC Brief (9 May 2024) <https://www.worldbank.org/en/topic/debt/brief/hipc> accessed 11 December 2025.

69 Additional information about the Global Fund is available at its website <https://www.theglobalfund.org/en/about-the-global-fund/> accessed 11 December 2025.

70 Additional information about CGIAR is available at its website <https://www.cgiar.org/> accessed 11 December 2025.

71 World Bank Policy on Trust Funds (note 15).

72 World Bank Operational Policy (OP) 14.40 (effective 1 July 2008) <https://documents1.worldbank.org/curated/en/932661468162558092/pdf/518940BR0CORR11C0disclosed011130191.pdf> accessed 11 December 2025.

73 World Bank Policy on Trust Funds (note 15), sec III(1).

74 Ibid, sec III(4).

75 Ibid, secs III(6), (8), and (9).

FIFs are a particular subset of trust funds where the Bank provides, at least as a minimum, services as a limited trustee, and that should present the following characteristics showing larger scale, complexity and need for coordination with a broader set of institutions:

(i) evidence of need for regional or global collective action to benefit the Bank's client countries;
(ii) determination that objectives cannot be reasonably addressed by alternative arrangements;
(iii) is consistent with the mandate, strategic priorities and comparative advantages of the Bank, and does not exceed the Bank's risk appetites and tolerances;
(iv) demonstrates assurance of large-scale funding with donor commitments of at least US$200 million in grants at entry, and at least three participating donors at initiation; and
(v) determination that, for global or regional partnership programs, large-scale and coordinated implementation is needed across a significant number of implementing entities.[76]

Concerning the financial terms and mechanisms of trust funds as regulated by the current policy framework, it is important to note that these trust funds are almost exclusively grant-based, meaning that both funds in and funds out are provided on a grant basis.[77] However, another sign of innovation and evolution related to the financial practices of trust funds is evidenced by one salient difference between the current World Bank Policy on Trust Funds and the prior OP 14.40 Policy[78] regulating trust funds: the absence of references in the 2021 policy to disbursements through 'grant accounts'[79] or 'grants'.[80] While

76 World Bank Directive on Financial Intermediary Funds (effective 26 February 2022), sec III(1)(a)(ii) <https://ppfdocuments.azureedge.net/d2658e30-3a2e-47d9-ad96-ea63e28581e0.pdf> accessed 11 December 2025.

77 Schermers and Blokker make the distinction between 'contributions' and 'gifts' for voluntary contributions to international organizations, noting that (i) in principle voluntary contributions are periodic (though amounts may vary) while gifts are usually for one occasion only; and (ii) voluntary contributions are made for programs and are not part of the regular budget of the organizations, whereas "most gifts" are income to the organization as a whole, and so are part of its regular budget. Schermers and Blokker, *International Institutional Law* (note 39), §1022, 655, 1302. In World Bank trust fund usage, a common term of 'contributor' is used for FIFs and 'donor' for World Bank Trust Funds (with some variations), more or less in line with the division as set out by Schermers and Blokker. 'Gifts' to the overall budget are more akin to replenishment cycles, such as of IDA.

78 World Bank Operational Policy (OP) 14.40 (note 72).

79 Ibid, sec 5.

80 Ibid, sec 6 and fns 6, 7, and 9.

most World Bank Trust Funds receive contributions in the form of grants, and disburse funds to recipients in grant terms, the more general wording of the Trust Funds Policy responds to the existence of discrete FIFs and World Bank Trust Funds that receive loan contributions and provide financing on loan terms.[81]

Governance is also a key part of trust funds. A core policy principle for trust funds is that the World Bank must have "decision-making authority on the use of funds adequate to fulfill its roles in administering the specific type of Trust Fund".[82] This equally assertive and flexible principle allows the Bank to agree with contributors on a wide range of governance frameworks. These span from a single governance structure for multiple trust funds combined under an Umbrella 2.0 Program,[83] to the bespoke governance structures of FIFs that comprise governing bodies either with separate legal personalities (such as the Green Climate Fund), or without separate legal personality but relying on the World Bank hosting their secretariats (such as the Pandemic Fund). This flexibility has allowed FIFs to function both as a mechanism that bypasses the creation of a new international organization, and as a provider of financial services that incubate new international organizations. Section 5.3 expands on this.

Responding to the more complex mix of institutions that compose each FIF, their governance structure may vary, and normally comprises the following four features: (a) a governing body, responsible for selecting and approving implementing entities and funding decisions, among other matters; (b) the World Bank acting as trustee; (c) multilateral development banks, the IMF or United Nations organizations (or a combination thereof) acting as implementing entities; and (d) a secretariat, that may or may not be hosted by the World Bank.[84]

---

81 See World Bank Group, 'Canada-World Bank Clean Energy and Forests Climate Facility' <https://www.worldbank.org/en/topic/climatechange/brief/canada-world-bank-clean-energy-and-forests-climate-facility>, and Climate Investment Funds, 'Clean Technology Fund: Clean Technologies' <https://www.cif.org/topics/clean-technologies> both accessed 11 December 2025.

82 World Bank Policy on Trust Funds (note 15), sec III(5)(d).

83 World Bank Group, 'Board Paper on Trust Fund Policy' (19 January 2021), 20, <https://documents1.worldbank.org/curated/en/987411611543659040/pdf/Trust-Fund-Policy.pdf> accessed 11 December 2025.

84 World Bank Directive on Financial Intermediary Funds (note 76), sec III(4)-(8).

5 International Trust Funds, Multi-Stakeholder Cooperation, and New Institutions

This section examining the way in which international trust funds may facilitate multilateral innovation is organized under the following headings: firstly, 'Partnership-Building'; second, 'Platforms to Innovatively Address Global Public Goods'; and third, 'Fragmentation and Proliferation of International Organizations'.

5.1 Partnership-Building

While, as already noted, the core functioning of a World Bank Trust Fund is as a financial mechanism to manage contributions from donors, they can also be viewed as providing a separate type of benefit: namely, harnessing partnerships to address the development challenges of present times. As noted by the World Bank:

> Partnerships are critical to ending extreme poverty and boosting shared prosperity on a livable planet. No single institution can address today's development challenges in isolation, and the World Bank Group is working with partners – [Multilateral Development Banks], the UN, sovereign governments, [Civil Society Organizations], [Non-Governmental Organizations], philanthropic organizations, and the private sector – to confront the current crisis in development.[85]

Stumpf has characterized trust funds as "international partnership programs, a particularly popular form of structured partnership for international collaborations".[86] They note that trust funds are "[a]ccounts managed by trustees on terms agreed with donors that support international partnership programs and are usually operated by international organizations outside of domestic laws".[87]

This concept that "[t]rust funds enable the [World] Bank Group to work with a variety of donors and partners to mobilize and direct funding when and where it is needed most, especially during emergencies and crises when

85 World Bank Group, '2024 Trust Fund Annual Report' (note 6), 2.

86 Andrea E Stumpf, *Designing International Partnership Programs: How to Structure for Sustainability, Efficiency, and Development Impact: A Primer for Partners* (Partnerships 2019), 14.

87 Ibid, 18.

speed matters", also allows donors and partners to work together.[88] They are essentially platforms for international cooperation, often at a technical level, that then can help build networks and collaborations, even at times when international cooperation is challenged. It is difficult to quantify, but 'small' collaborations at the Trust Fund and FIF level may create necessary linkages on areas of substance, in a way that is different from large-scale international organizations themselves. A partnership of highly qualified experts in a field – such as global public health experts at the Pandemic Fund – can accomplish a lot collectively and can encourage cooperation on other issues where the technical issues and the global demands might outweigh some of the politics one sees.[89]

Another advantage of trust funds and FIFs at the World Bank is that this provides multiple fora to discuss, debate, and address – or find innovative solutions to – emerging challenges in development by engaging a broader set of stakeholders beyond states as the members and governors of international organizations. For example, the Pandemic Fund is a FIF that incorporates recipients and civil society with a voting role within its Governing Board, acknowledging the importance of coordination in decision-making for the success of the prioritization strategy and financing of pandemic preparedness and response activities.[90] The key is that there is room in the governance arrangements to seek to accommodate concerns of a range of partners while still providing effective and efficient financing as needed to address development challenges.

5.2 Platforms to Innovatively Address Global Public Goods

One conceptual way to think about trust funds is the 'polycrisis' facing development agendas – and ultimately people.[91] This is daunting, including "geo-

88 World Bank Group, 'Understanding Trust Funds' (note 18), 4.

89 See Kenneth W Abbott and Duncan Snidal, 'Why States Act Through Formal International Organizations' (1998) 42 Journal of Conflict Resolution 3.

90 The Pandemic Fund, 'Governing Board' <https://www.thepandemicfund.org/who-we-are/board> accessed 11 December 2025.

91 The term 'polycrisis' was originally coined by the French philosopher Edgar Morin but brought into widespread use by Jean-Claude Juncker, President of the European Commission. See Adam Tooze, 'Polycrisis and the Fraying of U.S. Hegemony' (Hans Maeder Lecture Series, The New School for Social Research, November 2024) <https://youtu.be/b57bVILz6FM> accessed 11 December 2025 (referring to the Eurozone crisis of 2010–2015, Refugee crisis, Ukraine – Maidan crisis 2013–2014, and populist movements of Brexit and the initial rise of Trump). Adam Tooze then notes how the concept has taken off and been used by many others and is now in the more common discourse. They note the

political conflict, violence, fragility, inflation, supply chain disruption, food crises, challenges of climate change, under-serving healthcare and education systems and the under-achievement of the Sustainable Development Goals".[92] International trust funds are one tool to address these challenges, since they provide the ability to be targeted in different ways – narrowly to a country, sector, theme, or to be broader in cross-cutting ways. This flexibility is paired with the efficiency of the use of standardized forms and template agreements that donors and implementing entities are generally comfortable with, reducing the need for extensive negotiations. When the crises are many, it is critical to simplify how to address them in a more efficient, faster, and more transparent manner. It also allows room for – and indeed encourages – innovation in how to address the polycrisis.

The polycrisis calls for innovation, and international trust funds allow for experimentation in how to address it. As the World Bank notes, "FIFs have enabled the World Bank and the world community at large to engage in new and urgent corporate and global priorities, provide the flexibility for customization based on partnership needs, and allow the World Bank to develop innovative financing models."[93] A current example for trust funds is that the World Bank is moving towards more intentional fundraising and allocation of financing resources to deliver global public goods as part of its Global Challenges Program. The aim of this is to "[crowd] in public and private sector support and leverag[e] other development partners to help scale and replicate impactful programs that tackle global challenges related to climate change, fragility and conflict, pandemic prevention and preparedness, energy access, food and nutrition security, water security and access, digitalization, and bio-

views of Michael Geyer that the term refers in its essence to a knowledge crisis – to hold open the space. For Tooze's part, in terms of usage, they note they "appropriated" the idea of a "found concept" of the polycrisis from Edgar Morin. The use of a list here, however, is not to suggest that polycrisis only refers to a list of problems, and indeed the idea of polycrisis is that the convergence of these issues is distinct. It is a useful concept – even though it is amorphous, "underspecified" and "weak" or even "irritating" or "incomplete". See Adam Tooze, 'Polycrisis & the Critique of Capitalocentrism' (Chartbook 343, Substack, 6 January 2025) <https://adamtooze.substack.com/p/chartbook-343-polycrisis-and-the?utm_source=publication-search> accessed 11 December 2025.

92 Christopher Stephens, 'An Evolving Role for Law and Lawyers in Development' (World Bank Blogs – Voices, 6 November 2023) <https://blogs.worldbank.org/en/voices/evolving-role-law-and-lawyers-development> accessed 11 December 2025.

93 Main Messages for the Publication of the 2017 Trust Fund Annual Report <https://www.worldbank.org/en/publication/trust-fund-annual-report-2017> accessed 11 December 2025.

diversity and nature".[94] Whereas, as a unique type of international trust fund, FIFs' contribution to global goods is evidenced by the fact that the largest volume of FIF transfers also address global challenges related to health, climate change, education, the environment and food and nutrition security.[95]

5.3 Fragmentation and Proliferation of International Organizations

Already noted is that one of the benefits of international trust funds is that they provide a mechanism to address emerging challenges without the high levels of structure and administration that a new international organization, or even a new department or work program in an existing organization, would require. For example, the World Bank, beyond having established legal personality, privileges and immunities,[96] has systems in place that allow for the administration of trust funds and the provision of trustee and other financial services (including treasury management) to FIFs. This is complemented by the existing information technology systems, human resources, policies and procedures.

On the other end of this dynamic interaction between international trust funds and international organizations, FIFs can have flexible designs – within constructs – and can be ways to launch new global initiatives. In particular, a function of FIFs has been to incubate new ('soft') organizations that may ultimately move past only distributing donor resources.[97] This has happened on sufficient occasions such that it serves a predictable purpose for the partners to those initiatives. For example, the Global Environment Facility, the Adaptation Fund, the Global Climate Fund, and the Fund for Responding to Loss and Damage could have been established as fully independent international organizations at their founding. However, this would be accompanied by significant costs, time and efforts that starting new international organizations entails and for which there might not be sufficient resources. Instead, the FIF structure at the World Bank allows the 'international organization' to be incubated. If ultimately the establishing partners wish it to be the case, the FIF could become its own international organization (or if not treaty-based,

94 World Bank Group, '2024 Trust Fund Annual Report' (note 6), 13–14.

95 Ibid, 11.

96 IBRD Articles of Agreement (note 12), art VII; and IDA Articles of Agreement (note 12), art VIII.

97 See Jan Klabbers, 'Institutional Ambivalence by Design: Soft Organizations in International Law' (2001) 70 Nordic Journal of International Law 403. Klabbers identifies CGIAR – a World Bank FIF – as an example of such an organization. Ibid, 406.

otherwise attributed the privileges and immunities of an international organization) following a process that would be unique for each FIF.

This process of becoming a new organization has worked well for entities as diverse as the Global Fund to Fight AIDS, Tuberculosis and Malaria, the Global Environment Facility, and CGIAR.[98] Some of these entities act so independently that most people do not realize their origins with the World Bank or that they technically continue to retain the World Bank's trustee services as a FIF.

This feeds into the larger question of proliferation of international organizations, which has persisted to this date since this was directly addressed by Blokker and Schermers.[99] Even Shihata conceptualized the possibility of combining the parts of the World Bank Group – IBRD, IFC, and MIGA – and restructuring IDA to be a large international trust fund.[100] However, Shihata cites the expansion of the Bank's activities through international trust funds as a way of *avoiding* proliferation, in other words, to address these global issues without creating a truly new institution.[101] But the article cites the Global Environment Facility, the Secretariat of which is hosted at the World Bank, and which has been functioning almost like an independent international organization for many years. It was a creation between the World Bank, United Nations Development Program (UNDP), and United Nations Environment Program.[102] So, is it an example of constraining proliferation, or is it an example of proliferation itself? Shihata notes it was able to be established without a new treaty – despite serving a number of global climate treaties – and therefore did not constitute a new international organization since it also relies on the Bank's privileges and immunities. In many ways it does reduce the administrative burden of creating and running an international organization, even if it seeks to live somewhere in between the World Bank and a truly independent international organization. Indeed, this history applies to the

98 The status of these organizations as 'legal entities' and/or having 'international legal personality' is a different question. This grouping of soft organizations and their status are not 'unproblematic', despite the prevailing view Klabbers identifies: "[i]n line with the dominant positivist mode of thinking in international law, whatever status the founding fathers wish to endow their creations with must be possible". See Klabbers, 'Institutional Ambivalence by Design' (note 97), 409.

99 Niels Blokker, 'Proliferation of International Organizations: An Exploratory Introduction', in Niels M Blokker and Henry G Schermers (eds), *Proliferation of International Organizations* (Kluwer Law International 2001), 1.

100 Shihata, 'Techniques to Avoid Proliferation of International Organizations' (note 43), 119.

101 Ibid, 125, 133.

102 Instrument for the Establishment of the Restructured Global Environment Facility (May 2004, as subsequently amended) <https://www.thegef.org/newsroom/publications?topic=&agency=&title=instrument> accessed 11 December 2025.

IMF as well in terms of the discussion above on the Subsidy Account and Trust Fund, finding them as ways to not have to create a brand new institution.

For more traditional World Bank Trust Funds, there has also been a question of proliferation and how their large numbers generate fragmentation and inefficiencies in development finance. The World Bank's answer to these questions has been to consolidate its trust fund portfolio since 2020, reducing by 53 percent the number of standalone trust funds from a peak of 486, and consolidating fundraising through 67 large umbrella programs.[103]

6 Conclusion

Over the last few decades, international trust funds of the IMF and the World Bank have provided each institution with a flexible tool to address the needs of its memberships in response to emerging challenges, while staying within the mandate under its respective Articles of Agreement. As the use of each institution's own resources is limited or subject to specific restrictions, the use of trust funds to pool resources from donors and provide financing to member countries leverages each institution's capacity, facilitates tailored assistance to its members, and further advances its purposes. Some of these trust funds may have created the perception that they function separately from the host institution. However, in establishing and designing trust funds, the IMF and the World Bank have always evaluated very carefully this and other relevant factors to ensure that their trust funds fit within their broader mandates and adopt relevant measures of control to bring their trust funds 'under the tent'.[104] For the World Bank, there is additional and important nuance on the differences between its types of trust funds: the World Bank Trust Funds and FIFs, with the latter entailing the provision of financial services by the World Bank while incorporating more complex governance arrangements.

History has shown the balance between innovation and consistency within the respective mandates of the IMF and the World Bank, and in the view of the authors has in some ways helped counter the potential proliferation of new institutions and their accompanying costs and challenges. Ultimately inter-

103 World Bank Group, '2024 Trust Fund Annual Report' (note 6), 15.

104 For discussions on the mandate of the IMF and how its roles can evolve over time, see Kristalina Georgieva and Rhoda Weeks-Brown, 'The IMF's Evolving Role Within a Constant Mandate' (2023) 26 Journal of International Economic Law 17. See also, Andrew Giddings and Clifford Blair, 'The Adaptive Mandate of the International Monetary Fund: Challenges and Opportunities in the Time of COVID-19' (2021) 1 Rutgers International Law and Human Rights Journal 1.

national organizations are funded by sovereign state members, and proliferation of new organizations with staff and the like risks increasing the concerns about funds going to the organizational structure and staff rather than to the projects or issues at hand. Trust funds can be ways to address specific concerns of donors without adding standalone administrative structure.

This review of trust funds of the IMF and the World Bank is not intended to be exhaustive, but rather to highlight their importance, which is underappreciated by international organizations literature. The relevant purpose, structure, and operations of the IMF and World Bank trust funds are appropriately tailored in accordance with the mandates and functions of these institutions. The commonality is that international trust funds are established to address issues and problems in a way that the other functions of their host institutions were not able to address; so the continuing relevance of international trust funds is assured.

Sexual Misconduct and the United Nations: Organizational Tensions, Zero Tolerance and Unfinished Justice

*Brenda Costecalde Orpineda and Mohamed Abdou**

Abstract Has the United Nations (UN) fulfilled its commitment to combat sexual misconduct? Is the UN's legal framework and accountability mechanisms adequate to address sexual misconduct involving its own officials? For decades, the UN and other international organizations have faced persistent criticism for their inability to adequately respond to incidents of sexual exploitation, abuse and harassment. While such allegations were often reported at an office-based workplace, by the turn of the 21st century, they drew growing attention and public scrutiny across the wider UN operational landscape, particularly in field-based humanitarian and peacekeeping missions. As the UN enjoys treaty-based privileges and immunities, there has been an increasing belief that the organization had become not only unaccountable, but also complicit in cultivating and perpetuating a culture of complacency and institutional indifference towards presumably some of the most serious forms of misconduct. This article examines how the UN has responded to evolving challenges related to the handling of sexual misconduct cases involving its officials and assesses both the strengths and weaknesses of its regulatory responses. It concludes that the UN's evolving framework remains fraught with tensions, ambiguities and unresolved challenges as the organization faces the daunting task of managing competing priorities and interests, together with commitments and expectations to enforce a zero tolerance policy, adhere to a victim-centred approach and safeguard the due process rights of defendants. In doing so, the UN's ambition to achieve a coherent and credible accountability framework remains ongoing – and unfinished.

* Brenda Costecalde Orpineda, Legal Officer, Office of International Standards and Legal Affairs of the United Nations Educational, Scientific and Cultural Organization (UNESCO); Mohamed Abdou, Legal Officer, Office of International Standards and Legal Affairs of UNESCO. The contents of this article reflect the opinion of the authors and do not necessarily represent the views of UNESCO.

 | HTTPS://DOI.ORG/10.1163/9789004765672-006

1 Introduction

As is the case with multiple other international organizations, the United Nations (UN) faced significant criticism for its inaction and shortcomings in addressing sexual exploitation and abuse (SEA) and sexual harassment.[1] Public outcry over SEA allegations involving UN peacekeepers led to increased scrutiny and a transformative shift in policy, marking the beginning of a more proactive stance in ensuring accountability for sexual misconduct, not only in the context of external peacekeeping operations but also in the workplace. By examining the notion of sexual misconduct as an all-encompassing category of prohibited acts, and focusing on the accountability framework for UN officials, the effectiveness of the UN framework is put to the test and analysed through the lens of the most recent case law of the United Nations Appeals Tribunal (UNAT).

In the early 2000s, sexual misconduct within UN operations was often downplayed or ignored. A fragmented regulatory framework, coupled with a reluctance to acknowledge and investigate complaints, allowed perpetrators to act with little fear of consequence. Despite the existence of professional conduct standards, enforcement was sporadic, and responses were largely reactive, more concerned with protecting the institution's reputation than victim-centred.

1.1 The Early Days and Turning Point

The paradigm shift occurred at the turn of the millennium, largely in response to the scandals involving serious allegations of SEA perpetrated by UN peacekeepers in multiple countries. Conflict-related sexual violence emerged as a pressing issue in the international security agenda in the 1990s. The UN first confronted SEA as a major issue in peacekeeping during the UN Transitional Authority in Cambodia in 1993. The spike in the number of sex workers in Cambodia – from 6,000 to over 25,000 within a year of the peacekeepers' arrival – was accompanied by widespread sexual abuse and mistreatment directed at women and associated with a rapid rise of child prostitution.[2] The

1 Note, the scope of this article is limited to the UN Secretariat's operations, and does not encompass funds and programmes, nor Specialized Agencies, of the UN.

2 Sandra Whitworth, *Men, Militarism, and UN Peacekeeping: A Gendered Analysis* (Lynne Rienner Publishers, 2004), 67.

UN's initial response was largely reputational: the Head of mission dismissed the issue's significance by stating that "boys will be boys",[3] peacekeepers were advised to avoid wearing uniforms when visiting brothels or parking UN vehicles nearby, and 800,000 condoms were shipped to the country to prevent the spread of HIV.[4]

This disregard for the seriousness of SEA persisted into 1995 in Bosnia and Herzegovina, where peacekeepers were implicated in sex trafficking. Not long after, independent consultants raised alarms about SEA of local women and girls by UN and non-governmental organization (NGO) staff in refugee camps in Guinea, Liberia and Sierra Leone. In 2001, reports in West Africa further underscored the pervasive nature of the problem and prompted the UN to respond.[5]

Importantly, the standards of conduct applicable to UN officials did not apply to peacekeepers, who are seconded by Member States and subject to different oversight mechanisms. Instead, the conduct of peacekeepers was guided by other frameworks: the document 'We are United Nations Peacekeepers', which was released in 1998 and emphasized the protective and restorative nature of peacekeeping operations;[6] and the 'Ten Rules: Code of Personal Conduct for Blue Helmets', also released in 1998, outlining general expectations for peacekeepers to dress, think, talk, act, and behave in a manner that preserves the dignity of a disciplined force.[7] These codes were largely aspirational and lacked clear enforcement mechanisms or reference to sexual misconduct, failing to provide the accountability necessary to prevent abuse.

In April 2002, the Inter-Agency Standing Committee (IASC) – established by the UN General Assembly in 1991 as a humanitarian coordination forum of the UN system,[8] comprising members from within and outside the UN – issued a landmark policy statement on protection from SEA in humanitarian

3 Jasmine-Kim Westendorf and Louise Searle, 'Sexual Exploitation and Abuse in Peace Operations: Trends, Policy Responses and Future Directions' (2017) 93 International Affairs 365, 366, citing Judy Ledgerwood, 'UN Peacekeeping Missions: the Lessons from Cambodia' (1994) AsiaPacific Issues no 11 (Honolulu, East-West Center).

4 Ibid, 366, citing Olivera Simic, *Regulation of Sexual Conduct in UN Peacekeeping Operations* (Springer 2012), 41.

5 Ibid, 367.

6 United Nations, We Are United Nations Peacekeepers <https://pseataskforce.org/uploads/tools/weareunpeacekeepers_undpko_english.pdf> accessed 12 December 2025.

7 United Nations, Ten Rules: Code of Personal Conduct for Blue Helmets <https://www.un.org/en/ethics/assets/pdfs/ten_rules.pdf> accessed 12 December 2025.

8 United Nations General Assembly Res 46/182 (19 December 1991) UN Doc A/RES/46/182.

crises.[9] This statement marked a turning point by clearly affirming the collective responsibility of humanitarian agencies and explicitly prohibiting SEA by all IASC staff and implementing partners.

The IASC policy introduced six core principles, which later became foundational in codes of conduct across the humanitarian sector.[10] These included: (i) "sexual exploitation and abuse by humanitarian workers constitute acts of gross misconduct and are therefore grounds for termination of employment"; (ii) "sexual activity with children (persons under the age of 18) is prohibited regardless of the age of majority or age of consent locally. Mistaken belief regarding the age of a child is not a defence"; (iii) "exchange of money, employment, goods, or services for sex, including sexual favours or other forms of humiliating, degrading or exploitative behaviour is prohibited. This includes exchange of assistance that is due to beneficiaries"; (iv) "any sexual relationship between those providing humanitarian assistance and protection and a person benefitting from such humanitarian assistance and protection that involves improper use of rank or position is prohibited. Such relationships undermine the credibility and integrity of humanitarian aid work"; (v) "where a humanitarian worker develops concerns or suspicions regarding sexual abuse or exploitation by a fellow worker, whether in the same agency or not, he or she must report such concerns via established agency reporting mechanisms"; and (vi) "humanitarian workers are obliged to create and maintain an environment which prevents sexual exploitation and abuse and promotes the implementation of their code of conduct. Managers at all levels have particular responsibilities to support and develop systems which maintain this environment".[11] It also called on humanitarian agencies to develop and enforce internal codes of conduct that reflect minimum behavioural standards and include disciplinary mechanisms.

1.2 UN Officials

As key players in upholding the mission and values of the organization, UN officials are entrusted with significant authority and responsibility, and their conduct directly impacts on the credibility, effectiveness and legitimacy of the

9 Inter-Agency Standing Committee, IASC Policy Statement on Protection from Sexual Abuse and Exploitation in Humanitarian Crises (Rome, 4 April 2002 – updated in 2019).

10 Inter-Agency Standing Committee, IASC Six Principles Relating to Sexual Exploitation and Abuse (23 September 2019) <https://interagencystandingcommittee.org/inter-agency-standing-committee/iasc-six-core-principles-relating-sexual-exploitation-and-abuse-2019> accessed 12 December 2025.

11 Ibid.

UN system. It is therefore not surprising that UN officials became a primary subject of an increasingly detailed body of standards and rules governing sexual misconduct, as part of a wide effort to ensure that the personnel selected and retained by the organization meet the requisite highest standards of integrity, efficiency and competence as required under Article 101(3) of the UN Charter.

Initially, the first major effort to establish rules of conduct for UN officials came in 1954, when the International Civil Service Advisory Board, which preceded the establishment of the International Civil Service Commission (ICSC), introduced the first version of the Standards of Conduct for the International Civil Service, outlining a rudimentary framework of rules. These standards were later revised by the ICSC in 2001, 2013 and 2025.[12] While the original 1954 version and even early revisions provided general guidance and expectations on appropriate conduct at workplace, they notably did not explicitly address sexual harassment or SEA. It was only in more recent years – particularly with the 2013 revision – that the standards more clearly emphasized the prohibition of abusive behaviour, including harassment. The standards of conduct did not include any reference to sexual misconduct, be it SEA or sexual harassment, until the latest 2025 revision (effective 1 January 2026).

The articulation of a legal framework applicable to sexual misconduct occurred outside the scope of the long-standing and established norms of conduct for UN officials. In November 2002, the Secretary-General issued a bulletin on the 'Status, basic rights and duties of United Nations staff members', reaffirming the foundational ethical obligations of UN personnel, including the duty to uphold the highest standards of conduct and integrity.[13] While this instrument did not directly address SEA or sexual harassment, it played a normative role by reinforcing the expectations of ethical behaviour within the UN system.

Similarly, in April 2003, the UN General Assembly adopted a resolution "[e]xpressing its grave concern at incidents of sexual exploitation and abuse against vulnerable populations".[14] The resolution called upon the Secretary-General to apply preventive and remedial measures to all peacekeeping and humanitarian operations, ensuring that reporting and investigative proced-

12 ICSC, Standards of Conduct for the International Civil Service <https://icsc.un.org/Resources/General/Publications/standardsE.pdf> accessed 1 May 2026.

13 UN Secretary-General's Bulletin, Status, basic rights and duties of United Nations staff members (1 November 2002), ST/SGB/2002/13 (subsequently replaced by ST/SGB/2016/9 issued on 21 July 2016).

14 United Nations General Assembly Res A/RES/57/306 (15 April 2003), 1.

ures were in place, and maintaining data on SEA.[15] It also encouraged all entities of the UN system and NGOs working under cooperation agreements with the UN humanitarian and peacekeeping operations to adopt similar preventive and remedial measures, including the implementation of codes of conduct aimed at eliminating SEA. This signalled a clear expectation that those standards of conduct and accountability should apply not only to UN staff but also to contractors, implementing partners and other affiliated personnel involved in UN operations.

The same year, the Secretary-General issued the bulletin 'Special measures for protection from sexual exploitation and sexual abuse' (2003 Secretary-General's bulletin on SEA), marking the UN's first comprehensive policy explicitly prohibiting SEA.[16] This bulletin incorporated the IASC principles and applied them to all UN Staff and to all categories of personnel working in UN peacekeeping and other operations. Moreover, it required that cooperating partners and contractors ensure that their personnel comply with the standards set out in the bulletin. The 2003 Secretary-General's bulletin on SEA introduced a zero tolerance policy toward SEA – intended to signal a categorical shift in the UN's stance toward sexual misconduct. It established a comprehensive set of explicit standards governing sexual conduct for UN personnel for the first time, signalling to the global community that the UN was serious about addressing sexual misconduct and was committed to preventing further violations against the vulnerable populations it aimed to protect and assist.

This bulletin outlined three key rules. Firstly, it categorically prohibited all sexual activity with children (defining a child as any person under the age of 18, regardless of the age of majority or age of consent locally). Secondly, it prohibited the exchange of sex for money, employment, goods or service. Thirdly, it strongly discouraged sexual relationships with those receiving assistance, as such relationships "are based on inherently unequal power dynamics" and "undermine the credibility and integrity of the work of the UN". The bulletin also emphasized the responsibility of UN leadership to take active steps to hold perpetrators accountable, including through referrals of cases to national authorities for criminal prosecution where appropriate. Furthermore, it obligated all non-UN entities or individuals working in cooperation with the UN to adhere to these standards.

---

15 Ibid, 2.

16 UN Secretary-General's Bulletin, Special measures for protection from sexual exploitation and sexual abuse (9 October 2003) SG/SGB/2003/13.

Despite these developments, the adoption of a zero tolerance policy by the UN does not necessarily result in a zero occurrence reality. Its practical implications, such as clarity of definitions, enforcement procedures and due process safeguards, remain underdeveloped and significant challenges in implementation and enforcement persist.

This article now examines the UN's evolving framework for addressing sexual misconduct (Section 2), beginning with the development of zero tolerance policies and the adoption of a victim-centred approach (Sections 2.1–2.2). It then reviews key initiatives introduced by the Secretary-General to strengthen the institutional response (Section 2.3). The analysis turns to the definitional categories of sexual misconduct – SEA and sexual harassment, and highlights the limitations of this binary typology, particularly with respect to uncategorized acts (Section 2.4). The article then explores the legal concept of consent and its boundaries (Section 2.5), followed by an examination of investigative procedures, protective measures, and available remedies for victims (Section 2.6). Building on this framework, the article further provides a detailed legal analysis of SEA (Section 3), including its definition, the applicable legal tests, and key tensions in UNAT jurisprudence (Sections 3.1–3.3). A parallel discussion follows on sexual harassment (Sections 4.1–4.3). The final part assesses how due process guarantees are implemented in practice, focusing on procedural rights such as notice, disclosure, administrative leave, standard and burden of proof, proportionality of sanctions, the right of appeal (Sections 5.1–5.5), and persistent tensions between accountability and fairness within the UN's internal justice system (Section 5.6).

2 UN Framework for Addressing Sexual Misconduct

The following section explores the evolution of the UN's approach to sexual misconduct by addressing: (i) the zero tolerance policy as a foundation for institutional response; (ii) the adoption of a victim-centred approach to support affected individuals; (iii) the initiatives taken by the Secretary-General to strengthen accountability; (iv) an analysis of the UN's typology of sexual misconduct, highlighting the challenges posed by acts that fall outside the established categories of SEA or sexual harassment; (v) the complexities surrounding the concept of consent; and (vi) the investigation procedures, protective measures and remedies available to those affected.

2.1 Zero Tolerance

As the leading international organization entrusted with maintaining international peace and security, and promoting human rights, the UN bears a heightened institutional responsibility to model exemplary standards of conduct. This responsibility is not merely aspirational but firmly grounded in the UN Charter and operationalized through staff regulations, rules, policies and general principles of administrative law.

The UN Charter mandates the organization to promote and encourage respect for human rights. Article 1(3) affirms that one of the purposes of the UN is to "achieve international cooperation in solving international problems of an economic, social, cultural or humanitarian character, and in promoting and encouraging respect for human rights and for fundamental freedoms for all without distinction as to race, sex, language or religion". Furthermore, Article 101(3) states that "the paramount consideration in the employment of the staff [...] shall be the necessity of securing the highest standards of efficiency, competence, and integrity".[17]

In fulfilling its mandates, the UN is required to promote rights externally but also to safeguard them internally, including by preventing and addressing all forms of sexual misconduct. This responsibility is integral to the UN's duty of care, which imposes both a legal and a moral obligation to provide a safe, secure, and respectful working environment for all personnel, free from harassment, abuse, all forms of discrimination, and sexual misconduct. Staff Regulation 1.2(b) further codifies this duty, requiring that "[s]taff members shall uphold the highest standards of efficiency, competence and integrity. The concept of integrity, in this context, includes but is not limited to probity, impartiality, fairness, honesty and truthfulness in all matters affecting their work and status".

At the core of the UN response to sexual misconduct lies the notion of 'zero tolerance' which underscores the organization's commitment to ensuring that any credible allegation – whether involving sexual exploitation, abuse, or harassment – is taken seriously, thoroughly investigated, and met with timely and appropriate disciplinary or administrative action. This approach is grounded in the organization's legal framework. The zero tolerance policy was first formally introduced and codified in the 2003 Secretary-General's bulletin on SEA which sets out accountability mechanisms for peacekeepers and other per-

---

17 Charter of the United Nations (adopted 26 June 1945, entered into force 25 October 1945), art 101(3).

sonnel engaged in field missions. The notion builds on the requirements of Article 101(3) of the UN Charter, echoed in Staff Regulation 1.2(b).

The UNAT case law sheds further light on the rationale behind the zero tolerance approach with respect to sexual misconduct.[18] In *Claude Cahn v. Secretary-General of the UN*, the UNAT has recalled that "[t]here is a commitment that all international organizations must have 'zero tolerance' for harassment in the workplace and will not tolerate conduct that can be construed as harassment, sexual harassment or abuse of authority. [...] The 'zero tolerance' policy is aimed at providing a safe environment for all United Nations employees, free from discrimination on any grounds and from harassment at work, including sexual harassment".[19]

The Tribunal also emphasized that the policy serves both retributive and preventative aims: "[t]he 'zero tolerance' policy [...] aims to tackle the issue of harassment in the workplace mainly by two methods. The first and more immediate one has the corrective purpose of addressing any possible inappropriate behaviour and applying the necessary measures according to the situation. The second and broader one has the preventative aim of promoting a positive work environment and preventing inappropriate behaviour in the workplace".[20]

Zero tolerance is thus also a manifestation of the organization's duty of care to ensure a harmonious, safe and secure work environment, free of harassment and sexual abuse, and protect staff members from any harm through appropriate preventive and remedial measures in each specific case.[21] The duty of care is an inherent part of the employment relationship and a funda-

---

18 *Appellant v. Secretary-General of the UN*, UNAT Judgment No 2022-UNAT-1216, para 35. See also, *Mbaigolmem v. Secretary-General of the UN*, UNAT Judgment No 2018-UNAT-819, para 33.

19 *Claude Cahn v. Secretary-General of the UN*, Judgment No 2023-UNAT-1329, paras 35 and 36. See also, Sergio Baltazar Arvizú Trevino v. Secretary-General of the UN, Judgment No 2022-UNAT-1231, para 39.

20 *Claude Cahn v. Secretary-General of the UN*, UNAT Judgment No 2023-UNAT-1329, para 61.

21 *Melanne Civic v. Secretary-General of the UN*, UNAT Judgment No 2020-UNAT-1069, para 73. See also, *Delaunay v. Registrar of the International Court of Justice*, UNAT Judgment No 2019-UNAT-939, para 59; *Cheikh Thiare v. Secretary-General of the UN*, UNAT Judgment No 2021-UNAT-1167, para 42; *Haq and Kane v. Secretary-General of the UN*, UNAT Judgment No 2019-UNAT-922, para 31.

mental condition of service.[22] It must be fulfilled with due diligence and without delay.[23]

In the seminal *Mbaigolmem* case, the Tribunal held: "The [United Nations] is entitled and obliged to pursue a severe approach to sexual harassment. The message therefore needs to be sent out clearly that staff members who sexually harass their colleagues should expect to lose their employment".[24] While this statement is a clear confirmation that loss of employment would be the expected sanction for established acts of sexual misconduct, the UNAT clarified in a subsequent judgment that a sanction for sexual misconduct may still be reviewed in case it is "excessive, abusive, discriminatory, or absurd in its severity".[25]

The UN's zero tolerance policy emphasizes the need for profound cultural transformation and the promotion of a 'speak-up' culture.[26] Under this policy, even behaviours that some might dismiss as mere 'jokes' or minor improprieties may amount to actionable harassment under the organization's standards. A striking illustration of this principle emerged in a 2023 appeal arising from a UN Secretariat official's lewd remarks and display of a sexually explicit image to colleagues, the United Nations Dispute Tribunal (UNDT), serving as the first-instance tribunal, characterized the conduct as benign horseplay and downgraded the sanction imposed by the organization. On appeal, the UNAT emphatically reversed the UNDT's decision, stressing that puerile and unwelcome sexual comments, coupled with the display of graphic sexual images, manifestly violate the professional standards of dignity and respect owed in a professional workplace.[27]

This case demonstrates that while the UN's rigorous enforcement of its sexual misconduct policies is critical, the implementation of the zero tolerance policy may at times be controversial and even criticized as overzealous, prompting broader discussions on how to best reconcile robust enforcement with principles of fairness, proportionality and due process. A comprehensive

22 *Haq and Kane v. Secretary-General of the UN*, UNAT Judgment No 2019-UNAT-922, para 31.

23 *Cheikh Thiare v. Secretary-General of the UN*, UNAT Judgment No 2021-UNAT-1167, para 42.

24 *Mbaigolmem v. Secretary-General of the UN*, UNAT Judgment No 2018-UNAT-819, para 33.

25 *Balint Szvetko v. Secretary-General of the UN*, UNAT Judgment No 2023-UNAT-1311, para 45, citing *Samandarov v. Secretary-General of the UN*, Judgment No 2018-UNAT-859, paras 23–25.

26 United Nations, 'Report of the Secretary-General: Special measures for protection from sexual exploitation and abuse' (14 February 2024) UN Doc A/78/774, para 6.

27 *Balint Szvetko v. Secretary-General of the UN*, Judgment No 2023-UNAT-1311.

approach for combating sexual misconduct is based on prevention and incorporates a range of measures including screening, training, awareness-raising, and risk assessment. Two key components of this system-wide effort include enhanced training programs and the use of two important tools, namely, the ClearCheck system[28] and the Inter-Agency Misconduct Disclosure Scheme.[29]

The ClearCheck system, operational since June 2018, is an online platform of a centralized database designed to facilitate the sharing of information across UN entities, system-wide, about individuals against whom allegations of SEA or sexual harassment have been substantiated. It aims to prevent the hiring or re-hiring of such individuals within the UN system. The database also includes data on individuals with pending allegations who separate from the organization before investigation or disciplinary proceedings are concluded.

Similarly, the Inter-Agency Misconduct Disclosure Scheme enables participating organizations to exchange relevant information about individuals who were found to have committed SEA or sexual harassment. This mechanism supports informed decision-making in the recruitment process and helps prevent perpetrators from moving between organizations undetected.

Ultimately, the zero tolerance policy is a core expression of the UN's broader commitment to uphold the dignity, safety and rights of all individuals it serves and of those who serve within in. It affirms the UN's legal and ethical responsibility to maintain the highest standards of integrity, accountability and conduct, in accordance with the UN Charter and the principles of international civil service.

2.2 Victim-Centred Approach

Consistent with the duty of care and central to the UN's evolving response to sexual misconduct is its adoption of a victim-centred approach, designed to ensure that policies and practices prioritize the rights, dignity, interests and needs of individuals who have experienced SEA or sexual harassment. This commitment has been explicitly and repeatedly affirmed at the highest levels of UN leadership. In his 2017 report on special measures for protection from sexual exploitation and abuse, the Secretary-General stated:

---

28 UN System Chief Executives Board for Coordination, ClearCheck System <https://unsceb.org/screening-database-clearcheck> accessed 12 December 2025.

29 Inter-Agency Standing Committee, Inter-Agency Misconduct Disclosure Scheme <https://interagencystandingcommittee.org/sites/default/files/migrated/2018-11/inter-agency_misconduct_disclosure_scheme_final_draft_002.pdf> accessed 12 December 2025.

> Our priority first and foremost must be to strengthen the support that we give to victims of sexual exploitation and abuse [...]. I intend to provide victims a platform for their voice that the world will not be able to ignore. I will meet personally with victims to hear from them directly. I will let these survivors know that their protection is our priority and that going forward, the United Nations will be at their side to support them as they go through the healing process and rebuild their lives.[30]

2.2.1 Victim-Centred Approach in SEA

In the context of SEA, the primary aim of the UN's victim-centred approach is to empower victims, ensure that their voices are heard, and address the harm they have suffered while protecting them from retaliation, discrimination or re-traumatization.[31] This model implies that victims' choices are given central priority and that their informed consent is respected regarding their participation in addressing and resolving misconduct matters, as well as in assessing and determining protection and support measures.

The adoption of the Comprehensive Strategy on Assistance and Support to Victims of SEA in 2007 institutionalized these commitments by providing a coordinated framework for medical care, psychosocial support, legal assistance, and the provision of basic needs such as food, clothing, and shelter.[32] This strategy applies to a broad range of personnel, including UN staff, consultants, volunteers, contractors, peacekeepers and partner organizations.

In 2017, the Secretary-General's report on special measures for protection from SEA marked a new era with normative and operational changes brought about to address identified institutional deficiencies. Further advancing this agenda, in August 2017, the first Victims' Rights Advocate was appointed by the Secretary-General, and the Office of the Victims' Rights Advocate (OVRA) began its work in January 2018 with a specific mandate to ensure a system-wide, survivor-focused response.[33] OVRA's work aims to amplify victim's voices, monitor service delivery and coordinate assistance efforts with peacekeeping missions, UN country teams and local civil society partners. To operationalize these goals in field operations, Senior Victims' Rights Officers have

30 United Nations, 'Report of the Secretary-General: Special measures for protection from sexual exploitation and abuse' (28 February 2017) UN Doc A/71/818, paras 20–21.

31 United Nations General Assembly Res 62/214 (21 December 2007) UN Doc A/RES/62/214.

32 Ibid.

33 United Nations, Office of the Victims' Rights Advocate, Annual Report 2023 <https://www.un.org/preventing-sexual-exploitation-and-abuse/content/annual-reports-victims-rights-advocate> accessed 12 December 2025.

been appointed in several duty stations, to serve as primary points of contact with victims and survivors on the ground and play a critical role in ensuring that a victim-centred approach is fully integrated into the UN's support activities.[34]

These efforts complement the Trust Fund in Support of Victims of SEA that was established by the UN Secretary-General in March 2016.[35] The Trust Fund is not intended to provide individual compensation but rather serves to bridge service gaps by funding essential assistance to complainants, victims and children born as a result of SEA.

However, despite these institutional efforts, victim services remain underfunded and inconsistently implemented across different contexts and regions. Gaps in local capacity, fluctuating political will, and the lack of consistent long-term funding mechanisms continue to hinder the realization of a comprehensive, victim-centred response to SEA within the UN system.

2.2.2 Victim-Centred Approach in Sexual Harassment

While SEA typically arises in peacekeeping or humanitarian settings, the UN's approach to sexual harassment has also been restructured to incorporate a victim-centred orientation, particularly within institutional and professional environments. Recognizing systemic gaps, the Chief Executives Board (CEB) Task Force on Addressing Sexual Harassment within the organizations of the UN system was established in 2017 by the Secretary-General. Its mandate was to coordinate a system-wide strategy for preventing and responding to sexual harassment, ensuring consistency, transparency and accountability across agencies.[36]

The CEB Task Force delivered the following actions for UN system-wide implementation:

(a) a UN system model policy on sexual harassment;
(b) a system-wide screening database to prevent the rehiring of perpetrators of sexual harassment;

---

34 United Nations, Senior Victims' Rights Officers <https://www.un.org/preventing-sexual-exploitation-and-abuse/content/senior-victims%E2%80%99-rights-officers> accessed 12 December 2025.

35 United Nations, Trust Fund in Support of Victims of Sexual Exploitation and Abuse <https://www.un.org/preventing-sexual-exploitation-and-abuse/content/trust-fund> accessed 12 December 2025.

36 UN System Chief Executives Board for Coordination, Summary of Deliberations: First Regular Session of 2018 (24 July 2018) UN Doc CEB/2018/1, Annex III.

(c) a harmonized mechanism for system-wide collection and analysis of data;
(d) guidelines for managers on prevention of, and response to, sexual harassment in the workplace and helplines and hotlines for staff;
(e) a draft model code of conduct to prevent sexual harassment during and in relation to United Nations events; and
(f) a commitment to strengthening and harmonizing investigatory capacity and improving the quality of investigation, in the next phase of the work of the task force.[37]

One of the CEB Task Force's central outputs was the 2018 Model Policy on Sexual Harassment for the UN system, which outlines guiding principles including procedural fairness, confidentiality, support to complainants, and prompt disciplinary action.[38] Complementing this was the publication of the Secretary-General's bulletin on 'Addressing discrimination, harassment, including sexual harassment, and abuse of authority' (2019 Secretary-General's bulletin on addressing sexual harassment) which articulates the UN's organizational commitments to creating a safe and respectful workplace. It obliges managers to take protective measures for complainants, including adjustments to reporting lines, security arrangements and leave entitlements, while also guaranteeing access to support services and protection from retaliation.[39]

However, the implementation of victim-centred justice within the UN internal legal framework – especially in relation to sexual harassment – reveals inherent tensions between empowering victims and upholding due process rights. In line with victim-centred principles, the UNAT case law has stressed that in relation to complaints and grievances, it is the complainant, not the employing international organization, who has the right to choose the appropriate process although managers or supervisors are obligated to take all necessary action to address any known incident of sexual misconduct in the

37 UN System Chief Executives Board for Coordination, 'Addressing Sexual Harassment' <https://unsceb.org/topics/addressing-sexual-harassment> accessed 12 December 2025.

38 UN System Chief Executives Board for Coordination, UN System Model Policy on Sexual Harassment <https://unsceb.org/un-system-model-policy-sexual-harassment> accessed 12 December 2025. The UN System Model Policy on Sexual Harassment was endorsed by the UN System Chief Executives Board for Coordination in 2018. The CEB is the highest-level coordination forum of the UN system, composed of the executive heads of UN specialized agencies, funds and program. The Model Policy was developed by the CEB Task Force on Addressing Sexual Harassment within the Organizations of the UN Common System.

39 UN Secretary-General's Bulletin, Addressing discrimination, harassment, including sexual harassment, and abuse of authority (10 September 2019) ST/SGB/2019/8, secs 5.7–5.12.

workplace.[40] This may sometimes conflict with other legal requirements, particularly regarding the UNAT's recognition of the legal duty to report complaints or allegations of sexual misconduct so that they can be investigated, as this duty to report may limit the prospect of informal resolution in cases where the victim desires such a course of action.[41] Nonetheless, the 2019 Secretary-General's bulletin on addressing sexual harassment provides that where a formal report of possible sexual harassment is submitted by a person other than the affected individual, the investigators "shall normally seek the views of the affected individual before deciding whether to proceed with an investigation".[42]

The UNAT case law further clarifies that while affected persons have the right to bring their complaints to the competent authority within the organization and request action against the alleged offender, they may not, as a general rule, compel the organization to initiate disciplinary action or impose a specific measure on the alleged perpetrator.[43] This is explained by the fact that disciplinary sanctions are considered administrative decisions directed at the staff member who committed the misconduct, not the complainant. The organization retains discretion to conduct a fact-finding investigation, following a preliminary assessment, if there are sufficient grounds or reasons to believe that a staff member has engaged in prohibited conduct.[44] Similarly, the UNAT has consistently held that the administrative decision to impose sanctions or disciplinary measures on other staff members is a prerogative of the UN in the regular exercise of its administrative discretion, not of other staff members, even though they may also have been victims.[45]

Notwithstanding this, a complainant or affected person may challenge the outcome of an investigation process and in particular the findings as to whether or not sexual harassment occurred. The UNAT has affirmed that "once the investigation has been concluded, its outcome and administrative consequences, as well as any related acts or omissions, can be challenged in their own right via management evaluation and before the Dispute and

---

40 *Parker v. Secretary-General of the UN*, UNAT Judgment No 2010-UNAT-012, para 41.

41 *Richard Loto v. Secretary-General of the UN*, UNAT Judgment No 2023-UNAT-1362, para 94.

42 UN Secretary-General's Bulletin, Addressing discrimination, harassment, including sexual harassment, and abuse of authority (note 39 above), sec 5.5 (c).

43 *Mihai Nastase v. Secretary-General of the UN*, UNAT Judgment No 2023-UNAT-1373, para 34.

44 Ibid, para 35. See also, *Nadeau v. Secretary-General of the UN*, UNAT Judgment No 2017-UNAT-733/Corr. 1, para 33.

45 *AAJ v. Secretary-General of the UN*, UNAT Judgment No 2023-UNAT-1317, para 38.

Appeals Tribunals".[46] Once it is established that an affected individual has the right to appeal the outcome of an investigation, it then is necessary to determine the scope of procedural rights and information which should be made accessible to the complainant to enable meaningful review of the administrative decision.

While a victim of sexual harassment does not have standing to appeal the adequacy of a disciplinary sanction imposed on the offender, or lack thereof, the UNAT case law is clear that "in a case of a serious and reasonable accusation, a staff member [does] have a right to an investigation against another staff member, and this process may be subject to judicial review", and that they may appeal delays and flaws in the investigative processes or the lack of adequate protective measures following the filing of a complaint.[47] Thus, while complainants do not have the right to contest the specific disciplinary measures imposed, they have standing to challenge aspects of the process and findings, even when they perceive those measures as insufficient.

This reflects the structural limitations within the UN's administrative justice system, where victim-centred ideals are necessarily balanced against the rights of the alleged perpetrator and the procedural prerogatives of the UN. It underscores the continuing challenge of reconciling institutional accountability with victims and survivor's empowerment, and the need for clear procedural safeguards that do not dilute the principles of a victim-centred justice.

2.3 Secretary-General's Initiatives in Addressing Sexual Misconduct

The UN has undertaken a series of reforms and initiatives to address sexual misconduct, encompassing both SEA and sexual harassment. These efforts, spearheaded by successive Secretaries-General, aim to reinforce accountability, enhance victim support, and foster a culture of zero tolerance.

2.3.1 Early Reforms and Institutional Foundations

In March 2005, the Secretary-General commissioned the Zeid Report, which laid out a comprehensive strategy to eliminate SEA in UN peacekeeping oper-

46 *Auda v. Secretary-General of the UN*, UNAT Judgment No 2017-UNAT-786, para 35; *Masylkanova v. Secretary-General of the UN*, UNAT Judgment No 2014-UNAT-412, para 18.

47 *Nadeau v. Secretary-General of the UN*, UNAT Judgment No 2017-UNAT-733/Corr. 1, para 33.

ations.[48] The Zeid Report identified systemic issues related to a range of misconduct, including a lack of awareness of UN standards of conduct, unclear procedures for making complaints, incomplete data on misconduct and insufficient investigative capacity in peacekeeping missions. It recommended reforms for both the UN Secretariat and Member States. One of the first steps in response was the creation of the Conduct and Discipline Unit at UN Headquarters and with a presence at field missions in November 2005.[49]

In February 2008, the Secretary-General issued the bulletin 'Prohibition of discrimination, harassment, including sexual harassment and abuse of authority' (2008 Secretary-General's bulletin on prohibiting sexual harassment).[50] This bulletin formally prohibited misconduct in the workplace, including discrimination, harassment, sexual harassment and abuse of authority. It came in response to increasing awareness of workplace abuses and the need to ensure that all staff members and non-staff personnel are treated with dignity and respect and are aware of their role and responsibilities in maintaining a workplace free of any form of sexual harassment.

2.3.2 Strengthening Accountability and Victim Support

In 2015, the Secretary-General's report to the UN General Assembly on special measures for protection from SEA, introduced initiatives including enhanced personnel vetting, expanded training, creating new tools to enhance accountability and improved support for victims.[51] The 2016 Secretary-General's report to the UN General Assembly expanded on this by adding proposals for increased transparency and victim support and the need for Member States to be effective partners in achieving financial, administrative and criminal

48 United Nations, 'A comprehensive strategy to eliminate future sexual exploitation and abuse in United Nations peacekeeping operations' (24 March 2005) UN Doc A/59/710. Prince Zeid Ra'ad Zeid Al-Hussein, Permanent Representative of Jordan, acted as adviser to the UN Secretary-General and assisted him in addressing the problem of sexual exploitation and abuse by United Nations peacekeeping personnel.

49 The Conduct and Discipline Unit is a specialized office within the UN Secretariat, tasked with promoting high standards of conduct among UN personnel, particularly in peacekeeping operations and field missions, and with preventing and responding to misconduct including SEA.

50 UN Secretary-General's Bulletin, Prohibition of discrimination, harassment, including sexual harassment, and abuse of authority (11 February 2008) ST/SGB/2008/5.

51 United Nations, 'Report of the Secretary-General: Special measures for protection from sexual exploitation and sexual abuse' (13 February 2015, reissued on 18 March 2015) UN Doc A/69/779.

accountability for those who commit acts of SEA.[52] Notably, it marked the first time the UN disclosed the nationality of military and police personnel implicated in credible SEA allegations.

Another significant turning point occurred in 2015 following allegations of sexual violence by non-UN foreign forces in the Central African Republic. In response, the Secretary-General appointed an independent panel to review the UN's handling of these allegations, leading to recommendations for systemic reforms to prevent and respond to SEA.[53] In February 2016, the Secretary-General appointed, for a time-bound period, a Special Coordinator on Improving the UN Response to SEA, with a mandate to organize, unify and prioritize the UN system-wide measures for prevention and response.[54]

On 18 September 2017, the Secretary-General convened a High-Level Meeting on combating SEA to demonstrate solidarity of the international community in condemning and committing to combat this issue. The event recognized signatories to a 'Voluntary Compact between the UN and Member States', emphasizing shared principles and specific commitments for protection from SEA.[55] As of 15 December 2021, 105 Member States have signed the Voluntary Compact.[56] Additionally, the Secretary-General announced the 'Circle of Leadership on the prevention of and response to SEA in UN operations', comprising Heads of State and Government committed to ending impunity and strengthening preventive measures.[57]

52 United Nations, 'Report of the Secretary-General: Special measures for protection from sexual exploitation and sexual abuse' (19 February 2016) A/70/729.

53 Ibid, para 83.

54 Ibid, para 87.

55 The Compact is a demonstration of the political will to prevent sexual exploitation and abuse, demand accountability and provide meaningful support to victims. It sets out a statement of commitment based on shared values, as well as specific commitments on the part of both the United Nations and signatory Member States. See UN, 'Voluntary Compact' <https://www.un.org/preventing-sexual-exploitation-and-abuse/content/voluntary-compact> accessed 12 December 2025.

56 Member States Signatories to the Voluntary Compact with the Secretary-General of the United Nations on the Commitment to Eliminate Sexual Exploitation and Abuse (As of 15 December 2021) <https://www.un.org/preventing-sexual-exploitation-and-abuse/sites/www.un.org.preventing-sexual-exploitation-and-abuse/files/voluntary_compact_countries_list_15_december_2021.pdf> accessed 12 December 2025.

57 United Nations, 'Report of the Secretary-General: Special measures for protection from sexual exploitation and sexual abuse' (28 February 2017) A/71/818, para 18. See also, UN, 'Circle of Leadership' <https://www.un.org/preventing-sexual-exploitation-and-abuse/content/circle-leadership> accessed 12 December 2025.

2.3.3 Addressing Sexual Harassment across the UN System

In September 2019, the Secretary-General issued the 2019 Secretary-General's bulletin on addressing sexual harassment.[58] This bulletin superseded and replaced the earlier 2008 harassment policy[59] as part of the Secretary-General's efforts to strengthen accountability and improve internal practices in response to the 'Me Too' movement and increased demands for accountability, transparency, and a victim-centred approach.

Since 2016, there has been a marked shift in the UN's approach, most notably with the 2017 strategy launched by the Secretary-General. This strategy represented a necessary transformation from a framework aimed at minimizing reputational harm to the UN, to a model which is victim-centred and that acknowledges the UN's responsibility and accountability towards victims of SEA.

Despite the achievements made through the Secretary-General's initiatives, operationalizing the victim-centred approach on the ground continues to present significant challenges. Coordination mechanisms, while developed at the headquarters, are not always effectively translated into field practice. Inconsistencies in the implementation of policies, limited local resources, fragmented data collection and the persistence of siloed responses between UN entities and national actors have all hindered the ability to ensure equal access to justice and support for victims across contexts.

2.4 UN Typology of Sexual Misconduct and the Challenge of Uncategorized Acts

Throughout this article, the broad term 'sexual misconduct' is used as an all-encompassing notion covering all acts and behaviours of a sexual nature that breach the professional standards of conduct applicable to UN officials. However, under the UN legal framework, sexual misconduct is not an officially codified terminology. Rather, the UN's legal framework on sexual misconduct has a narrower scope, centred around two categories of prohibited acts, na-

58 UN Secretary-General's Bulletin, Addressing discrimination, harassment, including sexual harassment, and abuse of authority (note 39 above).

59 While the Secretary-General's Bulletin ST/SGB/2019/8 (note 39 above) is the current and applicable policy, the Secretary-General's Bulletin ST/SGB/2008/5 (note 50 above) may still be referenced in legal proceedings concerning incidents that took place prior to 10 September 2019.

mely SEA and sexual harassment. The binary categorization of sexual misconduct is reflected, respectively, in Staff Rules 1.2(e) and 1.2(f).[60]

Staff Rule 1.2(e) deals with SEA and provides that:

> Both sexual exploitation and sexual abuse are prohibited. Sexual activity with children (persons under the age of 18) is prohibited regardless of the age of majority or the age of consent locally. Mistaken belief in the age of a child is not a defence. The exchange of money, employment, goods or services for sex, including sexual favours or other forms of humiliating, degrading or exploitative behaviour, is prohibited. United Nations staff members are obliged to create and maintain an environment that prevents sexual exploitation and sexual abuse.

Staff Rule 1.2(f) deals with harassment and reads as follows: "[a]ny form of discrimination or harassment, including sexual or gender harassment, as well as abuse in any form at the workplace or in connection with work, is prohibited". Further internal policies set out in greater detail the definitions and the constitutive elements of these two forms of sexual misconduct, such as the 2003 Secretary-General's bulletin on SEA[61] and the 2019 Secretary-General's bulletin on addressing sexual harassment.[62]

There are noteworthy limitations to the UN's focus on only two main categories of sexual offences. As the organization operates across diverse contexts – including conflict-affected areas and vulnerable populations – it cannot be ruled out that other forms of sexual misconduct may emerge that fall outside the scope of the two currently defined categories.

One practical example involves acts of rape and sexual assault which, while indisputably constituting serious violations of the standards of conduct, are not specifically conceptualized within the UN's internal policies and legal instruments. A case heard by the UNAT involving two staff members of the United Nations Population Fund (UNFPA) exposes the inadequacy of the UN binary approach.[63] The case concerned a report of rape, sexual assault and harassment by a UNFPA staff member against another member of personnel. The complainant alleged that the offender had locked her in a hotel room

60 UN Staff Regulations and Staff Rules, including provisional Staff Rules of the UN (1 January 2023) <https://docs.un.org/en/ST/SGB/2023/1> accessed 12 December 2025.

61 UN Secretary-General's Bulletin, Special measures for protection from sexual exploitation and sexual abuse (note 16 above).

62 UN Secretary-General's Bulletin, Addressing discrimination, harassment, including sexual harassment, and abuse of authority (note 39 above).

63 *AAE v. Secretary-General of the UN*, UNAT Judgment No 2023-UNAT-1332.

preventing her from leaving and forcing her to engage in sexual intercourse. In characterizing the allegations, the Tribunal only contemplated the organization's rules on sexual harassment and SEA, even though there was no evidence of power differential justifying the invocation of the notion of SEA. The Tribunal ultimately found that the offender had engaged "in non-consensual sex with the Complainant, amounting to sexual assault".[64] The Tribunal's approach is questionable, as it is not unreasonable to argue that the facts alleged did not amount to SEA and that sexual harassment only formed part of the allegations. Hence, the gravity and intensity of the acts of rape and sexual assault were neither properly nor fully captured by the Tribunal's characterization of misconduct.

Importantly, the case highlights a broader policy issue – there remains considerable uncertainty as to whether every instance of rape or sexual assault would fall within the definitions of sexual harassment or SEA. Neither of these two categories captures the full range of non-consensual sexual acts or behaviours as their definitions are qualified by additional requirements that narrow their scope. Presumably, uncodified forms of sexual misconduct which are not explicitly listed in the internal rules or codes of conduct but nonetheless violate the core professional duties of UN officials may still be punishable, under 'catch-all provisions' which allow organizations to address misconduct not explicitly enumerated but clearly inconsistent with the values and duties of international public service. This is the case of UN Staff Regulation 1.2(b) which requires staff members to "uphold the highest standards of efficiency, competence and integrity". That being said, the formal adoption and codification of a more broadly defined concept of 'sexual misconduct' as an all-encompassing term into the UN Staff Regulations and Rules would not only align with the increasing use of the terminology by the UNDT and UNAT but also ensure consistency with the organization's messaging and unwavering commitment to tackle all forms of sexual misconduct, as serious breaches of professional and ethical standards.

2.5 Concept of Consent and Its Limits

A core common denominator to all forms of sexual offences is the unwelcome nature of the act or the lack of valid consent from the victim, or both. In this regard, consent must be informed, freely given, and continuous. Passive behaviour by the victim, such as silence or the absence of verbal or physical

64 Ibid, para 136.

resistance, is generally insufficient to establish consent.[65] Rather, consent must be demonstrated through unambiguous positive actions, and it requires "a voluntary agreement [...] to engage in the sexual activity in question in the form of actual statements, actions or other evidence".[66] In this context, the UNAT clarifies that "the law cannot take silence, passive, or ambiguous conduct as consent" which must be defined as a voluntary agreement, evidenced through statements, actions, or other forms of clear indication.[67] The Tribunal further acknowledges that the determination of consent to a given sexual activity will depend on the overall evidence and the specific circumstances of each case.

There are also circumstances where it cannot be argued that consent has been legally given. This includes, for instance, the case of child, early or forced marriage. Developments in this area are particularly noteworthy. Until 1 January 2023, Staff Rule 1.2(e) allowed recognition of a marriage of a staff member to a person under the age of 18, provided that the person in question had reached the age of majority or legal consent under the relevant national law.

In January 2023, the Secretary-General introduced temporary Staff Rules which removed the exemption of legally married persons under the age of 18 from the application of SEA rules.[68] The amendment to UN Staff Rule 1.2(e) was explained by the necessity of aligning UN personnel policies with the strict prohibitions set out in General Assembly resolution 73/153 on child, early and forced marriage, calling upon States to "develop and implement holistic, comprehensive and coordinated responses, strategies and policies to prevent and end child, early and forced marriage" and to protect the rights of affected individuals.[69] The provisional rules were confirmed and entered into effect on 1 January 2023.[70]

Reflecting this change, Staff Rule 1.2(e) provides that "both sexual exploitation and sexual abuse are prohibited. Sexual activity with children (persons under the age of 18) is prohibited regardless of the age of majority or the age of consent locally. Mistaken belief in the age of a child is not a defence".[71] The UN considers that valid consent cannot be presumed in situations involving children or any relationship marked by an inherent power imbalance. These situ-

65 Ibid, para 129.
66 Ibid, para 131.
67 *AAE v. Secretary-General of the UN*, UNAT Judgment No 2023-UNAT-1332, para 130.
68 UN Staff Regulations and Staff Rules (note 60 above), para 1.2.
69 United Nations General Assembly Res on Child, Early and Forced Marriage (17 December 2018) UN Doc A/RES/73/153, para 2.
70 UN Staff Regulations and Staff Rules (note 60 above), art XII.
71 Ibid, Rule 1.2(e).

ations are categorically prohibited and fall outside the scope of acceptable conduct under the UN's zero tolerance policy.

These amendments to UN internal rules on SEA, though representing a significant and abrupt policy change, do not appear to have received adequate attention. The absence of transitional measures and the potential retrospective effect of the amendments on situations previously covered by exemptions are particularly problematic. UN personnel legally married to a person under the age of 18 and exempted from the scope of UN Staff Rule 1.2(e) now fall under the reach of SEA rules and oddly find themselves in serious breach of their professional standards.

Aside from the legal age of marriage, the UNAT enumerated several other scenarios where consent cannot be deemed to have been satisfied, including: (i) when there has been no attempt to obtain consent, and the activity is clearly forced; (ii) where an individual not involved in the activity expresses consent on behalf of the complainant; (iii) when the complainant lacks capacity to provide consent; (iv) when an individual induces the complainant to engage in the activity by abusing a position of trust, power, or authority; and (v) where the complainant communicates, by words or conduct, an express lack of agreement to engage in or continue the activity.[72]

2.6 Investigation, Protections and Remedies

Importantly, as previously noted, the UN owes a duty of care towards its personnel and must honour its commitment to provide a safe and secure working environment, free from discrimination on any grounds and all forms of sexual misconduct. Protective measures must be effective, timely and available to both the complainant and any affected individuals, without requiring them to establish the veracity of their allegations as a precondition for receiving assistance.

In this regard, the 2019 Secretary-General's bulletin on addressing sexual harassment contemplates a range of interim measures, which may be implemented at any time following receipt of the report of misconduct, to protect the integrity of investigations, prevent the occurrence or repetition of possible prohibited conduct and address risks of possible retaliation.[73] These measures include physical separation of the alleged offender and the affected individual and reassignment of either person after having received their consent; insti-

72 *AAE v. Secretary-General of the UN*, UNAT Judgment No 2023-UNAT-1332, para 131.

73 UN Secretary-General's Bulletin, Addressing discrimination, harassment, including sexual harassment, and abuse of authority (note 39 above), sec 6.6.

tuting flexible working arrangements; granting or suggesting annual or special leave to either person; and implementing temporary changes in reporting lines or placement of the alleged offender on administrative leave.

Whether or not the UN is under an obligation to take protective measures, and the appropriateness and adequacy of any such measures may be subject to judicial review. The standard of judicial review, however, is not clear.[74] The UNDT recognized that while the UN is required to take protective measures, the nature and extent of such measures depend on the facts and circumstances. The Tribunal considered that these are administrative decisions subject to review for manifest excess of discretion or procedural irregularity but not automatically subject to reversal.[75]

Importantly, the UN has a duty to protect its staff from sexual misconduct and a failure to fulfil this duty may result in award of compensation. The organization's responsibility to implement adequate protective measures is distinct from the decision regarding the outcome of the investigative or disciplinary process. For example, in a case where the UN's response was found to be delayed or inadequate to prevent harm to a complainant, the UNAT awarded compensation for moral damages.[76] In another case, the complainant successfully demonstrated harm caused by the organization's failure to act promptly notwithstanding being made aware of a harmful working environment.[77]

Affected persons may also be awarded compensation for pecuniary losses and moral damages. The UNAT, however, imposes a significant limitation on compensation awards: it does not award damages for the actual harm suffered as a direct consequence from the sexual acts committed by the offender. Instead, compensation can only be awarded for harm stemming from a contested administrative decision found to be unlawful,[78] and even then, shall be supported by three elements: the existence of harm; an illegal administrative decision; and a nexus between the two. Furthermore, the UNAT imposes strict admissibility criteria for the establishment of harm. For moral damages, it refuses to give any weight to contemporaneous exchanges or statements by a complainant and requires that "there is evidence produced to the Tribunal, predominantly by way of a medical or psychological report of harm, stress or anxiety caused to the employee, which can be directly linked, or reasonably

74 *Appellant v. Secretary-General of the UN*, UNAT Judgment No 2021-UNAT-1137.

75 *Appellant v. Secretary-General of the UN*, UNDT Judgment No UNDT/2020/094, upheld by UNAT Judgment No 2021-UNAT-1137.

76 *Delaunay v. ICJ*, UNAT Judgment No 2019-UNAT-939.

77 *Claude Cahn v. Secretary-General of the UN*, UNAT Judgment No 2023-UNAT-1329.

78 See *Coleman v. Secretary-General of the UN*, UNAT Judgment No 2022-UNAT-1228, para 44.

attributed, to a breach of his or her substantive or procedural rights".[79] The UNAT's focus on medical evidence as the main source of evidence, to the exclusion of other forms of evidence, is questionable.

The multiple layers of restrictive requirements imposed by the UNAT in respect of damages place a high and often inaccessible burden on claimants, thereby precluding compensation as an effective remedy to victims. It may even be viewed as disincentivizing the reporting of harm, particularly in cases involving sensitive issues like harassment, SEA or emotional distress.

Whilst SEA first emerged as a critical issue in peacekeeping operations in 1993, incidents of SEA in subsequent peace operations prompted the continuous development of internal policies, evolving from prevention efforts to enforcement and accountability measures, and more recently, to approaches addressing the impact of SEA on survivors. A notable milestone in this policy evolution is the United Nations Protocol on the Provision of Assistance to Victims of Sexual Exploitation and Abuse, issued in December 2019.[80]

The Protocol establishes a coordinated, system-wide framework to ensure that victims receive immediate assistance and support in a manner that is "victim-centred, rights-based, age, disability and gender sensitive, non-discriminatory and culturally appropriate". It further emphasizes that "the rights and best interests of victims shall guide how assistance and support are designed and provided" and that such support to child victims (under age 18) shall be provided in a manner "consistent with the rights enshrined in the Convention on the Rights of the Child, in particular the 'best interests of the child'".[81]

To operationalize the Protocol, UNICEF led the development of a technical note providing practical guidance on implementation of the Protocol to Special Representatives of the Secretary General, Resident and Humanitarian Coordinators, UN Country Teams and Humanitarian Country Teams, PSEA coordinators and other relevant stakeholders involved in victim assistance

---

79 Ibid, para 42. See also, *Auda v. Secretary-General of the UN*, UNAT Judgment No 2017-UNAT-787, para 64 (holding that "[g]enerally speaking, the testimony of an applicant alone without corroboration by independent evidence (expert or otherwise) affirming that non-pecuniary harm has indeed occurred is not satisfactory proof to support an award of damages").

80 United Nations, United Nations Protocol on the Provision of Assistance to Victims of Sexual Exploitation and Abuse (12 December 2019) <https://www.un.org/en/pdfs/UN%20Victim%20Assistance%20Protocol_English_Final.pdf> accessed 12 December 2025.

81 Ibid, art 3.1.

for women and children.[82] These initiatives underscore the UN's commitment not only to preventing and responding to SEA, but also to upholding the dignity and rights of survivors through comprehensive support mechanism.

3 Sexual Exploitation and Abuse (SEA)

This section addresses SEA within the UN framework by examining (i) the definition and scope of such misconduct; (ii) the legal standards applied when addressing allegations of SEA; and (iii) the tensions and ambiguities that arise in practice.

3.1 Definition and Scope of SEA

SEA constitutes a category of sexual misconduct defined in the 2003 Secretary-General's bulletin on SEA.[83] Section 1 of the bulletin defines sexual exploitation as "any actual or attempted abuse of a position of vulnerability, differential power, or trust, for sexual purposes, including but not limited to, profiting monetarily, socially or politically from sexual exploitation of another" and sexual abuse as "the actual or threatened physical intrusion of a sexual nature, whether by force or under unequal or coercive conditions".[84] SEA constitutes acts of serious misconduct and is strictly prohibited under the UN regulatory framework. SEA violates universally recognized international legal norms and is explicitly prohibited under the regulatory framework of the UN and other international organizations. Since the issuance of the 2003 Secretary-General bulletin on SEA, the UN has established a zero tolerance approach to all forms of SEA.

Section 3.2(a) of the bulletin provides that in order to protect the most vulnerable populations, especially women and children, "[s]exual exploitation and sexual abuse constitute acts of serious misconduct and are therefore grounds for disciplinary measures, including summary dismissal". Section 3.2 (d) further provides that "[s]exual relationships between United Nations staff

---

82 UNICEF, Technical Note on the Implementation of the UN Protocol on the Provision of Assistance to Victims of SEA (October 2021) <https://www.un.org/preventing-sexual-exploitation-and-abuse/sites/www.un.org.preventing-sexual-exploitation-and-abuse/files/technical_note_on_the_implementation_of_the_un_protocol_on_the_provision_of_assistance_to_victims_of_sea_eng.pdf> accessed 12 December 2025.

83 UN Secretary-General's Bulletin, Special measures for protection from sexual exploitation and sexual abuse (note 16 above).

84 Ibid.

and beneficiaries of assistance, since they are based on inherently unequal power dynamics, undermine the credibility and integrity of the work of the United Nations and are strongly discouraged". The applicable legal framework governing SEA is further detailed in Staff Rule 1.2, which elaborates on the expected standards of conduct. As noted in Section 2.4 of this Article, Staff Rule 1.2(e) prohibits all forms of SEA and obliges UN staff to create and maintain an environment that prevents such misconduct.

This provision does not apply to all forms of sexual harassment or degrading behaviour, but more specifically to different forms of SEA. For example, while Staff Rule 1.2(e) governs misconduct involving beneficiaries and other vulnerable populations, including transactional sex and conduct marked by power imbalances, Staff Rule 1.2(f) focuses on sexual harassment and abuse in any form at the workplace or in connection with work. In interpreting these provisions, the UNDT clarified that Staff Rule 1.2(e) applies to "sexual relations exploiting systematic inequality, such as between peacekeepers and the local population, and particularly where transactional exchange is involved".[85] Conversely, the UNDT added that workplace relations between two staff members, even with uneven positions, are governed by Staff Rule 1.2(f). This position was further affirmed by the UNAT when considering that "[t]he UNDT did not err in deciding that in the present case, the conduct of sexual harassment by [the claimant], in the context of workplace relation between two staff members, even of uneven position, only amounted to a violation of Staff Rule 1.2 (f)".[86]

3.2 Legal Tests When Addressing Allegations of SEA

According to the UNAT case law, the UN has the onus to prove with clear and convincing evidence that a staff member engaged in SEA as contemplated in Staff Rule 1.2(e). This standard of proof requires that the alleged facts be highly probable, though not proven beyond a reasonable doubt. Accordingly, in SEA cases, the UN must provide clear and convincing evidence showing that the staff member: (i) abused a position of vulnerability for sexual purposes; (ii) abused a position of differential power for sexual purposes; (iii) abused trust for sexual purposes; (iv) exchanged money, employment, goods or services for

85 *Ali Hussein Haidar v. Secretary-General of the UN*, UNAT Judgment No 2021-UNAT-1076, para 17.

86 Ibid, para 58.

sex; or (v) engaged in some form of humiliating, degrading or exploitative sexual behaviour.[87]

In *Makeen*, the UNAT reaffirmed these standards and, importantly, clarified that consent is "immaterial" to the offence of SEA, particularly where a power imbalance or vulnerability exists.[88] It further emphasized that Section 1 of the 2013 Secretary-General bulletin on SEA "does not provide an exhaustive list of all types of sexual exploitation, it captures some common forms. The phrase 'but not limited to' is used expansively to indicate that the list is by far non-exhaustive. By parity of reasoning, undue benefit from the sexual act is not a cardinal requirement for the existence of sexual exploitation".[89] Instead, it is sufficient to establish that the staff member abused a position of vulnerability, differential power or trust for sexual purposes.

The Tribunal also confirmed that misconduct may arise from conduct occurring in a staff member's private life if such behaviour is incompatible with the duty to act with integrity expected of international civil servants. The obligation to act with integrity extends beyond the workplace, particularly in SEA cases, where victims are often vulnerable individuals in the local community. The Tribunal upheld the sanction of separation from service, finding it proportionate and lawful, and confirmed that due process must be observed throughout both the investigative and disciplinary processes.

In *Lucchini*, the UNAT held that disparities in contractual status between an internationally recruited staff member and a locally contracted national does not create an inherent situation of vulnerability nor does a disparity in earnings between two parties constitutes an inherent situation of abuse of power for sexual purposes on the part of the person earning more against the person earning less.[90] For instance, a staff member promising to inform another person about a job opportunity in exchange for sex does not appear to be a plausible case of sexual exploitation, "[a]gain, as the UNDT correctly pointed out, a comment of that order cannot by any reasonable stretch of the imagination be construed as a promise of employment in the sense that sex would have been a quid pro quo".[91]

---

87 *Alex Lucchini v. Secretary-General of the UN*, UNAT Judgment No 2021-UNAT-1121, para 45. See also, *Mihai-Tudor Stefan v. Secretary-General of the UN*, UNAT Judgment No 2023-UNAT-1375, para 69

88 *Hassan Makeen v. Secretary-General of the UN*, UNAT Judgment No 2024-UNAT-1461, para 50.

89 Ibid, para 47.

90 *Alex Lucchini v. Secretary-General of the UN*, UNAT Judgment No 2021-UNAT-1121, para 47.

91 Ibid, para 54.

Moreover, the UNAT case law makes clear that the standards for demonstrating SEA are not confined to interactions between UN employees and external beneficiaries of assistance or non-UN staff members. Rather, the prohibition and evidentiary standards governing SEA also apply to relationships between UN employees. This was explicitly reaffirmed in *Stefan*.[92] In that case, the Tribunal addressed whether an alleged romantic and sexual relationship between two UN employees could amount to SEA if it involved the exploitation of a position of vulnerability, trust, or differential power. Accordingly, the central question was not whether both parties were UN employees, but whether one party exploited the other's vulnerability or a power imbalance for sexual purposes. In *Stefan*, the UNDT had found that such exploitation occurred. However, the UNAT overturned this finding of misconduct due to the UN's failure to meet the "clear and convincing evidence" threshold.

This case also clarified the notion of 'vulnerability'. While not rigidly defined, the UNAT has established that a vulnerable person is generally defined as someone who is unable to protect themselves from harm or exploitation or may be unable to give consent or sufficiently understand decisions or exercise their legal rights. This vulnerability may result from several factors, including: (a) developmental, physical, medical or psychological conditions; (b) an unequal relationship with a person in a position of trust, authority or support; (c) chronic intoxication or drug use that results in incapacity or patterns of behaviour that may pose a danger to themselves; or (d) circumstances such as gender, orientation, ethnicity, economic or social status that put them in a state of dependency or risk.[93]

In *Stefan*, the UNAT found that the complainant's alleged mental health vulnerabilities were insufficiently corroborated. It criticized the UNDT for failing to obtain or require objective medical evidence of the complainant's condition; substituting independent internet-based research in place of expert or medical testimony (violating procedural fairness); ignoring or downplaying contradictory evidence undermining the complainant's credibility (including allegations found to be false or uncorroborated during investigation); and

92 *Mihai-Tudor Stefan v. Secretary-General of the UN*, UNAT Judgment No 2023-UNAT-1375, para 69.

93 Ibid, para 77. See also, United Nations Office on Drugs and Crime, Issue Paper: Abuse of a position of vulnerability and other "means" within the definition of trafficking in persons (2013) <https://www.unodc.org/documents/human-trafficking/2012/UNODC_2012_Issue_Paper_-_Abuse_of_a_Position_of_Vulnerability.pdf> accessed 12 December 2025.

overlooking the absence of any clear authority, supervisory role or power differential between the parties, which could support a finding of exploitation.[94]

The Tribunal reiterated that findings of SEA cannot be based on vague allegations or unsubstantiated claims of emotional or psychological instability and that serious disciplinary measures like termination or dismissal must be proven with "clear and convincing evidence".[95] This case serves as a reminder that not all unhealthy or dysfunctional relationships between staff members meet the threshold of SEA, even where they involve emotional distress, use of drugs or volatility.[96] To amount to misconduct, there must be a demonstrable abuse of a recognized form of vulnerability, evidenced to the requisite legal standard.

3.3 Tensions and Ambiguities

Although legally sound, the UNAT's judgment in *Lucchini* highlights potential normative limitations in identifying and addressing exploitative conduct, especially in contexts where power asymmetries are not formally defined but still operative. The Tribunal emphasized that neither a disparity in earnings nor contract type creates a presumption of exploitation without evidence of a fiduciary or supervisory relationship or abuse of vulnerability. It found that while the complainant, a woman, was generally a "vulnerable person" as contemplated by Section 3.2 of the 2013 Secretary-General bulletin on SEA, there was insufficient evidence to establish that her vulnerability was abused by the staff member. The Tribunal concluded that neither the complainant's status as a locally contracted national nor the respondent's status as an internationally recruited staff member created a presumption of an exploitative power dynamic. Importantly, it also found that a general offer to "look out for opportunities" did not rise to the level of an exploitative quid pro quo exchange under Staff Rule 1.2(e).

Legally, this interpretation is sound and consistent with the UNAT standard of proof required to impose a disciplinary measure. The UNAT made clear that Staff Rule 1.2(e) targets specific forms of exploitative conduct, including the abuse of a position of vulnerability, power, or trust for sexual purposes, and quid pro quo sexual arrangements. Without evidence of such conduct or a

94 *Mihai-Tudor Stefan v. Secretary-General of the UN*, UNAT Judgment No 2023-UNAT-1375, paras 78–85.

95 *Diabagate v. Secretary-General of the UN*, UNAT Judgment No 2014-UNAT-403, para 30.

96 *Mihai-Tudor Stefan v. Secretary-General of the UN*, UNAT Judgment No 2023-UNAT-1375, para 78.

relationship of authority, trust or dependency, the Tribunal was correct in declining to infer misconduct solely from general socio-economic or contractual disparities.

Nonetheless, the case may reveal a deeper structural concern. Current regulatory interpretations may insufficiently capture forms of coercion or exploitation that arise from contextual or structural vulnerabilities, especially in mission settings where institutional hierarchies, racial and gender dynamics, and precarious employment can shape perceived or actual dependency. For instance, a locally recruited staff member nearing contract expiration may perceive or internalize an international staff member's position as influential, even absent explicit promises. These perceptions can create subtle pressures that may challenge the validity of apparent 'consent'. The absence of direct coercion or promises does not eliminate the ethical complexity of such interactions, especially when viewed through the lens of the UN's duty to uphold the highest standards of integrity and protection for all individuals with whom its personnel interact.

Thus, while the UNAT rightly avoids generalizing assumptions of vulnerability, a rigid application of these evidentiary standards may fail to capture the full ethical complexity of such interactions. As the UN continues to refine its legal and policy approaches, a more context-sensitive understanding of vulnerability, power and consent may be needed to uphold its commitment to integrity and protection in all staff interactions.

4 Sexual Harassment

This section addresses sexual harassment by examining (i) its definition and scope; (ii) the legal tests applied to allegations of sexual harassment; and (iii) the key tensions and ambiguities involved.

4.1 Definition and Scope of Sexual Harassment

UN Staff Rule 1.2(f) provides that "[a]ny form of discrimination or harassment, including sexual or gender harassment, as well as abuse in any form at the workplace or in connection with work, is prohibited". Sexual harassment, as a category of sexual misconduct, is defined by four constitutive elements outlined in Section 1.5 of the 2019 Secretary-General's bulletin on addressing sexual harassment,[97] which closely follows the uniform definition proposed by the model policy of the UN System Chief Executives Board for Coordination.[98] These elements comprise (i) an unwelcome conduct; (ii) of a sexual nature; (iii) that might reasonably be expected or be perceived to cause offence or humiliation; and (iv) when such conduct interferes with work, is made a condition of employment or creates an intimidating, hostile or offensive work environment. Sexual harassment may occur either in the workplace or in connection with work.

Sexual harassment encompasses a broad range of conduct, varying from overtly sexual behaviours to more subtle actions. It may take the form of a gesture, verbal or physical conduct, sexual advances or requests for sexual favours. As a matter of threshold, to be punishable under UN's legal framework the identified conduct must rise to the level of causing offence or humiliation to a reasonable person. It is not enough that the allegations be found "inappropriate" by the organization, as the UNAT has made it clear that "no conduct automatically rises to the level of sexual harassment merely on the basis of its sexual overtones and lack of 'appropriateness' […] unless it involves the elements articulated in the relevant rules and jurisprudence".[99] In *Bagot*, the UNAT relied on an uncontested preceding social relationship between the alleged offender and the complainant as part of a group of colleagues who used to meet outside working hours, to find that the act of biting the complainant's "toe and thumb" did not amount to sexual harassment, particularly in the absence of any attempt to set boundaries by the complainant.[100]

Moreover, the constitutive elements of sexual harassment cannot be assessed in isolation from the relevant context.[101] For instance, whether a particular type of conduct is of a "sexual nature" requires consideration of the circumstances surrounding the conduct, the type of alleged conduct, the nature of the relationship between the complainant and the alleged offender, the institutional culture that is generally accepted under these circumstances, and the complainant's perception of the conduct.[102]

---

97 UN Secretary-General's Bulletin, Addressing discrimination, harassment, including sexual harassment, and abuse of authority (note 39 above).

98 UN System Model Policy on Sexual Harassment (note 38 above).

99 *Bagot v. UNRWA*, UNAT Judgment No 2017-UNAT-718, para 62.

100 Ibid, para 63.

101 *Gonzalo Ramos v. Secretary-General of the UN*, UNAT Judgment No 2022-UNAT-1256, para. 38.

102 *Appellant v. Secretary-General of the UN*, UNAT Judgment No 2021-UNAT-1137, para 58.

4.2 Legal Tests When Addressing Allegations of Sexual Harassment

To ascertain whether sexual harassment has occurred, an objective assessment is necessary to determine if the alleged conduct may cause offence or humiliation to a reasonable person. In a case where a staff member asserted that hugging and touching women by men was culturally acceptable, the UNAT ruled that such "actions were clearly sexual in nature and [...] not acceptable by or towards [UN] staff".[103] The existence of misconduct does not therefore rest on the subjective intent of the alleged offender, which is immaterial and may not constitute a valid defence.[104] It is also unnecessary to establish whether the alleged offender was aware that the alleged behaviour was offensive or that they were put on notice, which would otherwise preclude a single incident from constituting sexual harassment.[105]

Although sexual harassment typically involves a pattern of conduct, the UNAT clarified that it may also take the form of a single incident.[106] Additionally, the perspective of the person who is the target of the conduct shall be considered when determining the offensive or humiliating nature of the conduct complained of.[107] In a noteworthy precedent, the UNAT ruled that sexual harassment may exist even where the victim gives no warning or signal that the behaviour is unwelcome and delays in reporting the conduct until they feel safe to report it with the support of other victims.[108] Furthermore, the fact that the behaviour of the offender has ceased does not negate the existence of misconduct for previous acts.[109]

Regarding the unwelcome nature of sexual harassment, the burden is not on the victim to indicate that sexual advances are unwanted. Rather, it is the responsibility of the alleged offender to ensure that their behaviour is welcomed before engaging in any such conduct, particularly in cases where there is a power imbalance.[110] A close relationship between colleagues does not justify unwanted and inappropriate sexual advances, especially in situations

103 *AAN v. Secretary-General of the UN*, UNAT Judgment No 2023-UNAT-1366, para 48.

104 *Appellant v. Secretary-General of the UN*, UNAT Judgment No 2021-UNAT-1137, para 58.

105 *Gonzalo Ramos v. Secretary-General of the UN*, UNAT Judgment No 2022-UNAT-1256, para 39.

106 Ibid, para 30.

107 *Flamur Kazazi v. Secretary-General of the UN*, UNAT Judgment No 2023-UNAT-1382, para 92.

108 *Andry Adriantseheno v. Secretary-General of the UN*, UNAT Judgment No 2021-UNAT-1146/Corr. 1, para 50.

109 Ibid.

110 *AAT v. Secretary-General of the UN*, UNAT Judgment No 2024-UNAT-1412, para 101.

between a supervisor and supervisee.[111] In the latter case, it was recognized that a supervisor has an obligation to "recognize [a] power imbalance and its impact on the professional and social relationship, and to act accordingly in his dealings with a supervisee".[112]

Importantly, sexual harassment can occur regardless of the scale or the impact for the affected person. The mere acceptance of an apology by a victim does not negate the existence of sexual misconduct, nor does it preclude the victim from filing a complaint of misconduct at a later time.[113]

4.3 Tensions and Ambiguities

The UNAT case law reflects a welcome liberal interpretation and expansive definition of the four constitutive elements of sexual harassment. However, this liberal approach is not without any risks. It may well be argued that an expansive view of what constitutes sexual harassment unduly lowers the applicable threshold for misconduct, allowing allegations of harassment to be accepted without sufficiently rigorous scrutiny. In assessing the appropriateness of a particular conduct, the UNAT often leans towards an abstract maximalist approach of the standards expected of UN personnel, presumably grounded in the UN values and "ethos expected by the Organisation from those responsible for executing its mandate".[114] This seemingly uniform approach overlooks the unique interpersonal, behavioural, social and cultural contexts of individual cases – especially in multicultural settings where norms and expectations can vary significantly.

An additional concern arises from the UNAT's lack of articulation of consistent standards and thresholds regarding the four constitutive elements of sexual harassment. In one judgment, the UNAT acknowledged that there are varying "degrees of severity to sexual harassment misconduct", acknowledging that "drawing the line between acceptable flirtation and sexual harassment is never easy".[115] In that case, the Tribunal seemed to require that the conduct go "beyond the limits of acceptable flirtation or playful banter" for sexual harassment to be satisfied.[116] This may signal an effort to place some boundaries on an otherwise expansive interpretive approach, yet it also in-

111 Ibid, para 81.
112 Ibid, para 82.
113 Ibid, para 95.
114 *Szvetko v. Secretary-General of the UN*, UNAT Judgment No 2023-UNAT-1311, para 55.
115 Ibid, para 48.
116 Ibid, para 55.

troduces tension with the seemingly uncompromising position previously adopted by the UNAT.

5 Due Process

Due process serves as a fundamental pillar of the legal framework for addressing allegations of sexual misconduct within the UN. It ensures fairness, transparency and impartiality in disciplinary procedures, safeguarding the rights of both the complainant and the accused. This section explores the key dimensions of due process in sexual misconduct cases, focusing on (i) the right to notice and disclosure obligations; (ii) the use of administrative leave pending investigation and disciplinary proceedings; (iii) the burden and standard of proof in disciplinary proceedings; (iv) the proportionality of sanctions imposed; (v) the right to appeal before a tribunal; and (vi) ongoing tensions and ambiguities in the application of these principles.

5.1 Notice and Disclosure

The UNAT has affirmed a range of procedural rights designed to guarantee fairness, transparency and impartiality in disciplinary proceedings – principles that are equally applicable in cases involving allegations of sexual misconduct. It consistently recalls the notion of presumption of innocence and highlights its implications, namely, that the UN bears the burden of establishing that the alleged misconduct for which a disciplinary measure has been taken, had occurred.[117] The principle of legality of sanctions is also firmly established with respect to sexual misconduct, as "it is not open to the [UN] to impose a sanction, whether disciplinary or administrative, without a finding that some misconduct has occurred".[118]

Furthermore, the UNAT has affirmed that staff members who are the subject of allegations of misconduct are entitled to a reasonably prompt conclusion of the investigation or disciplinary process. Specific time limits are instituted for the conclusion of the disciplinary case and identification of specific grounds and limits for re-opening the investigation. Compensation may be awarded if there is excessive delay in undertaking specific actions or proceedings, taking into consideration the specific circumstances of each case as well as the nature and complexity of the allegations. However, sexual misconduct

117 *Abdulhamid Al Fararjeh v. UNRWA*, UNAT Judgment No 2021-UNAT-1136, para 11.
118 *Sajiv Nair v. Secretary-General of the UN*, UNAT Judgment No 2023-UNAT-1394, para 59.

cases are often complex and may require more time compared with other types of disciplinary cases.[119]

The scope of due process rights evolves at different stages of the proceedings. During the investigation phase, only limited due process rights apply,[120] with the UN being mainly required to objectively and impartially assess and review the allegations of misconduct, offering the defendant an opportunity to respond to those allegations orally in the course of an interview and, where applicable, in writing.[121] The right to be heard entails not only that a staff member who is subject of an investigation be notified of the allegations against them, but also provided a reasonable opportunity to contest the allegations.[122] However, this does not imply that the subject will have the right to comment on every piece of evidence which could have a negative impact on his case during an investigation.[123] In this regard, the UN may conduct supplemental investigative steps after a subject interview is concluded, and may decide to withhold certain items of evidence in the interest of the investigation, provided that such measures are reasonable. Once an investigation is completed and a disciplinary process instituted, the defendant is entitled not only to receive written notification of the allegations but also be afforded the opportunity to review and assess the evidence produced against them.

In cases involving sexual misconduct, the UN may exceptionally withhold the identity of certain witnesses if maintaining anonymity is necessary for their protection and the evidence relates to facts that "are seriously prejudicial to the work, functioning and reputation of the Organization".[124] In such situations, due process requirements will be satisfied if the defendant can comment and effectively challenge the anonymous witness statements containing incriminating evidence against them, provided that it is possible to verify the circumstances surrounding the preparation of those statements.[125] This is

119 *AAE v. Secretary-General of the UN*, UNAT Judgment No 2023-UNAT-1 332, paras 78–81.

120 *Powell v. Secretary-General of the UN*, UNAT Judgment No 2013-UNAT-295, para 24.

121 *Hassan Makeen v. Secretary-General of the UN*, UNAT Judgment No 2024-UNAT-1461, para 71.

122 *Hasmik Egian v. Secretary-General of the UN*, UNAT Judgment No 2023-UNAT-1333, para 114.

123 *Samer Mohammed v. UNRWA*, UNAT Judgment No 2022-UNAT-1195, para 42.

124 *Oh v. Secretary-General of the UN*, UNAT Judgment No 2014-UNAT-480, para 32, citing *Liyanarachchige v. Secretary-General of the UN*, UNAT Judgment No 2010-UNAT-087, para 19.

125 *Oh v. Secretary-General of the UN*, UNAT Judgment No 2014-UNAT-480, para 40, citing *Applicant v. Secretary-General of the UN*, UNAT Judgment No 2013-UNAT-302, paras 33–34 and 38–39.

essentially a case-by-case assessment as procedural fairness is a variable concept and necessarily context-specific.

As for the consequences for breaching due process rights, the UNAT clarified that only substantial procedural irregularities will render a disciplinary measure unlawful.[126] The so-called "no-difference" principle applies in situations where the outcome of a decision-making process is highly likely to have been unaffected by a procedural flaw, even where the identified error renders the decision unlawful.[127] Hence, due process violations would in principle be insufficient to set aside a disciplinary measure if it appears that better due process would have led to a similar result. For example, a failure to strictly adhere to the provisions of an investigation's manual may have no impact on the substantive findings of the investigation report relied on in reaching the contested decision.[128]

5.2 Administrative Leave Pending Investigation and Disciplinary Proceedings

Significant concerns about due process arise in the context of administrative leave decisions pending the resolution of sexual misconduct cases. In this regard, the UNAT recognized that "[w]hile the emphasis placed by the [UN] on the identification and elimination of sexual exploitation and abuse is very important, so too are the human and due process rights of staff members who have not yet at least, been adjudged guilty of that misconduct. These factors must be carefully balanced in making decisions about administrative leave and particularly if this is to be without pay and for prolonged periods".[129]

The legality of administrative leave is thus assessed by reference to several factors, including its length and impact on the staff member, particularly the economic consequences in case of placement on administrative leave without

---

126 *Samer Mohammed v. UNRWA*, UNAT Judgment No 2022-UNAT-1195, para 37; See also, *Flamur Kazazi v. Secretary-General of the UN*, UNAT Judgment No 2023-UNAT-1382, para 100.

127 *James Wan v. ICAO*, UNAT Judgment No 2024-UNAT-1436, para 40.

128 *Nadasan v. Secretary-General of the UN*, UNAT Judgment No 2019-UNAT-918, para 57, citing *Michaud v. Secretary-General of the UN*, UNAT Judgment No 2017-UNAT-761, para 60.

129 *James Okwakol v. Secretary-General of the UN*, UNAT Judgment No 2022-UNAT-1293, para 54. It is important to note that a decision to place a staff member on unpaid administrative leave constitutes a separate administrative decision that may be challenged independently of the disciplinary process. The UNAT, in *Okwakol*, reviewed the legality of the unpaid administrative leave decision as a stand-alone issue, notwithstanding the ongoing nature of the underlying disciplinary investigation.

pay. The Tribunal recognized that in addition to economic hardship involved, staff members suffer from the "shame, stigma, humiliation, loss of dignity and other similar less tangible but nevertheless real consequences attaching to being suspected of serious misconduct".[130] These factors acknowledge the significance of proper use of administrative leave and safeguarding the subject's fundamental right to due process.

UN Staff Rule 10.4 sets out the conditions for placing staff members on administrative leave pending investigation and disciplinary proceedings. The UNAT analysed the applicable conditions identifying two main safeguards: the first, applicable to all forms of administrative leave, requires the organization to specify in writing both the reasons for the decision and its probable duration. The UNAT has emphasized that this obligation applies irrespective of whether the leave is without pay, and that the UN must have "good reasons" for the decision.[131] Further it is incumbent upon the UN to undertake and complete its investigation and decision-making process in a "timely and thorough" manner.[132]

The second safeguard relates to the presumption that administrative leave will normally be on full pay unless exceptional circumstances warrant placement on unpaid leave. The first exception to this presumption, directly relevant to sexual misconduct, is where there is probable cause or reasonable grounds to believe that the subject has engaged in SEA. In such case, placement would be on unpaid leave.[133] The second and independent ground for exceptional placement of a staff member on leave without pay is where the Secretary-General "decides that exceptional circumstances exist which warrant the placement of the staff member on administrative leave with partial pay or without pay", pursuant to Staff Rule 10.4(c)(ii).[134]

The UNAT clarified that the applicable standard of "probable cause" for placement on unpaid administrative leave in SEA cases was defined as "a practical, non-technical standard asking whether the proven circumstances permit a reasonable inference".[135] Given that the existence of probable cause is ultimately a question of fact to be proven, it is legitimate to ask whether a staff member can be placed on administrative leave without pay before the conclusion of the fact-finding or investigation process.

130 Ibid, para 53.
131 Ibid, para 56.
132 Ibid.
133 Ibid, para 57.
134 Ibid, para 59.
135 *Muteeganda v. Secretary-General of the UN*, UNAT Judgment No 2018-UNAT-869, para 38.

In this regard, the UN may conduct a separate factual and evidentiary assessment for the sole purpose of determining the appropriate modalities for administrative leave, without being required to await the conclusion of another process. Based on this assessment, it may reasonably conclude that sexual misconduct is probable, thereby justifying withholding all or part of the staff member's pay. In any case, any such interim assessment must remain subject to regular review to ensure its legality and compliance with the applicable due process safeguards.

5.3 Burden and Standard of Proof

In disciplinary proceedings, the burden of proof lies with the party making the allegation of misconduct or inappropriate conduct.[136] Specifically, where a disciplinary measure is imposed on a staff member, the UN bears the burden of proving that the alleged misconduct occurred.[137] When a staff member challenges the imposition of a disciplinary sanction, the organization must produce sufficient evidence to support the factual allegations upon which the sanction is based.

The applicable administrative instruction, ST/AI/2017/1, provides for two distinct standards depending on the disciplinary measure contemplated: (i) clear and convincing evidence where termination or dismissal is proposed, and (ii) preponderance of the evidence for other, less severe disciplinary sanctions. The latter is a lower threshold, requiring that it is more likely than not that the alleged facts occurred.

The UNAT and other international administrative tribunals have developed jurisprudence establishing varying standards of proof depending on the severity of the misconduct and the potential consequences for the staff member. These standards are fundamental to ensuring fairness and proportionality in the disciplinary process.

As for the applicable standard of proof by the UNAT, its case law requires that misconduct be established by "clear and convincing evidence" when termination or dismissal are considered as a possible sanction, which would typically be the case in situations involving sexual misconduct. This is a height-

136 *Fedorchenko v. ICAO*, UNAT Judgment No 2018-UNAT-867, para 58.

137 *Diabagate v. Secretary-General of the UN*, UNAT Judgment No 2014-UNAT-403, para 30. See also, *Liyanarachchige v. Secretary-General of the UN*, UNAT Judgment No 2010-UNAT -087, para 17.

ened evidentiary threshold, requiring that "the truth of the facts asserted is highly probable".[138]

The UNAT provides further guidance on the meaning of "clear and convincing evidence" by clarifying that

> [C]lear and convincing evidence of misconduct, including serious misconduct, imports two high evidential standards. The first ('clear') is that the evidence of misconduct must be unequivocal and manifest. Separately, the second standard ('convincing') requires that this clear evidence must be persuasive to a high standard appropriate to the gravity of the allegation against the staff member and in light of the severity of the consequence of its acceptance. Evidence, which is required to be clear and convincing, can be direct evidence of events, or may be of evidential inferences that can be properly drawn from other direct evidence.[139]

Other international administrative tribunals apply differing standards of proof, which reflect distinct institutional practices and philosophies of procedural fairness. The International Labour Organization Administrative Tribunal (ILOAT) historically applied a "beyond reasonable doubt" standard in particularly grave cases. The Tribunal held: "[a]lthough the proceedings are not criminal, the seriousness of the charges and the concomitant penalty demand that before there can be a finding against the complainant, the charges must be proved beyond reasonable doubt".[140] Since 2010, the ILOAT has confirmed that this stringent standard applies to all cases of misconduct, regardless of the disciplinary sanction imposed.[141] Importantly, the standard is applied at the disciplinary decision-making phase, typically by the executive head or a designated disciplinary board and not at the investigation stage.[142]

The World Bank Administrative Tribunal (WBAT) has developed a flexible, yet elevated, evidentiary approach. The Tribunal ruled that in disciplinary

138 Ibid. However, to date, the preponderance standard for lesser sanctions has not been explicitly adjudicated by UNAT, and thus its precise interpretation remains judicially untested.

139 *Mohammad Yahya Al Othman v. UNRWA*, UNAT Judgment No 2022-UNAT-1196, para 57. See also, *Neguisse v. Secretary-General of the UN*, UNAT Judgment No 2020-UNAT-1033, para 45.

140 *Navarro V. WHO*, ILOAT Judgment No 969 (1989), consid 16.

141 *Ms. C. C. v. WIPO*, ILOAT Judgment No 2879 (2010), consid 11; See also, *R. v. UNIDO*, ILOAT Judgment No 3725 (2017), consid 15.

142 *R. v. UNIDO*, ILOAT Judgment No 3725 (2017), consid 17; See also, *N. L. v. ICC*, ILOAT Judgment No 3862 (2017), consids 23–24; and *H. (No. 24) v. EPO*, ILOAT Judgment No 4047 (2018), consid 9.

cases, the standard must be "higher than a mere balance of probabilities".[143] In subsequent decisions, the WBAT has reiterated the requirement of "substantial evidence" to support the finding of facts which amount to misconduct.[144] For cases involving sexual harassment, the Tribunal has stated that the evidentiary standard must be clear and convincing evidence.[145]

To discharge its burden of proof, the UN must show that it was highly probable that the alleged offender engaged in prohibited conduct.[146] In sexual misconduct cases, this evidentiary threshold is not satisfied "where the probabilities are equipoised" and the UN, who bears the onus of proof, may simply lose the case on the basis that it failed to meet the applicable evidentiary threshold.[147]

Sexual misconduct cases present unique challenges, as they pertain to incidents typically occurring in closed settings with little or no independently verifiable evidence. In these cases, factfinders must therefore thoroughly assess the credibility of the various accounts and decide between conflicting versions of events and testimonies. Given the seriousness of sexual misconduct allegations and grave implications for the staff member's reputation and employment prospects, factfinders must reach reasoned conclusions with respect to any disputed facts and satisfy themselves of the credibility and reliability of the evidence.[148] Importantly, the victim's testimony will not automatically be considered more credible and reliable than that of the accused. Instead, the credibility, reliability and weight of all evidence must be deter-

143 *Dambita v. IBRD*, WBAT Decision No 243 (2001), para 21; and *Arefeen v. IBRD*, Decision No 244 (2001), para 42.

144 *Carew v. IBRD*, WBAT Decision No 142 (1995), para 32; *Planthara v. IBRD*, WBAT Decision No 143 (1995), para 25; *Mustafa v. IBRD*, WBAT Decision No 207 (1999), para 17; *CK v. IBRD*, WBAT Decision No 498 (2014), para 58; and *CB v. IBRD*, WBAT Decision No 476 (2013), para 31.

145 *M v. IBRD*, WBAT Decision No 369 (2007), para 60. It is worth noting that, effective 17 May 2023, the World Bank amended its Principles of Staff Employment to establish the 'preponderance of the evidence' as the applicable standard of proof for misconduct. While the WBAT affirmed that it was within the Bank's power to amend the applicable standard in disciplinary proceedings, it held that the 'substantial evidence' standard remains applicable in reviewing misconduct determination in respect of acts occurring before the effective date of the new standard. See *HQ v. IBRD*, WBAT Decision No 707 (2024), paras 123 and 125; *HR v. IBRD*, WBAT Decision No 708 (2024), paras 135 and 137.

146 *AAC v. Secretary-General of the UN*, UNAT Judgment No 2022-UNAT-1264, para 41.

147 Ibid, para 37.

148 *AAE v. Secretary-General of the UN*, UNAT Judgment No 2023-UNAT-1332, para 102.

mined considering the totality of the evidence and the circumstances of each case.[149]

In assessing the reliability and weight to be attributed to the evidence, it is relevant to consider multiple factors such as the overall consistency or inherent contradictions of the evidence; the witness' latent and blatant bias; the witness' familiarity with the events such as the opportunities for experiencing or observing the events and the quality, the integrity and independence of their recollection abilities; and the witness' candour and demeanour in case of oral testimony.[150]

Yet, the UNAT's approach to evidence has not been harmonious and consistent. In one case, it controversially held that self-corroboration in the form of previous consistent statements by witnesses or victims are normally irrelevant and inadmissible evidence. It further noted that it "does not ordinarily add anything to the value of a witness' evidence to be told that the witness had always adhered to the same view".[151] This holding seems to depart from the more widely accepted and consistent principles focusing on "internal and external inconsistencies in the witnesses' evidence", and the understanding that a reliable first report made by the complainant within a reasonable time of the incident is admissible, as it pertains to the truthfulness of a particular given encounter.[152]

The standard of proof required to open an investigation or to initiate disciplinary proceedings is less clear. The wording of UN Staff Regulation 10.1 and Staff Rule 10.3(a) is permissive providing that the Secretary-General "may" initiate the disciplinary process where the findings of an investigation indicate that misconduct may have occurred. Such authority to initiate a disciplinary proceeding is discretionary and not conditional upon a prior finding of possible misconduct by an investigative body.[153] Hence, the disciplinary authority may, upon review and assessment of an investigation report, validly pursue a case of sexual misconduct even if the investigation body did not reach any finding of misconduct.[154] The disciplinary authority can request additional

149 *AAO v. Secretary-General of the UN*, UNAT Judgment No 2023-UNAT-1361, para 71; see also *Applicant v. Secretary-General of the UN*, UNAT Judgment No 2022-UNAT-1187, para 67.

150 *AAC v. Secretary-General of the UN*, UNAT Judgment No 2022-UNAT-1264, para 36.

151 *AAO v. Secretary-General of the UN*, UNAT Judgment No 2023-UNAT-1361, para 64.

152 *AAE v. Secretary-General of the UN*, UNAT Judgment No 2023-UNAT-1332, paras 108–109.

153 It is worth noting that UN investigators are expressly not meant to be the arbiters of whether the conduct was misconduct, simply establishers of fact. This is reflected in section 6.1 of ST/AI/2017/1 on Unsatisfactory conduct, investigations and the disciplinary process: "The investigator(s) shall not make a legal determination about the established facts".

154 *AAE v. Secretary-General of the UN*, UNAT Judgement No 2023-UNAT-1332, paras 64–66.

information, clarification or evidence following the conclusion of the investigation.[155]

In granting the organization wide discretion to proceed with disciplinary process without a clear evidentiary threshold, the UNAT's approach may be seen as opening the door to subjective assessment or inconsistent application. Without further defined criteria, UN personnel may be exposed to disciplinary action even where evidence is weak or ambiguous, raising due process concerns. This can be particularly detrimental to respondents in politically sensitive or reputationally charged cases involving allegations of sexual misconduct, where procedural safeguards and rigor are especially important.

5.4 Proportionality of Sanctions

Fairness and natural justice considerations command that the principle of proportionality of sanctions be observed by international organizations to ensure that any disciplinary measure imposed corresponds to the severity of the misconduct and is adapted to the circumstances of the case. This core tenet of justice is enshrined in Staff Rule 10.3(b), which provides that "[a]ny disciplinary measure imposed on a staff member shall be proportionate to the nature and gravity of the staff member's misconduct".

While sexual misconduct is considered as a grave and serious offence, the UNAT has acknowledged the necessity to distinguish between the various manifestations of sexual misconduct by reference to their degree of severity, thereby admitting that some incidents or situations may be less serious than others. This implies that the sanctioning authority may vary and contemplate a "gradation" of possible sanctions.[156]

As explained above, in the UNAT's view, the existence of a zero tolerance policy for sexual harassment does not mean that the most serious penalty must be imposed in every case; rather, zero tolerance merely refers to the obligation for the organization to promptly and adequately address sexual misconduct.[157] Similarly, while previous disciplinary measures in similar cases are relevant, they serve no more than guidance as the UN retains a margin of discretion to impose different sanctions provided that they fall within a reasonable range of proportionate options. The most serious forms of sexual misconduct will necessarily lead to termination of the staff member's employment. For instance, a finding that a staff member committed rape or sexual

155 Ibid, para 69.

156 *Balint Szvetko v. Secretary-General of the UN*, UNAT Judgment No 2023-UNAT-1311, para 48.

157 Ibid.

assault is "undeniably serious misconduct that must lead to an end of the employment relationship between the staff member and the Organization".[158]

The UN Dispute and Appeals Tribunals have established significantly stringent standards for reviewing the proportionality of disciplinary measures, interfering only with the organization's choice of the appropriate sanction if the latter "is blatantly illegal, arbitrary, adopted beyond the limits stated by the respective norms, excessive, abusive, discriminatory or absurd in its severity".[159] There are very few precedents of rescission of disciplinary measures on grounds of proportionality.[160] In a sexual misconduct case, the UNAT removed the imposition of a fine together with separation from service on the grounds that the former did not bear any rational connection with either the retributive or preventive purpose of a disciplinary measure, resulting in the rescission of the fine due to its significant financial onerousness on the sanctioned person.[161]

The UNAT's excessively deferential standard undermines meaningful judicial oversight of the UN's exercise of discretion, thereby weakening accountability mechanisms, particularly in sensitive and complex cases such as sexual harassment. It also fails to align with the strict requirement under Staff Rule 10.3(b) that a disciplinary measure "shall be proportionate".

In identifying the appropriate disciplinary measure, it is necessary to distinguish the constitutive elements of sexual misconduct from the legal factors relied on to determine the severity or leniency of a sanction. This is because such factors, while not forming part a constitutive element of the misconduct, must be evaluated to ensure fair and proportional administrative and disciplinary actions.[162] Aggravating factors in sexual offences include the persistent and continuous nature of sexual acts, their length and impact on the affected person(s), and if established, may warrant the imposition of the strictest dis-

158 *AAE v. Secretary-General of the UN*, UNAT Judgment No 2023-UNAT-1332, para 144.

159 *Appellant v. Secretary-General of the UN*, UNAT Judgment No 2022-UNAT-1216, para 45.

160 *Turkey v. Secretary-General of the UN*, UNAT Judgement No 2019-UNAT-955, para 39. In this case, the purpose of progressive or corrective discipline was invoked by the UNAT in a drunk driving case to uphold a UNDT judgment rescinding the sanction of separation from service with compensation in lieu of notice and termination indemnity and replacing it with demotion by one grade together with the withdrawal of a driving permit for one year.

161 *Ali Hussein Haidar v. Secretary-General of the UN*, UNAT Judgement No 2021-UNAT-1076, para 60.

162 In this regard, it must be noted that the constitutive elements of misconduct may not be relied upon as mitigating or aggravating factors. See *Turkey v. Secretary-General of the UN*, UNAT Judgment No 2019-UNAT-955, para 40.

ciplinary measure, the dismissal.[163] Likewise, lack of cooperation in the investigation may be considered as an aggravating circumstance. Depending on the circumstances of each case, it may be necessary to distinguish between passive lack of cooperation and active hampering of an investigation.[164] In assessing the proportionality of a sanction, evidence regarding the record of service of the staff member is also a relevant consideration.[165]

5.5 Right of Appeal

A key element of due process is the ability of the accused to appeal an administrative decision or disciplinary measure before an impartial system of justice. For UN staff members, appeals with respect to decisions related to sexual misconduct will be submitted to the UNDT and, if necessary, to the UNAT. The judicial review process is focused on addressing mainly four questions: (i) whether the facts for which the disciplinary measure was imposed have been established (either by a preponderance of evidence or through clear and convincing evidence in cases where termination of employment is a possible outcome); (ii) whether the established facts constitute a breach of the applicable norms and thus amount to misconduct; (iii) whether the sanction is proportionate; and (iv) whether the staff member's due process and other procedural rights have been respected.[166] Importantly, judicial review will be limited to the facts asserted and relied upon in the disciplinary decision, not allegations which may have been dropped by the UN in the course of disciplinary proceedings.[167]

There is still considerable uncertainty in the UNAT case law with respect to the scope and manner in which judicial review is to be conducted in sexual misconduct cases. For instance, in one case, the UNAT overruled the UNDT's finding that the latter did not have the jurisdiction to conduct an entirely new (*de novo*) investigation into a harassment complaint and substitute its own decision for that of the UN.[168] In a separate non-disciplinary matter, however, the UNAT clarified that while the UNDT had no jurisdiction to investigate

---

163 *Appellant v. Secretary-General of the UN*, UNAT Judgment No 2022-UNAT-1216.

164 *AAE v. Secretary-General of the UN*, UNAT Judgment No 2023-UNAT-1332, para 140.

165 *Richard Nsengiyumva v. Secretary-General of the UN*, UNAT Judgment No 2020-UNAT-1057, para 41.

166 *Mubashara Iram v. Secretary-General of the UN*, UNAT Judgment No 2023-UNAT-1340, para 47.

167 Ibid, para 57; See also, *Khamis Ali Khamis v. Secretary-General of the UN*, UNAT Judgment No 2021-UNAT-1178.

168 *Sarwar v. Secretary-General of the UN*, UNAT Judgment No 2018-UNAT-868.

harassment complaints under its Statute, it may nonetheless examine allegations of harassment for the sole purpose of determining if a contested administrative decision is improperly motivated.[169] In the UNAT's view, such scenario is distinct from *a de novo* investigation into a complaint of harassment.

Additionally, there is ongoing debate about whether a judicial review of sexual misconduct cases requires the holding of an oral hearing. In one judgment, the UNAT indicated that the UNDT, as the UN judicial body responsible for carrying out first-instance review, should generally not consider cases solely on the basis of written submissions and documentary evidence but must also hear from witnesses in person, finding that it can benefit considerably from the physical or even virtual presence of individuals who are familiar with the specific circumstances of the case.[170] Crucial to this determination was the Tribunal's recognition that a challenge to the lawfulness of the dismissal of a staff member constitutes the first opportunity for a staff member to have their appeal heard and considered by a neutral judicial body independent of the Secretary-General's administration of the UN.[171]

The requirement for an oral hearing was emphasized in sexual misconduct cases where the UNDT must base its finding on "sufficient, cogent, relevant, and admissible evidence permitting appropriate factual inferences", which in the UNAT's view "normally occurs after an oral hearing of the involved parties and witnesses with the opportunity for cross-examination".[172] In those cases where an oral hearing is required, the UNDT is required to make a full and systematic analysis of the evidence presented, setting out explicitly the reasons for accepting or rejecting a testimony.[173] If witnesses are available to testify, there should be compelling reasons before disallowing such evidence and substituting it with evidence of a lesser weight and relevance.[174]

Nevertheless, the UNAT has also refused to overturn UNDT judgments for absence of an oral hearing, including in sexual misconduct cases, ruling that

169 *Dawas v. UNRWA*, UNAT Judgement No 2016-UNAT-612, para 23, citing *Mashhour v. Secretary-General of the UN*, UNAT Judgment No 2014-UNAT-483, para 45.

170 *AAK v. Secretary-General of the UN*, UNAT Judgment No 2023-UNAT-1348, para 71.

171 Ibid, para 85.

172 *AAE v. Secretary-General of the UN*, UNAT Judgment No 2023-UNAT-1332, para 102. See also *AAC v. Secretary-General of the UN*, UNAT Judgment No 2023-UNAT-1370, para 40, where the UNAT clarified that "real" and "genuine" factual disputes that are "irreconcilable on the papers" would normally have to expand to obtaining oral evidence under oath for examination and cross-examination to allow for reasoned findings on credibility, reliability and probability.

173 *AAO v. Secretary-General of the UN*, UNAT Judgment No 2023-UNAT-1361, para 54; see also *AAC v. Secretary-General of the UN*, UNAT Judgment No 2023-UNAT-1370, para 45.

174 *Appellant v. Secretary-General of the UN*, UNAT Judgment No 2022-UNAT-1210, para 42.

facts could "in certain circumstances" be established by the UNDT without an oral hearing and that due process requirements do not always necessitate that a staff member subject to a disciplinary measure of separation be afforded the right to confront and cross-examine their accusers.[175] In reaching this conclusion, the UNAT recalled its established jurisprudence that due process rights are satisfied so long as the staff member has been afforded a meaningful opportunity to mount a defence and question the veracity of the statements against them.[176]

A closely related question is the admissibility and weight of hearsay evidence, which was the subject of significant scrutiny in cases involving sexual misconduct. In this respect, the UNAT recognized that hearsay evidence is "intrinsically unreliable and of little weight, unless substantially corroborated, because its probative value depends largely on the credibility of a person (the complainants) other than the person giving such evidence".[177] The person making a statement might have deliberately lied, been mistaken, or may have narrated the facts in a misleading fashion. Hearsay, if admissible, must be received with caution as it does not allow for facts to be scrutinized through cross-examination, which is an important safeguard available to the parties to expose possible deficiencies in the evidence.[178]

Equally significant is the unsettled question of the value to be accorded by a UN tribunal to an investigation report in the context of a challenge against a disciplinary measure. In this regard, it was ruled that an investigative report in a sexual misconduct case, while relevant, is not a substitute for a judicial determination and does not absolve the tribunal from re-assessing the weight and reliability of the evidence relied upon to impose the contested sanction.[179] To properly discharge its judicial review function, it will not suffice that a tribunal repeat in its judgment findings quoted from an investigation report without further critical discussion or analysis. The function of the UNDT is to determine if the facts constituting sexual misconduct actually exist and not to review whether the determination of the facts by the internal investigator was reasonable and procedurally fair.[180] In *AAC*, the UNAT cast serious doubt on the weight and probative value of investigation reports, going as far as to say that their contents are usually "hearsay, unless the rele-

175 *Abdulhamid Al Fararjeh v. UNRWA*, UNAT Judgment No 2021-UNAT-1136, para 40.
176 Ibid, para 43.
177 *Applicant v. Secretary-General of the UN*, UNAT Judgment No 2022-UNAT-1187, para 73.
178 Ibid.
179 *Appellant v. Secretary-General of the UN*, UNAT Judgment No 2022-UNAT-1210, para 57.
180 *AAC v. Secretary-General of the UN*, UNAT Judgment No 2023-UNAT-1370, para 39.

vant witnesses themselves testify before the UNDT and their statements in the report are admitted into evidence in the course of their testimony".[181]

5.6 Tensions and Ambiguities

The above analysis reveals three gaps and inconsistencies that significantly impact the fairness, transparency and overall perception of legitimacy of the UN internal justice system.

Firstly, the lack of effective judicial oversight concerning the proportionality of disciplinary sanctions, with the UNAT imposing an exceptionally high threshold for judicial review. As a result, it has become virtually impossible to overturn disciplinary sanctions on proportionality grounds, even when the facts suggest mitigating circumstances or inconsistency with prior practice. On the one hand, this approach may erode accountability and undermine the rationale of judicial review. On the other hand, the current stance of the Tribunal appeared to have paid very little attention to the stated purpose of "progressive and corrective" discipline, including its rehabilitative function, by failing to scrutinize whether the imposed sanctions are adequate and truly commensurate with the established misconduct.

Second, the UNAT appears to have failed to articulate clear or consistent evidentiary standards for initiating disciplinary proceedings, effectively leaving it to the discretion of the Secretary-General's administration of the UN. Such level of discretion and the lack of oversight create uncertainty and risks of arbitrary or inconsistent application, which is particularly problematic in high-stakes or reputationally sensitive cases, such as those involving sexual misconduct.

Third, the UNAT has issued conflicting rulings on the necessity of oral hearings, even in disciplinary cases involving serious allegations. While the Tribunal has emphasized the importance of assessing witness credibility in sexual misconduct cases, it has also upheld decisions rendered solely on the basis of documentary evidence and denying requests for oral hearings. Likewise, the Tribunal's interpretation and application of this standard have been inconsistent, particularly in respect of the admissibility of previous statements, hearsay and uncorroborated testimonies. There is limited transparency in how this threshold is evaluated, which raises concerns about fairness and evidentiary sufficiency, particularly in cases involving severe sanctions such as summary dismissal or separation.

181 Ibid, para 49.

These gaps, taken together, weaken the procedural safeguards intended to uphold due process, especially the right of an accused staff member to confront and cross-examine their accuser. In disciplinary cases involving allegations of sexual harassment, where issues of credibility are often central and testimonies may be contested, denying an oral hearing can fundamentally impair the staff member's right to a fair defence.

6 Conclusion

Despite the UN's sustained efforts to combat sexual misconduct through its zero tolerance policy and the adoption of a victim-centred framework, its regulatory response remains fragmented, incoherent and incomplete. The organization's current approach continues to suffer from conceptual, procedural and normative ambiguities that undermine both its credibility and effectiveness.

At the heart of this regulatory uncertainty lie the definitional limits of the UN's dichotomous treatment of sexual misconduct, which classifies all such conduct into only two categories: SEA and sexual harassment. While these categories reflect distinct legal and operational standpoints, they fail to comprehensively capture the full range of unwelcome or non-consensual sexual conduct encountered in UN operations. This narrow binary framework not only leaves certain types of misconduct unaddressed, creating protection gaps, but also constrains the organization's ability to respond effectively to the lived experiences of victims. Compounding this problem is the very notion of 'victim', which remains loosely defined in the UN legal framework, often conflated with the terms of 'complainant' or 'affected person', resulting in inconsistent access to remedies, support services and justice.

The organization's embrace of a victim-centred justice – symbolized by the establishment of the Office of the Victims' Rights Advocate and other institutional reforms – reflects a normative shift toward rights-based responses. However, the operationalization of this model remains uneven and continues to face significant structural and cultural challenges. Despite rhetorical commitments, victim-centred policies are frequently shaped more by institutional risk management and compliance considerations, than by the rights, needs and voices of survivors. Furthermore, accountability mechanisms for sexual misconduct continue to focus on individual perpetrators, without sufficient attention to the organization's responsibility for systemic failures in prevention, redress and cultural change. A genuinely victim-centred approach requires more than policies and procedural reforms; it demands a cultural transformation that embeds principles of safety, inclusion, dignity and accountability into the core of organizational practice.

The evolving jurisprudence of the UNAT illustrates further gaps in the implementation of due process guarantees. Rights such as timely notice, fair access to evidence, oral hearings and proportionate disciplinary measures are not always fully upheld. These challenges are amplified by the excessively deferential stance by the UNAT, affording the UN a quasi-absolute authority to initiate disciplinary actions and determine the adequate sanctions. Although the Tribunal has sought to expand the scope of judicial review, the lack of procedural rigor and inconsistent holdings risk delegitimizing these efforts and eroding trust in the UN's internal justice system.

Ultimately, the UN's ambition to develop a coherent and credible accountability framework for addressing sexual misconduct remains an unfinished project. Meaningful progress requires addressing the shortcomings of definitional clarity, structural implementation and cultural resistance. Moving beyond policy to effect transformative change will require not only regulatory refinement and stronger institutional support but also a more consistent judicial oversight and guidance from the UNAT in enforcing fairness. Only then can the UN truly honour its commitments to uphold human rights and restore trust in its efforts to prevent and address sexual misconduct.

PART 2

Materials

POSITION PAPER

A Proposal for 'Conditional Immunity': A New Approach for Resolving Private Claims against International Organizations

*David P. Stewart**

Abstract The expanding activities of international organizations increasingly affect private individuals and entities, raising persistent questions about the proper scope of their jurisdictional immunities. While functional immunity from domestic courts is widely regarded as necessary to preserve institutional independence, it may also deny injured parties meaningful access to remedies. This position paper examines the tension between immunity and access to justice through a realistic hypothetical involving large-scale harm resulting from regulatory action by an international organization. After reviewing existing domestic and international mechanisms for resolving private claims, this position paper argues that current practice lacks coherence and balance. It proposes a framework of conditional, function-based immunity, under which immunity from domestic jurisdiction would depend on the availability of adequate and effective internal or international claims-resolution mechanisms, situating the proposal within contemporary international law on the accountability of international organizations.

1 Introduction

As the number of international organizations[1] continues to grow, so does the scope of their activities worldwide. Inevitably, those activities increasingly

* Professor from Practice, Georgetown University Law Center, David.Stewart@law.georgetown.edu.

1 The focus of this article is on 'public international organizations' – that is, those international organizations established by (and whose membership consists of) States and that have 'international legal personality'. Typically, they are created by treaty or other international agreement and engage in international regulation and standard setting. They include such entities as the United Nations, the Organization of American States, the African Union, the World Trade Organization. the Asian Development Bank, the Inter-

HTTPS://DOI.ORG/10.1163/9789004765672-007

affect the interests of private (non-State) entities and individuals, who in turn may seek relief from, or compensation for, harm allegedly attributable to the organizations' activities or failures to act. Where, how and under what law such claims should be resolved in turn raises questions about the scope of the jurisdictional immunities that should be accorded to international organizations in the evolving international arena.

These questions juxtapose competing interests. On the one hand, as supranational entities charged by the international community with addressing, managing and resolving 'communal' problems at the global level, international organizations must be accorded substantial independence from the differing (and sometimes conflicting) domestic laws and procedures of their Member States – in particular through broad jurisdictional immunity from suit in their domestic courts. Otherwise, they will simply be unable to perform the tasks assigned to them by the international community. On the other hand, as their activities increasingly affect private individuals, entities and interests around the globe, it would clearly be unjust to insulate them entirely from the domestic law and jurisdiction of Member States if the result would be to preclude claimants from having any effective opportunities to challenge their actions and obtain compensation or other effective remedies in appropriate cases.

The issues are practical, pressing and consequential. They implicate the question of the jurisdictional immunities to which international organizations are (and should) be entitled under international law. At present, however, there is no single or agreed response to those questions. Practice varies from one international organization to another, and from one domestic jurisdiction to another. The resulting disparities pose problems for both the organizations and the claimants.

This position paper addresses some of the issues raised by the lack of a consistent (much less coherent) approach to the problem and considers several possible approaches for addressing those issues, as illustrated by a realistic hypothetical situation. In an effort to balance the competing interests, it suggests consideration of a new approach – that, for claims by private individuals and entities arising from an international organization's core functions and purposes, the organization would have 'conditional' immunity from the jurisdiction of domestic courts and tribunals dependent on the provision of

---

national Bank for Reconstruction and Development, the International Monetary Fund, the International Finance Corporation, and the Inter-American Development Bank, to name only a few. By some estimates, several hundred such entities exist today. For a list of those invited to participate as Observers in the sessions and work of the UN General Assembly, see 'Intergovernmental and Other Organizations' <https://www.un.org/en/about-us/intergovernmental-and-other-organizations> accessed 13 December 2025.

adequate and effective internal (or international) mechanisms for addressing the relevant claims. The aim would be to provide claimants with effective and expeditious avenues for the resolution of claims, while protecting the organization's ability to conduct its 'core functions' without undue involvement by domestic law and courts.

2 A Hypothetical

To illustrate the problem, imagine that the international community has created a new international body to regulate issues related to the geostationary orbit (or GSO). Established by a multilateral convention open to all UN Member States, this new entity (the Organization) has been charged with managing the use of (and activities in) the GSO by all States and private entities.

This is obviously an important task with significant real-world consequences, clearly suited for a coordinated international approach. The geostationary orbit is that point 22,236 miles above the equator in which a satellite's 'orbital period' is equal to the Earth's rotation, so that the satellite remains over a given point above the surface and thus appears to the Earth-bound observer to be stationary in the sky. As a result, it can be immensely useful for weather, navigation, data transmission and other communications purposes. Indeed, most of us benefit from its advantages every day without realizing it.

The GSO is, however, an inherently limited resource, since satellites require some separation to function properly and to avoid interference or collision. Accordingly, it is a competitive space. Technologically advanced States able to place satellites in this orbit have generally claimed the freedom to do so, while States that lack that capability fear exclusion. Even though it is outside any country's 'territorial jurisdiction',[2] subjacent equatorial States have, on occasion, asserted independent authority to regulate (license) the use of the GSO above their respective national territories.[3]

---

2 The international community has not agreed on a clear dividing line between 'airspace' (subject to national regulation) and 'outer space' (not subject to such regulation). The most commonly proposed demarcations would place the boundary somewhere between 80 and 100 kilometers above the Earth's surface. See, e.g., Phil Plait, 'Where Does Outer Space Begin' (*Scientific American*, 2 February 2024) <https://www.scientificamerican.com/article/where-does-outer-space-begin> accessed 13 December 2025.

3 Generally, see Stephen Gorove, 'The Geostationary Orbit: Issues of Law and Policy' (1979) 73(3) American Journal of International Law 444; UN Committee on the Peaceful Uses of Outer Space, 'Report of the International Telecommunication Union on the use of the geostationary orbit and other orbits' (30 January 2024) UN Doc A/AC.105/C.1/2024/CRP.19.

The purpose of the Organization is to manage these competing interests on behalf of the international community as a whole, protecting the interests of States that are able to use the GSO as well as those not yet able to do so, in accordance with principles of international law. For that reason, we assume that the Organization has been accepted as a 'specialized agency' within the UN system.[4]

We also assume that, for political as well as symbolic reasons, the headquarters of the new organization has been established in Quito, Ecuador – the largest city on the equator and one of only two in the world that directly overlap the equatorial line. Clearly, the Organization must have both political and legal independence from its 'host' (the Ecuadorian government) in order to carry out the functions assigned to it by the international community. The same is true for its senior leadership, its professional and support staff, as well as the duly designated representatives of its Member States and their staff (both those assigned to Member State missions at its headquarters, and those who travel to the headquarters for meetings).

At the same time, the Organization will necessarily interact with private entities and individuals in conducting its work – not just at headquarters but around the globe. Inevitably, disputes will arise. Individuals and entities claiming to have been harmed or wronged by the Organization's actions or inactions must have avenues of effective recourse. The challenge is where to draw the line between respecting the Organization's supranational status and its need for independence and self-administration on the one hand, and providing access to justice where required on the other. This is a practical question with significant implications.

Consider this (disastrous) hypothetical scenario: despite all its accumulated expertise and professional due diligence, the staff of the Organization proposed a regulation concerning the placement and performance of satellites in the GSO that contained a serious but hidden flaw. Notwithstanding the most careful review by their own experts, the Member States failed to identify the error and officially approved, adopted and implemented that regulation in their GSO activities. Accordingly, the States complied. However, as a direct consequence of the flaw, several of those satellites collided – including two that were nuclear-powered. Not only did the re-entering debris cause direct injury and damage to people, facilities and activities on the Earth's surface (in one case, destroying an aircraft in flight, with substantial loss of life), the result-

4 'Specialized agencies' are independent international organizations working within the UN system pursuant to special agreements concluded with the UN Economic and Social Council in accordance with articles 57 and 63 of the UN Charter.

ing disruption in global services (such as weather, communications, data transmissions) was even more consequential.

One result would be a sizable number of substantial claims by private individuals, entities and businesses against the Organization, seeking compensation for death, personal injury, pain and suffering, property damage, business loss and other damages – all suffered through no fault of their own. Basic notions of justice would require that those harmed as a result of the Organization's activities be afforded an effective forum in which to pursue their claims and, when justified, to receive appropriate compensation. Where and under what rules (legal principles) might those claims best be addressed?

3 Possible Claims Settlement Mechanisms

Several possible avenues may be identified for addressing claims arising from the Organizations activities. These avenues fall broadly into two categories: (i) procedures before domestic courts that would apply if the Organization were treated as a private entity, and (ii) procedures at the international level, including those involving specialized international tribunals. In addition, at both levels there exist alternative mechanisms that may be used to supplement or substitute for formal judicial processes.

3.1 Domestic Litigation

Domestic avenues may be divided between (i) the ordinary judicial procedures that would apply if the Organization were a private entity, and (ii) alternative mechanisms that private entities sometimes use to consolidate or expedite claims. As set out below, however, pursuing any form of domestic recourse may face significant legal impediments given the Organization's jurisdictional immunities.

3.1.1 Domestic Court Litigation

If the Organization were a private entity (say, a corporation),[5] the primary avenue for the injured parties would presumably be through civil litigation to recover damages. Such actions could be brought in various domestic courts, for instance where the responsible entity was incorporated or headquartered, where the claimants reside, where the damage or injuries in question had

5 For the sake of simplicity, we can leave aside questions of insurance coverage.

been incurred, or perhaps in other jurisdictions where the responsible entity did significant business or where it had assets (individual or collective).

Even in the best of circumstances, however, such proceedings could face significant challenges. The outcomes in those various fora would likely vary because of differences in the applicable law (jurisdictional, substantive and procedural). Pursuing any of those options would surely be a lengthy, complicated and costly endeavor. Even where the claimants might succeed in obtaining judgments or awards, enforcing them against assets of the private entity in other jurisdictions (wherever such assets might be found) would surely face additional legal hurdles given significant differences in relevant national laws.

What about the domestic courts of the private entity's state of incorporation? Assuming that in our example it would be Ecuador, its courts would presumptively have jurisdiction to adjudicate the claims. Centralizing the claims adjudication process at the entity's headquarters would surely provide practical advantages. Claims might also be pursued in the domestic courts and under the domestic laws of the various countries in which the claimants reside, where the damage or injuries in question had been incurred, or perhaps even in other jurisdictions depending on the relevant law. Variations in the applicable jurisdictional requirements, substantive laws and approaches to calculating compensable damages in these different legal systems would virtually guarantee disparate results. Enforcement of those results would also face significant challenges.

3.1.2 Alternative Domestic Procedures

A private corporation faced with the task of responding to a large number of claims arising from the same facts in different jurisdictions, and the possibility of resulting judgments, might agree to some sort of collective (third-party) claims adjudication or arbitration process to consolidate, simplify and expedite matters. Even in the best of circumstances, however, such a process would be complicated, lengthy and expensive, and not all of the claimants would likely receive prompt compensation.

3.1.3 Challenge to Pursue Domestic Recourse

In any event, pursuit of such alternatives in our hypothetical would face another and even more significant challenge: unlike private entities, international organizations are typically afforded a substantial level of 'immunity' from national laws and regulations and the jurisdiction of domestic courts, precisely to enable them to carry out their assigned missions independently and without undue interference in all the various countries in which they operate.[6] While the extent of immunity provided to such organizations varies from one to another, the prevailing rule grants them some form of 'restricted' or 'functional' immunity – that is, exempting them from domestic jurisdictions with regard to the functions (or purposes) for which they were created.

In the case of the United Nations, for example, the Charter itself provides that the UN "shall enjoy in the territory of each of its Members such privileges and immunities as are necessary for the fulfilment of its purposes" and that UN officials and representatives of Member States "shall similarly enjoy such privileges and immunities as are necessary for the independent exercise of their functions in connection with the Organization."[7] These provisions were subsequently elaborated in a separate convention that accords a broader scope of immunity.[8] As a specialized agency of the United Nations, the Organization would be covered by the provisions of yet another related instrument with similarly broad language.[9]

In this regard, the law in the United States has recently become complicated. Textually, the International Organizations Immunities Act (IOIA),[10] adopted in 1945, granted organizations of which the United States is a member (and which have received Presidential designation) a limited set of privileges and immunities, including from suit and judicial process, in order to permit them to carry out their functions. The statute did not, however, fully define the precise contours of that immunity but instead said, somewhat curiously, that

6 By distinction, most States recognize foreign States and governments as entitled under international law to 'sovereign immunity', a doctrinally separate approach typically understood to embrace broader (if no longer 'absolute') exemption from national (domestic) jurisdiction.

7 Charter of the United Nations (signed 26 June 1945, entered into force 24 October 1945), art 105.

8 Convention on the Privileges and Immunities of the United Nations (adopted 13 February 1946, entered into force 17 September 1946) 1 UNTS 15 (sometimes referred to as the 'General Convention'), which inter alia gives the UN, its property and assets "immunity from every form of legal process except insofar as in any particular case it has expressly waived its immunity."

9 Convention on the Privileges and Immunities of the Specialized Agencies (adopted 21 November 1947, entered into force 2 December 1948) 33 UNTS 261. Art III, s 4 of that Convention provides: "The specialized agencies, their property and assets, wherever located and by whomsoever held, shall enjoy immunity from every form of legal process except in so far as in any particular case they have expressly waived their immunity. It is, however, understood that no waiver of immunity shall extend to any measure of execution."

10 International Organizations Immunities Act 1945, 22 USC § 288 (USA).

international organizations would "enjoy the same immunity from suit and every form of judicial process as is enjoyed by foreign governments."[11]

At the time the IOIA was adopted, foreign States were generally entitled to 'absolute' immunity under customary international law as understood and applied in US courts.[12] However, that is no longer the case; the prevailing approach today is one of 'restricted' or 'restrictive' immunity under which foreign States and their organizational components ('agencies and instrumentalities') lack immunity inter alia for their 'commercial activities'.[13] That rule had been codified earlier in US law by the 1976 Foreign Sovereign Immunities Act (FSIA).[14]

In 2019, the US Supreme Court adopted a very literal reading of the IOIA so that international organizations are now entitled in US law to the same immunity granted to foreign States and governments – meaning the FSIA.[15] The decision has introduced a measure of uncertainty into the issues, since international organizations are not like – and do not operate the same ways as – foreign States or governments.[16]

In any event, applying the generally accepted 'functional immunity' standard to the situation described in the hypothetical, it would be difficult to conclude that the Organization's activities had not been carried out within, and as part of, its 'core responsibilities' – meaning the specific purposes for which it was created. Accordingly, the Organization would presumptively be entitled,

---

11 22 USC 288a(b) provides that "[i]nternational organizations, their property and their assets, wherever located, and by whomsoever held, shall enjoy the same immunity from suit and every form of judicial process as is enjoyed by foreign governments, except to the extent that such organizations may expressly waive their immunity for the purpose of any proceedings or by the terms of any contract."

12 Generally, see Tom Ruys and others (eds), *The Cambridge Handbook of Immunities and International Law* (Cambridge University Press 2019).

13 See, for example, the 2004 UN Convention on Jurisdictional Immunities of States and Their Property, adopted by UNGA Res A/59/38 (24 December 2004, not yet in force). See also David P. Stewart, 'The UN Convention on Jurisdictional Immunities of States and Their Property,' 99 American Journal of International Law 194 (2005).

14 Foreign Sovereign Immunities Act 1976, 28 USC. §§ 1330, 1602 et seq. (USA) ('FSIA').

15 See *Jam v. International Finance Corporation*, 586 US 199 (2019). For discussions of the *Jam* decision and the questions it has raised, see Chimène I. Keitner and Scott Dodson, 'Jam v. International Finance Corp.' (2019) 113 American Journal of International Law 805; Rishi Gulati and Philippa Webb, 'The Legal Accountability of Transnational Institutions: Past, Present and Future' (2023) 34 King's Law Journal 411.

16 For instance, the most often invoked exception to the immunity of foreign states concerns their 'commercial activities'. It would be a rare case indeed when the activities of an international organization – especially its 'core' activities – would fall within that exception.

as a matter of international law, to immunity from the jurisdiction not only of the Ecuadorian courts but also those of all other Member States, even those where damage occurred, claimants resided, or (had the Organization been a private entity) claims might otherwise have been brought.[17] Voluntary waiver of such immunity (presumptively requiring the assent of all Member States) would be highly unlikely.

Assuming that to be the case, and that basic principles of justice nonetheless require some possibility of compensation or remediation for those injured or damaged, where (or how) else might the claimants in this instance (and those injured in analogous situations in the future) seek relief? In this regard, legal procedures at the international level, including by recourse to a specialized international tribunal or an arbitral mechanism, may offer viable and effective avenues for obtaining remedies.

3.2 International Tribunals

At the international level, two broad avenues may be considered: (i) creation or use of a supranational judicial body, and (ii) international arbitration mechanisms. Each offers theoretical advantages over domestic proceedings, but each also presents significant legal and political obstacles.

3.2.1 A Specialized Supranational Tribunal

One might contemplate the establishment of an 'internationalized' court for this particular situation, with jurisdiction over all international organizations – or perhaps with jurisdiction to adjudicate all such claims against international organizations in the future – to the exclusion of litigation in national courts and in which the organizations would not be able to invoke immunity. Such an approach might prove more convenient for the organizations themselves and more likely to provide consistency of results in similar cases. Among other challenges, however, it could well be difficult to obtain broad agreement of the Organization's Member States – or the international organizations community as a whole – to accept such oversight and to ensure consistent determination of the applicable *substantive* law to be applied by such a court for claims arising in different countries, although in principle it could be internationally agreed or determined by a specified 'choice of law' formula.

---

17 While it does not appear that any US court has yet addressed the issue, it would seem that the Court's approach in *Jam* could result in an expansion of the immunities afforded to specialized agencies in US courts.

Additionally, creating and maintaining such a tribunal would unquestionably be expensive and cumbersome. Whether all or even most international organizations – or their Member States – would agree to submit to its jurisdiction and procedures seems doubtful. Many would surely argue that all international organizations are not the same, and because the nature and scope of their international mandates differ widely, their various activities simply cannot be judged by a single uniform or 'universal' standard. In any event, any agreement to subject their activities to such an integrated procedure would likely require substantive amendments to their 'charters' or other constituent instruments, and obtaining the necessary agreement of their Member States would be difficult.[18]

3.2.2 A Specialized Arbitral Body

Another alternative might be to forego formal judicial 'litigation' in any domestic judicial system or international 'court' in favor of some agreed form of international arbitration. At least in theory, arbitration has the potential to provide simpler, more expedient and less expensive resolution of claims than domestic litigation, including greater freedom to specify the relevant law. Among the issues that would have to be addressed in creating such a procedure are (i) consent of the claimants and the organizations in question to forego other possible remedies in favor of arbitration, (ii) determination of the applicable law, and (iii) obligations of States in regard to enforcement of the resulting award.

4 A Proposal for 'Conditional Immunity'

As suggested earlier, one might imagine the eventual creation of a court, arbitral body or standing commission with global reach and specifically dedicated to addressing claims by private entities and individuals seeking compensation for harms allegedly attributable to the activities of international organizations in general – either on a 'first instance' basis or (more plausibly) as an appellate

---

18 All international organizations are, of course, unique in various ways, reflecting the differences in their purposes and the areas or activities they were created to regulate. Because the particular governance structures of various international organizations represent different geopolitical bargains, a single 'world international organization court' would face significant challenges in setting uniform rules for governance and liability.

body empowered to review relevant decisions of the international organizations themselves.

Short of that, another possibility exists to promote the international community's interests in achieving a more effective and harmonized regime for resolving such claims expeditiously while preserving the independence of international organizations from the domestic laws and procedures of their host countries or Member State: namely, the adoption of a new rule providing that, for claims arising from their 'core' functions and purposes, the organizations would have immunity dependent upon the provision of adequate and effective internal mechanisms for addressing claims arising from matters falling within the scope of the unique purposes and functions for which that organization was created by the international community. Under such an approach, the entitlement of an international organization to 'functional immunity' from other adjudicative processes – especially in the domestic courts of various States – would rest on its affirmative commitment to address claims concerning its 'core' functions and purposes through effective and efficient internal procedures.

Among the advantages of such an approach might well be (relative) speed, efficiency and consistency. Allowing the organizations themselves to consider such claims and (where justified) to remedy the wrongs is certainly consistent with their supranational status and, in at least some circumstances, would be more likely to have a positive (ameliorative) effect on the organizations in question. From a practical and logistical standpoint, requiring all claimants to present their claims at the organizations' headquarters (or retaining counsel to do so)[19] would certainly be more efficient for the organizations themselves and, depending on the circumstances, might well be less burdensome for the claimants. It could also promote consistency in approach.

Many governments in fact provide analogous processes in their domestic laws,[20] and some form of arbitral or adjudicative process has already been used by many international organizations to resolve various types of internal

19 Some of these challenges could be mitigated through use of online procedures permitting remote access and participation.

20 In the United States, for example, the Federal Tort Claims Act authorizes plaintiffs to obtain compensation from the federal government for the torts of its employees through an administrative process. The statute is codified at 28 USC §§ 1346(b), 2671–80. Generally, see Michael D. Contino and Andreas Kuersten, 'The Federal Tort Claims Act: A Legal Overview' (Cong. Research Sev. R45732, 17 April 2023) <https://www.congress.gov/crs-product/R45732?q=%7B%22search%22%3A%22The+Federal+Tort+Claims+Claim+A+Legal+Overview%22%7D&s=1&r=1> accessed 13 December 2025.

employment-related disputes, in preference to having those disputes submitted to host country courts and law.[21]

From the claimants' perspective, the obvious concerns would be permitting the alleged wrongdoers to sit in judgment of their own actions, the possible challenges of enforcing 'internal' decisions or awards against recalcitrant international organizations,[22] and the possibility of substantively inconsistent judgments from one international organization to another.[23] These concerns can be resolved, however. The first, for instance, could be addressed by including independent (outside) authorities as members of the tribunals. The second could be resolved by the international organization's explicit agreement to comply with relevant decisions. The third, while more challenging, might plausibly be addressed by the various international organizations' adoption of 'standardized' guiding principles.

The scope of such immunity might be described as 'core-function-plus' – to reflect that it would extend beyond requiring clear evidence that a ruling by the domestic court on the matter in question would demonstrably *prevent* the international organization from carrying out the 'core mission' assigned to it by the international community. It would also encompass matters that would *interfere* (unduly or unreasonably) with the organization's functions or burden it in doing so.

This somewhat more flexible standard might prove beneficial (and therefore attractive) to claimants and the international organizations alike. It would give domestic courts greater leeway in providing a measure of justice to deserving claimants by reducing the threshold for exercising their jurisdiction. It would not, however, allow the organization to frustrate a resolution of the claims merely by asserting immunity or contending that the issue in question concerned a 'function' or responsibility of the organization.

At the same time, the exercise of such jurisdiction would be dependent on the claimants showing that the concerned international organization had not in fact offered 'adequate and effective' internal procedures for resolving the claim or claims in question, or that the international organization had previ-

---

21 See, for example, International Law Commission, 'Report of the International Law Commission on the Work of its Sixty-eighth Session' (2016), UN Doc A/71/10 at 387, Annex A (Sir Michael Wood, 'The Settlement of International Disputes to Which International Organizations are Parties').

22 Absent a specific waiver of immunity in respect of such decisions.

23 It is standard practice, of course, for international organizations to use such internal mechanisms to resolve disputes brought by their employees. Ensuring consistency in applying the relevant rules and principles to claims by 'outsiders' such as private individuals and in respect of substantive issues is likely to present greater challenges.

ously and consistently denied similar claims, or that in denying the claim it had abused or exceeded its authority. Under such conditions, recourse to external judicial remedies – that is, to the host country's courts (or those of third countries) or to other kinds of remedies such as arbitration – would be available only when the required internal mechanisms were not available or had proved nonfunctional. The impetus would thus be placed on the international organization to provide effective avenues for claimants to pursue their interests through the organization's internal procedures before taking their claims outside, whether to the host country courts or the judicial system of a third country.

Admittedly, this broad proposal leaves several important details unresolved. They include, for instance, how to define an international organization's 'core' purposes and functions, what kinds or categories of claims might be excluded in favor of other remedies, what an abuse of authority might mean, whether dissatisfied claimants would have a right to an appeal and, if so, to what court or body, and how application of the 'functional' approach might be coordinated across differing organizations and areas of regulation.

Different arrangements might well be appropriate for different types of claims or families of organizations (for example, global vs. regional, human rights vs. scientific, technical vs. commercial). Some of these issues could be addressed in (i) a standardized dispute settlement procedure that international organizations could themselves adopt and (ii) a model law for adoption by individual 'host countries'.

5 Conclusion

As the role and importance of international organizations in the global community continue to grow, the kinds of risks suggested in the hypothetical situation described above also increase. Providing international organizations with a substantial measure of immunity from domestic laws, courts and procedures may be necessary for them to accomplish their missions successfully, but it should not result in impunity or a lack of responsibility for righting wrongs where justified.

The challenge is to determine the appropriate balance between these competing goals: on the one hand, to protect the integrity, independence and ability of international organizations to accomplish the work (the 'core functions') they were created to accomplish, without undue interference from host country laws and courts, while, on the other hand, to provide effective avenues for the resolution of claims by individuals and entities claiming to have been harmed in one way or another by an international organization's actions (or inactions).

Contemporary international law and practice, however, do not provide a uniform approach to this challenge. Typically, the immunity of the international organization in question is determined without regard to the interests of claimants but instead by the organization's needs and circumstances, and reflected in its constitutive instrument, a separate agreement between its Member States addressing its privileges and immunities, or (perhaps most concretely) a 'headquarters agreement' or other formal arrangement between the organization and its host State.[24] The thrust of the current proposal is simple: to condition the availability of 'core functions' immunity from domestic jurisdiction upon the availability of alternative procedures or mechanisms for claims resolution.

For any given organization, it may be possible to articulate and adopt separate rules and procedures for different types of claims, distinguishing for instance between claims arising from (i) the organization's substantive policies and programs or other actions, (ii) internal personnel or disciplinary matters, (iii) 'commercial' dealings with outside contractors and suppliers, and (iv) local 'torts' such as automobile accidents or allegations of libel and slander. In some situations, host State laws and regulations may be applicable, requiring (as a matter of public policy) referral to local law and procedures. In other circumstances, it might be possible to condition the organization's agreement to engage with local (host country) procedures on a requirement that the claimant first engage with available internal processes and procedures.

---

24 See, for example, the Agreement between the United Nations and the United States Regarding the Headquarters of the United Nations (signed 26 June 1947, entered into force 21 November 1947), 11 UNTS 11. Other countries have adopted such statutes, including inter alia the United Kingdom, Canada, The Netherlands, Switzerland, Australia, Thailand, Singapore, Malaysia and Papua New Guinea, to name only a few.

MANUAL

How to Be a Good Employer? The Duties of International Organizations Constituted by the ILO Administrative Tribunal

*Dražen Petrović and Bianca Carrer**

Abstract This manual presents the case law of the Administrative Tribunal of the International Labour Organization (ILOAT), up to the 139th session, analysing what would be relevant for international organizations in their role of employers. It is an attempt to identify major trends in the case law, so that decision-makers and legislative bodies in the organizations under the jurisdiction of the ILOAT may be guided on how to avoid liability before the ILOAT. As the ILOAT is often cited by other international administrative tribunals, this manual may help inform their case law. What is said by the ILOAT could be considered as best practice in the law of the international civil service. The manual is divided in three major categories, covering together 13 major duties of international organizations.

1 Introduction

The Administrative Tribunal of the International Labour Organization (hereinafter ILOAT or the Tribunal) has a unique position in the law of the international civil service. As its jurisdiction covers some 60 international organizations, it can influence significantly their procedures and policies and can indirectly harmonize their internal systems, although they remain autonomous. The judgments of the ILOAT formally bind only the parties to a dispute (*inter partes* effect) but, in reality, every judgment is widely discussed within the organizations concerned and the effects of the judgments are much larger. As a result, internal rules and procedures are often adjusted or amended and

* Respectively former Registrar and Legal Officer at the Registry of the ILOAT. The views expressed herein are those of the authors and do not necessarily reflect the views of the International Labour Organization, nor of its Administrative Tribunal.

 | HTTPS://DOI.ORG/10.1163/9789004765672-008

the arguments arising from the case law are often used in negotiations between the organizations and staff representatives. Nevertheless, organizations sometimes do not take into account the Tribunal's case law and do not amend their internal rules following the latest judgments of the Tribunal. This may be due to the lack of political will, ignorance or misunderstanding. As such behaviour creates an unnecessary legal risk for the organization, it is always useful to learn what the case law of the ILOAT is. Since the ILOAT case law is often referred to by other international administrative tribunals, this manual may also contribute to harmonizing the international civil service law.

The general idea of this manual is to offer readers a summary of the case law on several topics that are relevant for internal governance of international organizations, for example, on how to draft internal staff rules (the rules of the interpretation applied by the ILOAT may be used as a guidance for the way rules should be drafted), the notion of acquired rights, what is the extent of the duty of care in different situations, what principles must guide internal justice systems, and how to handle contract management (especially the non-renewal of contracts), and so forth. The jurisprudence of the ILOAT with over 5,000 judgments is not easy to grasp by decision-makers, and this manual may help to identify both stable case law and some recent trends, and to open up avenues for reflection on possible measures that organizations can take in specific areas where nothing exists yet or improvements can be made.

There are several areas where the case law of the ILOAT made clear what is expected from international organizations under its jurisdiction, as employers. In order to facilitate reading, we will group them into three major categories.

The first category deals with shaping an internal legal order. It comprises three principal duties:

(i) duty to create an internal legal system and comply with it;
(ii) duty to create an efficient mechanism for dealing with the claims of staff members in an internal justice system; and
(iii) duty to properly manage employment contracts.

The second category covers the ways to observe the officials' substantive rights. It outlines four principal duties:

(i) duty to respect the acquired rights;
(ii) duty to ensure a safe, adequate and healthy, harassment-free work environment for staff members;
(iii) duty to provide remedies when non-compliance with the rules caused damage to staff members; and
(iv) duty to provide social protection to staff members.

The third category explains how to comply with procedural requirements. It comprises six principal duties:

(i) duty to take individual administrative decisions in a transparent and lawful manner;
(ii) duty to respond to officials' queries and do it in a timely manner;
(iii) duty to assess performance of officials in a transparent and fair manner;
(iv) duty to comply with basic rules and principles applicable in the case of restructuring;
(v) duty to guarantee due process rights in disciplinary proceedings; and
(vi) duty of assistance with respect to host States.

It is important to note that the underlying rationale in all those areas is the general duty of international organizations towards their staff members, which exists in all fields of law and at all levels, and is manifested through concrete examples. In all those areas, there is an overarching rule: organizations' internal rules must be respected. On the one hand, while those rules may be outdated, obsolete or the organizations may be hesitant to propose new rules to the governing bodies or negotiate them with the staff representatives, until they are amended or repealed, the organizations have to abide by them, in accordance with the principle *tu patere legem quam ipse fecisti* ("[a]ny authority is bound by the rules it has itself issued until it amends or repeals them").[1] On the other hand, all officials are expected to know their rights and the rules and regulations to which they are subject, and ignorance or misunderstanding of the law is no excuse (*ignorantia juris non excusat*).[2]

This manual aims at providing a general framework and forms part of a longer process of study aimed at identifying what, according to our analysis and understanding of the ILOAT case law,[3] may constitute the elements enabling all parties involved in the employment relationship to act in the best possible way and in accordance with what is required of them.

---

1 Judgment 4312, consid 2; Judgment 4506, consid 5 and Judgment 4310, consid 9 (for references purposes, all Judgments referred to in the present manual are those of the ILOAT, unless explicitly stated otherwise).

2 Judgment 4777, consid 6; Judgment 4673, consid 16; Judgment 4573, consid 4; Judgment 4324, consid 11; and Judgment 4032, consid 6.

3 Our selection is inevitably subjective and non-exhaustive. It must be emphasized that everything written in this manual expresses personal opinions of the authors, and not the views of the ILOAT judges. One should bear in mind that the case law is constantly developed, which means that our analysis stops at the latest judgments delivered by the ILOAT at its 139th session, but that developments are possible, and even inevitable, in the years to come. Therefore, the case law database of the Tribunal, TRIBLEX <https://webapps.ilo.org/dyn/triblex/triblexmain.bySession?p_lang=en&p_all=N> (accessed 13 December 2025), remains the main tool to keep track of developments in the ILOAT case law.

We do hope that readers will find the entire manual interesting and will be able to read it from start to finish. However, as the manual is intended to serve as a practical guide and assist readers when dealing with specific situations, each section is self-contained and may be read separately.

2 Shaping an Internal Legal Order

It is now generally accepted that international organizations can and should create their own internal legal systems. Leaving aside the debate about the exact nature of these legal systems (namely, whether they form part of international law, or constitute a *sui generis* body of law), this section focuses on three areas in which the ILOAT case law is relevant. The first deals with the duty to create an internal legal system, determining its sources of law, hierarchy between them, the way the norms are interpreted, as well as the importance of the duty to comply with them, for reasons of legal stability, transparency and accountability. The second emphasizes the duty to create an efficient mechanism for dealing with claims of staff members in an internal justice system, which constitutes part of the general duty to create an internal legal system but has its own importance for the immunity from national jurisdiction. The third area focuses on the importance of employment contracts, as one of the sources of the international civil service law, and the duty of an organization to properly manage them.

2.1 Duty to Create an Internal Legal System and Comply with It

The independence of international organizations from national legal orders creates the need for them to develop their own internal legal systems. Although the internal legal systems of international organizations can rely on national laws in a few exceptional circumstances,[4] they are distinct from national laws, have their own sources of law and their own hierarchy and are frequently rather complex.[5]

---

4 For example, when the internal rules refer to national laws specifically, or when there is a need to clarify some notions that the internal rules do not define, or to identify general principles of law (see Section 4.6). For more discussions, see Dražen Petrović, 'Domestic Law and International Administrative Tribunals' in Jorge Viñuales and others (eds), *The International Legal Order in the XXIst Century, Essays in Honour of Professor Marcelo Gustavo Kohen* (Brill Nijhoff 2023), 611–627.

5 Santiago Villalpando, 'The Law of International Civil Service' in Jacob Katz Cogan, Ian Hurd and Ian Johnstone (eds), *The Oxford Handbook of International Organizations* (OUP 2016).

Importing merely what is stated in national laws is not a good idea, since the national legal systems have many mechanisms to ensure their compliance, development and enforcement. Without those mechanisms, simply copying national laws in the internal rules of the organizations risks compromising the effectiveness of the rules. It is better for the organizations to create their own internal legal systems. While this is within the discretion of the governing organs of each organization, it is limited by several parameters. The first is the constituent instrument of each organization. The second consists of general principles of international law, since international organizations are subjects of international law and are bound by international law comparable to States.[6] The third parameter concerns the general principles of law developed by judicial bodies whose jurisdiction has been accepted by the organizations, together with their case law of general applicability. This is particularly important for the case law of international administrative tribunals, although some other courts, such as the International Court of Justice, may also be relevant.

When creating their internal legal systems, the organizations must be mindful of the hierarchy of norms and certain rules that flow from it, for example, that lower-level norms cannot derogate from the higher-level norms,[7] or that the principle *lex specialis derogat generali* (namely, a specific rule prevails over a general one) does not apply to the rules of different hierarchical level.[8] This is important to keep in mind since there is sometimes a tendency to comprehensively deal with an issue in an administrative instruction, guideline or internal office notice, while overlooking that a higher norm already dealt with it or at least announced a general principle. As such, written norms should be drafted keeping in mind that their interpretation will be subject to the following rules:[9]

(i) words are to be given their obvious and ordinary meaning;[10]
(ii) the meaning of words must be construed objectively in their context and in keeping with their purport and purpose;[11] and

---

6 Kristina Daugirdas, 'How and Why International Law Binds International Organizations' (2016) 57 Harvard International Law Journal 325.

7 Judgment 4316, consid 13; Judgment 3322, consid 6; and Judgment 1631, consid 15.

8 Judgment 3339, consid 3.

9 See also cases cited by Laurent Germond, *Les Principles généraux selon le Tribunal administratif de l'O.I.T.* (Pedone 2009), 20–21.

10 Judgment 4827, consid 5; Judgment 4681, consid 5; Judgment 4639, consid 3; Judgment 4477, consid 4; Judgment 4145, consid 4; Judgment 3310, consid 7; and Judgment 2276, consid 4.

11 Judgment 4796, consid 3; Judgment 4639, consid 3; Judgment 4066, consid 7; Judgment 4031, consid 5; and Judgment 3744, consid 8.

(iii) the context must be discerned from the provision and not just from a phrase "taken in isolation".[12]

Where the language of the text is clear and unambiguous, the words must be given effect without looking outside of the text to determine the meaning.[13] The rules that are ambiguous will be interpreted according to the *contra preferentem* rule: a clause in a document should be interpreted in favour of the party who did not draft the clause (in this case the staff member), and not in favour of the party who did draft the clause, sought the inclusion of the clause or possibly in whose interests the clause was intended to operate.[14] If the interpretation concerns the regulations or rules of an international organization, it must in principle be construed in favour of the interests of its staff and not those of the organization itself.[15] When a provision is capable of more than one interpretation, the interpretation favouring a broader application for the benefit of staff members, rather than that of narrower application which could deprive staff members of the benefit, should be adopted.[16]

When the text exists in more than one language – as is often the case in international organizations – and there is no express mention that a particular version of the text is authentic and that others are only translations, or that one linguistic version prevails,[17] all linguistic versions shall be deemed to bear the same meaning. If a comparison of those versions reveals a point of divergence, the interpretation that should prevail is the one that, having due regard to the purpose of the text, best reconciles the different versions.[18]

As there is no perfect legal text, some issues may not be covered by it. In that case, there may be a need to identify implied terms in the rules.[19] But more importantly, it is the ILOAT case law that should be taken into account in such situations. For example, the internal rules of an organization are often

---

12 Judgment 4477, consid 4; and Judgment 4145, consid 4.

13 Judgment 3701, consid 4. In particular, there is no need to look at the preparatory works or supposed intent of the lawmaker. On this point, see Judgment 4818, consid 18.

14 Judgment 4057, consid 3.

15 Judgment 4921, consid 3; Judgment 4639, consid 3; Judgment 3539, consid 8; Judgment 3355, consid 16; Judgment 2396, consid 3(a); Judgment 2276, consid 4; and Judgment 1755, consid 12.

16 Judgment 3539, consid 8.

17 For an example see Judgment 4931, consid 12.

18 Judgment 853, consid 5.

19 Judgment 2805, consid 7: "Where regulations and rules or other written documents are silent as to a matter, a term dealing with that matter may be implied, but only if it is so obviously comprehended within the text used in the regulations and rules or other document that its statement is unnecessary, or, if the term to be implied is necessary to give effect to some other term."

silent about the damage to be awarded in the case of its negligence, as the organization does not want to admit that they could be negligent. In such situations, the ILOAT ruled that the payment of damages was due in addition to what is already foreseen in the rules for a non-fault injury or illness. In Judgment 4222, the Tribunal dealt with the claim for damage of a staff member of the United Nations Educational, Scientific and Cultural Organization (UNESCO) who fractured her ankle on the organization's premises. The accident was recognized as work-related, and, as provided for in the internal rules, all medical expenses directly related to the injury were settled by UNESCO. However, the official claimed additional damage. The ILOAT found that the accident was caused by the negligence of UNESCO and that, according to its case law, an organization may incur liability in negligence where it fails to take reasonable steps to prevent a foreseeable risk of injury.[20] Pursuant to the principle that full compensation is due in respect of injuries caused by negligence, the ILOAT determined that the complainant was entitled to compensation for injuries not already compensated under the Staff Compensation Plan.[21]

Another example of what is due when the rules are silent concerns moral injury in relation to a service-incurred illness or accident. In Judgment 4239, the ILOAT examined a claim for compensation of a former staff member of the World Health Organization (WHO) who suffered a brain injury in a car accident while on duty in India. As a result of the brain injury, she became permanently unable to perform her previous professional activity or any professional activity. WHO recognized it as a service-incurred accident, and compensated it accordingly, but the ILOAT found that, in addition, WHO had an ongoing responsibility to do all it could to mitigate the effects of the accident as part of a more general obligation to protect the health and ensure the safety of its staff. Although the Tribunal did not find that WHO was negligent, it concluded that there was a possibility that the breach of WHO's duty of care towards the complainant when she returned to Geneva had led or contributed to the professional and personal circumstances in which the complainant found herself. The Tribunal stated:

> An inference can readily be drawn that the complainant knows that, had she received appropriate treatment immediately on her return to Geneva, her grave present predicament, arising so early in her adult life, might not have come about and also she believes WHO should have done more to support and help

20 Judgment 4222, consid 16, referring to Judgment 3733, consid 12; Judgment 3215, consid 12; and Judgment 2804, consid 25.

21 Judgment 4222, consid 17.

> her. It cannot be doubted that these matters have caused and will continue to cause the complainant considerable distress.[22]

In addition to all amounts statutorily due in the case of a service-incurred illness, the Tribunal awarded the complainant 180,000 United States dollars in moral damages. In Judgment 4602, the ILOAT examined the case of a victim of harassment who was denied compensation by the World Trade Organization (WTO) on the grounds that this was not provided for in the internal rules. The Tribunal rejected this argument saying that:

> [T]he WTO's assertion, to the effect that no provision in the internal regulations, rules or policies directly provides for the possibility of a compensation to the individuals who filed a harassment complaint, is in tension with and indeed ignores [the Tribunal's] rather clear case law which recognises the right to such compensation when properly supported.[23]

As a result, the Tribunal awarded the complainant 10,000 Swiss francs for moral damages. An organization can also import into its legal system legal texts adopted by other entities. This is the case of organizations belonging to the United Nations common system, which relies on the International Civil Service Commission (ICSC) for the establishment of certain salary scales and entitlements. The ILOAT determined that in such situations the organization has to assess the lawfulness of those standards before implementing them.[24]

There are always situations where written rules do not cover all the issues that may arise in the functioning of an organization and where some unwritten rules may apply. The ILOAT has admitted that administrative practice can be a source of law.[25] However, the party who relies on a practice bears the burden to prove its existence.[26] Moreover, the practice cannot contravene a

---

22 Judgment 4239, consid 26.

23 Judgment 4602, consid 14.

24 See, for example, Judgment 2420, consid 11; Judgment 1765, consid 8; and Judgment 1265, consid 24.

25 See recent Judgment 4994, consid 6, and the case law cited therein. In general, see Christian Rohde, 'Organizational Practice as a Source of Law' in Dražen Petrović (ed), *90 Years of Contribution of the Administrative Tribunal of the International Labour Organization to the Creation of International Civil Service Law* (ILO 2017) <https://www.ilo.org/sites/default/files/wcmsp5/groups/public/%40dgreports/%40trib/documents/meetingdocument/wcms_613945.pdf> accessed 13 December 2025 (90 Years of Contribution of the ILOAT), 53–73.

26 Judgment 4716, consid 11, and the case law cited therein.

specific written rule already in force[27] and the change of practice must be clearly announced.[28]

Whenever the rules can be identified, the most important rule for an organization is that "as long as the rules are neither amended nor repealed, the principle *tu patere legem quam ipse fecisti* [namely, any authority is bound by the rules it has itself issued] requires the Organization to apply them".[29] There are sometimes situations in which the organization decides to ignore their own rules. Whatever argument may be presented in favour of doing that, it is difficult to convince a tribunal, such as the ILOAT, that a specific rule should be ignored. If there are legitimate reasons why the rule should no longer apply, the organization should amend or repeal it through the proper procedures.

2.2 Duty to Create an Efficient Mechanism for Dealing with Claims of Staff Members in an Internal Justice System

International organizations under the ILOAT's jurisdiction should – whenever possible – create internal conflict-resolution mechanisms to settle disputes that may arise with their employees.[30] Internal remedies constitute an important safeguard of staff rights, in addition to their right of appeal to a judicial authority, and social harmony.[31] The ILOAT considers that the internal appeal process is an extremely significant element of the entire system of review of administrative decisions affecting the rights of staff employed by organizations which have accepted its jurisdiction.[32] This is especially true since internal appeal bodies may normally allow an appeal on grounds of fairness or advisability,[33] whereas the Tribunal must essentially give a ruling on points of law.[34] The review of a disputed decision in an internal appeal procedure may well suffice to resolve a dispute, one of the main justifications for such a procedure

27 See Judgment 4770, consid 14; Judgment 4555, consid 11; Judgment 4026, consid 6; Judgment 2959, consid 7; and Judgment 2556, consid 12.

28 Judgment 4425, consid 7.

29 Judgment 4506, consid 5.

30 Renuka Dhinakaran and Alex P Haines, 'Internal Justice Systems of International Organisations - Legitimacy Index 2018' (International Administrative Law Centre of Excellence 2018) <https://rm.coe.int/internal-justice-systems-ofinternational-organisations-legitimacy-ind/1680952638 accessed 13 December 2025, 7.

31 See, for example, Judgment 3253, consid 15; Judgment 3184, consid 15; and Judgment 1317, consid 31.

32 Judgment 3253, consid 15; and Judgment 3222, consid 9.

33 Judgment 3732, consid 2.

34 Judgment 4923, consid 5.

is to enable the final decision-maker within the organization, and the Tribunal, in the event that a complaint is ultimately lodged, to have before them the findings of fact, items of information or assessment resulting from the deliberations of appeal bodies, especially those whose membership includes representatives of both staff and management, as is often the case.[35] The 'encouragement' to create internal conflict-resolution mechanisms derives, implicitly but clearly enough, from Article VII, paragraph 1, of the Tribunal's Statute, which must be complied with both in terms of time limits and of the procedural rules which are laid down.[36]

Most international organizations have set up a more or less complex system of internal recourse. For some of them, this system comprises several stages (sometimes also including an informal mechanism which may even be mandatory or left to the initiative of the parties involved), constituting a sort of "double (or even triple) degree of reconsideration" of contested decisions, omissions or actions.[37] These stages can even be combined with specific preliminary procedures for particular areas such as harassment, disciplinary proceedings or medical matters. If, on the face of it, the multitude of stages ensures that the guarantees granted to officials will be strengthened – assuming that these steps are carried out objectively and without bias – there are nevertheless obvious downsides, such as longer timeframes for dealing with disputes, additional costs if officials consult lawyers, or even a possible increase in the material or moral damage suffered by the official depending on the issues at stake. The risk for the organizations is to be 'caught at their own game' with the multitude of procedures when, for example, unforeseen events arise in terms of workforce, workload or even environmental context (considering the COVID-19 pandemic as an example), which makes it difficult for them to comply with their own rules. Practical difficulties cannot exonerate an organization from its responsibility. It is up to the organization to overcome a shortage of human or financial resources, so that no staff member who is waiting for a decision suffers undue delay, which constitutes a denial of a staff member's right to have their requests handled with due diligence.[38]

---

35 Judgment 3732, consid 2, and the case law cited therein.

36 See, for example, Judgment 4929, consid 4; Judgment 4927, consid 3; Judgment 3296, consid 10; Judgment 3027, consid 6; and Judgment 1653, consid 6.

37 Laurence Fauth, 'Due Process and Equality of Arms in the Internal Appeal: New Developments from Judgments 3586 and 3688' in Petrović (ed), *90 Years of Contribution of the ILOAT* (note 25), 184–185.

38 Judgment 4924, consid 17; Judgment 4923, consid 18; Judgment 4922, consid 22; Judgment 4748, consid 7; Judgment 4284, consid 8, and the case law cited therein.

In the end, the 'not-so-obvious' task facing international organizations which provide for internal redress mechanisms is to find the right balance between, on the one hand, creating and operating an efficient internal justice system that guarantees the rights of the parties involved and, on the other hand, respect their own rules and not penalize the parties involved with procedural, time or financial constraints. In this sense, it is firmly established in the case law that, as part of their duty of care, organizations have an obligation to maintain a properly functioning appeal system that adheres to the established rules and regulations.[39]

This obligation takes various forms, some of which go well beyond simple compliance with internal rules, for example, when filing an internal claim or appeal. It is true that the rules of procedure set up by the organizations should ordinarily be strictly complied with, but they must not set traps for officials who are defending their rights and therefore they must not be construed too pedantically.[40] For example, when an official submits an appeal to the wrong authority, it is for that authority to forward it to the one which is competent, within the organization, to hear it.[41] In such a situation, it is not sufficient for the authority merely to inform the official that it is not competent and to suggest that they apply to the competent authority.[42] Or, when an internal appeal is tainted with a flaw other than late submission, which prevents it from being considered as properly filed, it is for the internal appeal bodies, in the exercise of their duty of care, to enable the appellant to correct the appeal by granting them a reasonable period of time in which to do so.[43] In the same vein, with regard to the form of an appeal lodged by an official, organizations need to be 'open-minded' in their interpretation of the document addressed to them, meaning that, for a letter or an e-mail to constitute an appeal, it is sufficient that the official clearly expresses therein their intention to challenge the decision adversely affecting them and that the request thus formulated can be granted in some meaningful way.[44] If the organization feels that the appeal does not contain sufficient details for it to be able to examine it, it should ask the official for additional information.[45]

---

39 Judgment 4748, consid 6; and Judgment 4384, consid 7.

40 Judgment 3034, consid 15.

41 Judgment 4542, consid 3; Judgment 4517, consid 6; Judgment 3424, consid 8(b); Judgment 3027, consid 7, and the case law cited therein.

42 Judgment 3595, consid 10.

43 Judgment 4028, consid 2; Judgment 3943, consid 5; and Judgment 3127, consid 10.

44 Judgment 4461, consid 5; Judgment 3829, consid 6; Judgment 3068, consid 16; Judgment 2572, consid 9; Judgment 1172, consid 7; and Judgment 461, consid 3.

45 Judgment 3067, consid 16.

As to the possibility to settle disputes amicably, mechanisms for an informal, voluntary and amicable resolution of disputes are not always expressly provided for in the internal rules of international organizations. And yet, this is an option which exists in any event, even in the absence of any provisions on the subject. Indeed, dialogue is a faculty inherent in the management power of organizations and, more specifically, their administration, but it is also an aptitude inherent in the status of civil servants. As explained in 'A Staff Member's Guide to Resolving Disputes' at the United Nations, which can undoubtedly be transposed to the system of organizations under the jurisdiction of the Tribunal:

> Taking an informal approach to resolving a dispute can be preferable for the staff member and any other party that is involved. Informal dialogue is often less stressful than formal legal action, offers more control of the outcome and often creates mutually beneficial solutions. The outcome is agreed to by both parties, as opposed to cases brought before the Tribunal whose judgment may be in favour of one party only. It can also take much less time to discuss finding a solution to a grievance than it takes to work the case through the formal system.[46]

The ILOAT strongly encourages the use of informal, voluntary and amicable dispute resolution mechanisms.[47] According to its case law:

> It is now almost universally recognised that the settlement of legal disputes is, in many cases, a preferable outcome than the full ventilation of legal and factual issues in contested litigation to be resolved by the adjudication of a court of justice. Some cases, by their very nature, will take that path. However, many others are more appropriately resolved by discussion and agreement. The parties control the terms of an agreed outcome even if, as is almost always the case, it involves some reciprocated compromise. There appears to be a regrettable attitude amongst some parties before the Tribunal, both individual complainants and defendant organisations alike, not to entertain the possibility of settlement by agreement. It should be otherwise.[48]

---

46 United Nations, 'A Staff Member's Guide to Resolving Disputes' <https://www.un.org/en/internaljustice/assets/pdf/StaffMembersGuideToResolvingDisputes.pdf> accessed 13 December 2025, Ch 3.

47 See, for example, Judgment 3901, consid 11; Judgment 3900, consid 11, and the case law cited therein.

48 Judgment 3731, consid 7. See also Judgment 3901, consid 11; and Judgment 3900, consid 11.

The settlement may be subject to some conditions, for example, to keep confidential the terms of the settlement agreement or to waive the right to challenge the final settlement in an appeal. When the legality of such conditions were questioned before the Tribunal, it clearly stated that "the subject conditions are usual in negotiated settlement agreements, and [...] it is entirely acceptable for an official to waive a right to appeal or to file a complaint in return for the benefits gained from a settlement".[49]

If there is no agreed settlement, internal appeal bodies play a crucial role within the internal justice system.[50] Several guiding principles may be identified to ensure their proper functioning:

(i) The composition of the internal appeal bodies must comply with the procedural rules in force at the time of the examination of the appeal[51] and must be balanced in representation, composed not only of members appointed by the organization, but also of those elected by the staff. The members from both groups should participate in the work of an appeal body.[52]

(ii) Impartiality and independence of the internal appeal bodies' members should not be in doubt.[53] Because officials do have a right to a fair procedure and that due process rights should be ensured, internal appeal bodies should treat them fairly.[54] In this regard, the Tribunal has stated that:

> An internal appeal procedure that works properly [...] necessarily encompasses the requirement that the members of an internal appeal body should not only be impartial and objective in fact, but that they should so conduct themselves and be so circumstanced that a reason-

---

49 Judgment 4395, consid 4.

50 For a detailed presentation of the case law, see Bianca Carrer, 'La procédure de recours interne précédant la saisine du Tribunal administratif de l'Organisation internationale du Travail: du côté des organes paritaires' (Institut luxembourgeois des droits de l'homme) <https://4d9506f4.isolation.zscaler.com/profile/c74b2a4e-bf34-49a3-99e2-b37b8f0318e7/zia-session/?controls_id=3bca35d1-c8dd-4d4b-af12-d92e23a2f927&region=was&tenant=17f781a9f280&user=3afce6b0ee9413fb956ec7592b45b7907d0132a1e1b561af98533c4e88bfd623&original_url=https%3A%2F%2Fildh.lu%2F2021%2F10%2F04%2Fla-procedure-de-recours-interne-precedant-la-saisine-du-tribunal-administratif-de-lorganisation-internationale-du-travail-du-cote-des-organes-paritaires-bianca-carrer%2F&key=sh-1&hmac=9c7ac360f765f9c774eb6e1a7925e9baea61834c7ddbab90497606019ee432c2> accessed 13 December 2025.

51 Judgment 3896, consid 4; Judgment 3895, consid 4; and Judgment 2667, consid 5.

52 See, in this regard, Judgment 4318, consid 6; and Judgment 4049, consids 5–6.

53 Judgment 1127, consid 8.

54 Judgment 2667, consid 5.

> able person in possession of the facts would not think otherwise. [Hence], it is necessary only to observe that staff confidence in internal appeal procedures is essential to the workings of all international organisations and to preventing disputes from going outside those organisations.[55]

In the event of a conflict of interest, organizations should establish mechanisms for disqualification and recusal.[56]

(iii) As to the scope of the power of review of internal appeal bodies, it extends to the overall re-examination of all matters submitted to it and, as such, is not subject to the same restrictions that might apply to the judicial review by the Tribunal.[57] The only exception to this is if the rules governing the review body provide for such restrictions.[58]

(iv) In order to ensure the officials' right to an effective internal appeal, the appeal bodies do have a duty to review all claims and pleas raised by the officials.[59]

(v) This obligation to review all claims and pleas goes hand in hand with the duty of the internal appeal bodies to give reasons, in fact and in law, in their opinions and reports. They must demonstrate that they have carried out a balanced and thoughtful analysis of the issues raised in the internal appeal to be able to issue justified and rational recommendations.[60] In particular, there should be consistency between the findings of the internal appeal body and its recommendations.[61]

(vi) Depending on the statutory and regulatory provisions specific to different organizations, the internal appeal bodies may, if they consider it necessary, summon and hear witnesses as part of their examination of a case. If they decide to do so, they are responsible for assessing the reliability of the evidence adduced, keeping in mind that a full appreciation of the evidence can only occur "in circumstances where individuals whose interests may have been adversely affected have an opportunity not only to be present to hear the evidence but also to

---

55 Judgment 2671, consid 11, citing Judgment 1317, consid 31. See also Judgment 4915, consid 7, and the case law cited therein.

56 Judgment 4140, consid 4.

57 Judgment 5003, consid 5; Judgment 4923, consid 5; Judgment 3318, consid 5; and Judgment 3423, consid 12.

58 Judgment 5003, consid 5; and Judgment 3318, consid 5.

59 Judgment 4170, consid 6; Judgment 4169, consid 5; Judgment 4063, consid 5; and Judgment 3284, consid 27.

60 Judgment 4999, consid 6; Judgment 4180, consid 7; Judgment 4010, consid 7; Judgment 3400, consid 6; Judgment 3284, consid 27; and Judgment 2295, consid 10.

61 Judgment 4170, consid 5; Judgment 3934, consid 4.

test the evidence through cross-examination."[62] Officials may also request that certain witnesses be heard. Should the internal appeal body decide to refuse such request, its decision must be based on valid grounds.[63]

(vii) The appellants' right to be heard must be guaranteed but that does not necessarily mean that a hearing is mandatory when requested. All that the right to a hearing requires is that the appellants be free to put their case, either in writing or orally; the appeal body is not obliged to offer them both possibilities.[64] If the internal appeal body considers that it had gleaned sufficient information about the case from the parties' written submissions and documentary evidence, it is under no obligation to invite the appellants to put their case orally, or indeed to accede to any request to that effect.[65]

(viii) Because officials must, as a general rule, have access to all evidence on which the authority bases or intends to base a decision affecting a personal interest worthy of protection,[66] the internal appeal bodies must communicate to them all relevant documents received in the course of the examination of a case. Disclosure of documents and information permits to ensure the adversarial principle.[67] The Tribunal has held that:

> Under normal circumstances, evidence cannot be withheld on grounds of confidentiality unless there is some special case in which a higher interest stands in the way of the disclosure of certain documents. But such disclosure may not be refused merely in order to strengthen the position of the [organization] or one of its officers.[68]

(ix) The scope of the appeal bodies' power of review in responding to officials' procedural requests – such as requests for recusal of its members,[69] for the disclosure of evidence, to be assisted or represented,[70] to use a particular language,[71] to have certain documents translated, to submit further evidence, to waive or extend dead-

62 Judgment 3108, consid 9; and Judgment 2513, consid 11.
63 See, in this regard, Judgment 5003, consid 5; and Judgment 4111, consid 3.
64 Judgment 3447, consid 8, and the case law cited therein.
65 Judgment 4398, consid 4.
66 Judgment 3755, consid 10, and the case law cited therein.
67 See Judgment 4961, consid 13; and Judgment 4960, consid 3.
68 Judgment 3688, consid 29, and the case law cited therein.
69 Judgment 2940, consid 3(b).
70 Judgment 3994, consid 11.
71 Judgment 2598, consid 6.

lines[72] – depends principally on the applicable rules and regulations. Nevertheless, the internal appeal bodies must always guarantee due process, including respect for the adversarial principle,[73] equality of arms, transparency and the officials' right of defence.[74]

(x) Regarding the question of delay in the internal appeal proceedings, due diligence and promptness are the key.[75] In this regard, the Tribunal has stated that:

> [I]nternational civil servants are entitled to expect their cases to be examined by the internal appeal bodies within a reasonable time and failure to deal with them expeditiously constitutes misconduct on the part of the organisation concerned [...]. [T]he amount of compensation liable to be granted under this head ordinarily depends on two essential considerations, namely the length of the delay and the effect of the delay on the employee concerned.[76]

Even if it is true that the internal rules of each international organization take precedence and that, thus, the Tribunal has no power to impose the creation of an internal appeal mechanism within the organizations, it considers that it is highly desirable to have such a mechanism established and does not hesitate to say so. In Judgment 4313, for example, the Tribunal recalled its constant case law dealing with the "fundamental role" of internal appeal procedures in the resolution of disputes[77] and expressed regret to the fact that, following a review of the Staff Regulations of the International Labour Organization (ILO) on the procedure to be followed in cases of harassment, it was no longer possible for staff members to bring an internal appeal against a harassment-related decision before the Joint Advisory Appeals Board, even though it was normally the rule at the ILO for such an appeal to be available.[78]

The internal appeal mechanism normally finishes with the final decision taken by the executive head or, by delegation of authority, on their behalf. As properly formulated findings and recommendations warrant a "considerable

72 Judgments 3267 and 4035.

73 Judgment 4408, consid 4; and Judgment 3447, consid 8.

74 Judgment 4960, consid 3, and the case law cited therein.

75 Judgment 4100, consid 7, and the case law cited therein. See also Judgment 4947, consid 17.

76 Judgment 4727, consid 14, and the case law cited therein. See also Judgment 4997, consid 8; Judgment 4962, consid 22; Judgment 4635, consid 8; Judgment 4178, consid 15; and Judgment 4100, consid 7.

77 Judgment 4313, consid 3.

78 Judgment 4313, consid 3. See also, in this regard, Judgment 4168, consid 2.

deference",[79] their rejection by the executive head must be properly motivated.[80] It is important to stress that the internal appeal body's work is not a simple formality before the decision is taken, but it is supposed to assist fully the executive head in making an informed decision.

2.3 Duty to Properly Manage Employment Contracts

The law of international civil service consists of general norms, such as staff regulations and rules, administrative instructions or general policies, administrative practices, and individual employment contracts. This is complemented by general principles of law identified by international administrative tribunals. Thus, the contract between an individual and the organization plays a significant role in the determination of the official's conditions of employment.

The employment contract should be written, and not merely oral.[81] For the contract to be concluded, not only has it to be signed by both parties,[82] but the offer may be subject to certain conditions. The contract becomes effective only once those conditions are fulfilled. One of the frequent conditions is to obtain medical clearance of a competent medical practitioner. Another may be the need to successfully undergo security clearance. Yet another may be to obtain entry visa to a country where the official is supposed to be posted.[83]

Most individual employment contracts make specific reference to staff regulations and rules. They represent an overall context in which the contract is concluded, and provisions of those rules become contractual terms as well. Although this may be tempting, the organizations cannot include in the contract terms that would be incompatible with the staff regulations and rules. In Judgment 4018, the Tribunal explained:

> [A]n international organisation cannot lawfully conclude an employment contract containing a clause that is contrary to its existing staff rules and regulations. The organisation must abide by the provisions it has itself laid down and they therefore take precedence over the clauses of contracts concluded between it and its officials [...]. It follows that a clause which [...] contravenes the staff

79 Judgment 4999, consid 6; Judgment 4953, consid 23; Judgment 4923, consid 5; Judgment 4180, consid 7; and Judgment 3417, consid 4.

80 See Section 4.1. See notably Judgment 5000, consid 9; Judgment 4962, consid 21; and Judgment 4930, consid 3, and the case law cited therein.

81 Judgment 675, consid 8.

82 Judgment 3112, consid 2.

83 See, in this regard, Judgment 3938.

> rules and regulations is unlawful and therefore cannot apply, even if the contracting parties clearly intended it to do so. Were that not the case, an organisation could evade compliance with its staff regulations on a case-by-case basis, which would seriously undermine the legal framework to which they belong and, in particular, would breach the principle of the equal treatment of officials.[84]

One important element of the contract, which can determine the application of general rules regarding entitlements, is whether an official was recruited locally or internationally. As the Tribunal said:

> [A]ccording to consistent precedent the distinction between international and local staff is a fundamental one inherent in the very nature of an international organisation. It is due to the peculiar circumstances in which such organisations work and it is concurred in, with both its advantages and its drawbacks, by anyone who seeks employment with them, be it in one category of staff or in the other. Each category of staff offers career prospects and conditions of recruitment and pay that differ according to its own requirements, and a staff member may not plead breach of equal treatment if treated differently because he belongs to one category rather than to the other.[85]

This determination cannot rely solely on the applicable internal rules, but must take into account the legislation of the host State, as the State authorities need to issue an identity document to the official concerned. Host States normally refuse to issue such document to an official recruited locally if the person concerned does not reside legally within that State.[86] Certain individuals may agree to a local status when they join the organization but may try to challenge that status later.[87] Their lack of awareness of the implications of the determination that they are recruited locally is not a valid reason to obtain the change in the status after the fact. It is up to each individual to ask the organization about the implications of this important clause of the offer they were invited to accept, on points decisive for their future career and salary.[88]

84 Judgment 4018, consid 7, reiterated in Judgment 4149, consid 13. See also Judgments 1539 and 1189.

85 Judgment 1196, consid 19.

86 See also Judgment 3141.

87 Judgments 4021 and 3603.

88 Judgment 2667, consid 11.

The organization can also rely on the affirmation in the job application about the resident status in a country.[89]

Another important element of each employment contract is the grade of the official concerned. The grading of the post should correspond to the level of duties performed. If the official is asked to perform duties at a higher level than that of the actual post being encumbered, this may be considered as "an affront to [their] dignity and a breach of the principle of equal pay for work of equal value".[90]

Beyond its specific clauses, the employment contract contains several implicit terms. One of them is the freedom of association.[91] Another is the obligation of the organization to provide a safe, healthy, harassment-free work environment to its staff.[92] Yet another is the principle that any employee is entitled, in the event of a dispute with their employer, to the safeguard of some appeals procedure.[93] These implicit terms were identified in the ILOAT case law and the organizations must take this into account.

The employment contract has to be respected by the parties according to its terms. In some instances, one of the parties may argue that an administrative or material error occurred, that the text does not reflect the parties' intentions and that the contract should be amended. If the argument is accepted by the other party, the contract may be amended: "the trite and consistent principle [is] that a written contract or a provision therein may be revoked or amended for error or mistake where the minds of the parties meet in agreement that what is expressly provided does not reflect their real intention".[94] But, if there is a disagreement, this process may be complicated, and some basic rules apply:

> The Tribunal has often stated that the function of a court of law is to interpret and apply a contract in accordance with the real intention of the parties as expressed in the language of the contract. It is basic principle that when a term of employment is clear and unambiguous the parties are bound by that term unless there is evidence that warrants looking behind the mere wording of

89 Judgment 1189, consid 5.

90 See Judgment 2931, consid 11.

91 See Judgment 4971, consid 6; Judgment 4550, consid 4; Judgment 4482, consid 5; Judgment 3414, consid 4; and Judgment 496, consid 6. For a more detailed analysis, see Dražen Petrović, 'Freedom of Association and International Civil Service' (2024) 21 International Organizations Law Review 304.

92 See Section 3.2.

93 See Judgment 122.

94 Judgment 3483, consid 9.

> the text to ascertain the parties' real intention (see, for example, Judgment 1385, under 12). The Tribunal has also stated that where any term of employment is expressed in writing, the intention of the parties is to be ascertained from the documents that are produced. A contract or term therein may be vitiated or varied if there is overwhelming evidence that the parties had a contrary intention to that which is expressed in the text (see, for example, Judgment 1634, under 21).[95]

At the beginning at least, the employment contracts are generally concluded for a limited duration. The rights attached to those contracts are not the same depending on their type. As an example, the Tribunal noted:

> [A] short-term contract ordinarily ends automatically, without prior notice, on the expiration date of the period for which it was concluded. It is true that, according to the case law, an international organisation is nevertheless obliged to give a reasonable period of prior notice where a staff member has been employed continuously under such contracts for a period of time exceeding that which corresponds to a purely temporary assignment.[96]

Although fixed-term contracts also have an expiry date, the rights attached to them are different if the official occupies a post of longer duration. As far back as 1955, the ILOAT said that:

> An official who combines all the necessary qualities has a legitimate expectancy of being offered a new appointment in the position which he occupied [...]. That not only is such an almost absolute quod plerumque fit [as is almost always the case] but also in thus acting the [organization] has as its objective to create a permanent body of officials experienced in their duties, who are destined to follow a career in the organisation.[97]

In case there is an underlying decision not to renew a contract, it must be notified with a reasonable notice[98] and needs to be properly motivated.[99]

---

95 Judgment 3483, consid 1.

96 Judgment 3362, consid 16, referring to Judgment 2104, consid 6; and Judgment 2531, consid 9.

97 Judgment 21 (emphasis in original).

98 Judgment 4877, consid 9, and the case law cited therein.

99 Judgment 4877, consid 2 (holding that "a non-renewal decision must also be based on objective, valid reasons, and not on arbitrary or irrational ones [...]. Those reasons must

One of the valid reasons is the lack of financing for the post.[100] Another valid reason is bad performance:

> If the reason given is the unsatisfactory nature of the performance of the staff member concerned, who is entitled to be informed in a timely manner as to the unsatisfactory aspects of his or her service, the organisation must base its decision on an assessment of that person's work carried out in compliance with previously established rules.[101]

There may also be a termination of the contract before its expiry. The most frequent reason is disciplinary sanction of dismissal.[102] However, there may be some other reasons, such as those of health.[103] If the staff member disagrees with the decision to terminate their employment for health reasons, the organizations must be aware that under a general principle of international civil service law, established by the Tribunal's settled case law, the administrative status of a staff member cannot be unilaterally altered to their detriment by the employing organization without that staff member having been given the opportunity to comment on the proposed measure beforehand.[104]

Another reason for early termination may be a resignation of the staff member.[105] In Judgment 4053, the Tribunal recalled its previous Judgment 856 and identified several principles arising from that judgment, which are relevant to assessing the legality of a resignation:

> The first is that a resignation comes into effect when it is accepted by the employer. The second is that once the resignation has come into effect it cannot be withdrawn unless the offer to resign was tainted with some flaw that renders it void. If the alleged flaw is that the individual purporting to resign was suffering from a psychological illness, then the individual, as a complainant, has

---

also be communicated to the staff member concerned [...], although they need not necessarily appear in the decision itself").

100 For example, it is possible that the funds are not allocated by the donor to continue to fund an extra-budgetary post when its term expires. In that case, there is no obligation to use funds that may be still available from the regular budget of the organization. See Judgment 4953, consids 21–22, referring to Judgment 3586.

101 Judgment 2991, consid 13. See also Section 4.3.

102 For the obligations of the organizations, see Section 4.5.

103 See, for example, Judgments 4850, 4622, 4177 and 3687.

104 Judgment 4622, consid 10, referring to Judgment 3124, consid 3; Judgment 1817, consid 7; and Judgment 1484, consid 8.

105 See, for example, Judgments 4595, 4053 and 1818.

to adduce precise, cogent and consistent evidence to show that the consent was lacking.[106]

3 Observing Officials' Substantive Rights

The ILOAT case law has identified some substantive rights for all the officials, which can be claimed as individual rights. They are peculiar for the law of international civil service and are not simple transposition of what could be found in national laws. We have identified four such rights and corresponding duties of the organizations: (i) the duty to respect the acquired rights; (ii) the duty to ensure a safe, adequate and healthy, harassment-free work environment for the staff members; (iii) the duty to provide remedies when non-compliance with the rules caused damage to the staff members; and (iv) the duty to provide social protection to staff members.

3.1 Duty to Respect the Acquired Rights

The acquired rights are one of the main guarantees of the international civil service. Although the same expression may be used in national laws, there is no automatic equivalence in substance. That is why some decision-makers, especially those representing member States in international organizations, and even some newly appointed judges of international administrative tribunals, have difficulties understanding this concept. Nevertheless, most of those tribunals declared it applicable in the terms defined almost 100 years ago by the League of Nations Administrative Tribunal (LoNAT). The only notable exception is the United Nations Appeals Tribunal (UNAT) which, in Judgment 2018-UNAT-840, *Lloret-Alcañiz et al.*, emptied it of all the substance, thereby putting at risk one of the essential elements of the United Nations common system.

The acquired rights concept was announced in the very first judgment rendered by an international administrative tribunal. In re *Di Palma Castiglione*,[107] from January 1929, the LoNAT rejected the argument of the League that it has the power, based on the general provision allowing it to modify the staff regulations during an official's appointment (Article 117 of the Staff

---

106 Judgment 4053, consid 6.

107 *In re di Palma Castiglione v. International Labour Office*, League of Nations Administrative Tribunal Judgment No 1 (1929).

Regulations), to modify the conditions of service of an official. The LoNAT explained that:

> Such an article could not have been intended to expose officials to arbitrary decisions of the [organization] since, on the contrary, the existence of staff regulations stems from the need to afford staff members legitimate guarantees as to the stability and terms of their employment both now and in the future.[108]

The LoNAT explained that such a general provision must be construed "as referring only to conditions of application or ancillary matters and not to the substantive rights enjoyed by the staff".[109] The LoNAT declared that "[t]he [organization] is at liberty to establish for its staff such regulations as it may see fit, provided that it does not in any way infringe the acquired rights of any staff member".[110]

In one of its early judgments, the ILOAT explained:

> A right is acquired when he who has it may require that it be respected notwithstanding any amendment to the rules. In particular, it may be either a right which arises under an official's contract of appointment and which both parties intend should be inviolate, or a right which is laid down in a provision of the Staff Regulations or Staff Rules and which is of decisive importance to a candidate for appointment.[111]

The ILOAT's case law recognizes that international civil servants' conditions of employment existing at the time of recruitment are not immutable and need not, of necessity, be applied to them throughout their careers.[112] However, some modifications may go too far and the ILOAT has examined arguments alleging violation of acquired rights on many occasions. That case law has triggered considerable interest from practitioners.[113] The ILOAT examines whether an amendment to the rules to an official's detriment and without their consent disturbs the structure of their contract of appointment or

108 Ibid.

109 Ibid.

110 Ibid.

111 Judgment 366, consid 6.

112 See, for example, Judgment 4465, consids 5–8.

113 For a detailed presentation of the case law, see Dr Eva-Maria Gröniger-Voss, A. Kristen Baxter and Arthur Nguyen Dao, 'The Principle of Acquired Rights with Particular Focus on the Jurisprudence of the Administrative Tribunal of the International Labour Organization' in Petrović (ed), *90 Years of Contribution of the ILOAT* (note 25), 109–128.

impairs "an essential term of employment which induced the complainant to accept the appointment and to stay on".[114] If yes, there is a breach of acquired rights. In Judgment 4711, the ILOAT recently re-affirmed the principle of acquired rights in the following terms:

> According to the Tribunal's case law [...], the amendment of a provision governing an official's situation to [their] detriment constitutes a breach of an acquired right only when such an amendment adversely affects the balance of contractual obligations, or alters fundamental terms of employment in consideration of which the official accepted an appointment, or which subsequently induced her or him to stay on. In order for there to be a breach of an acquired right, the amendment to the applicable text must relate to a fundamental and essential term of employment. [...] The test is as follows:
> (1) The nature of the altered term: "It may be in the contract or in the Staff Regulations or Staff Rules or in a decision, and whereas the contract or a decision may give rise to acquired rights the regulations and rules do not necessarily do so."
> (2) The reason for the change: "It is material that the terms of appointment may often have to be adapted to circumstances, and there will ordinarily be no acquired right when a rule or a clause depends on variables such as the cost-of-living index or the value of the currency. Nor can the finances of the body that applies the terms of appointment be discounted."
> (3) The consequence of allowing or disallowing an acquired right and the effect it will have on staff pay and benefits, and how those who plead an acquired right fare as against others.[115]

The answer is not given in the abstract and the outcome depends on specific facts. For example, the ILOAT found in Judgment 4381 that changes in benefits and entitlements of internationally recruited staff did not violate acquired rights. In Judgment 1912, the Tribunal found that the lack of automatic indexing of the salaries does not violate acquired rights. However, in Judgment 1264 the Tribunal set aside a new salary scale for the General Service category in Geneva because it violated acquired rights. Concerning promotion, the Tribunal found that staff rules providing for the grant of promotion within an international organization do not confer any acquired rights

114 Judgment 4898, consid 10.
115 Judgment 4711, consid 8 (internal citations omitted).

on staff, unless the new rules substantially deprive staff of their former prospects for advancement.[116]

As for pensions, in Judgment 4277, the ILOAT concluded that acquired rights were not violated when the organization introduced a "pension point" and did not adjust that point for one year. In an important old judgment, 832 (*Ayoub*), the Tribunal also rejected argument that changes in the pension regime violated acquired rights. However, the Tribunal found that the right to a pension is a fundamental and essential term of the conditions of appointment,[117] and hence the elimination of this right would be violation of acquired rights. In Judgment 986, the Tribunal found the violation of acquired rights when the scale of pensionable remuneration in the ILO was reduced.

As far as it concerns indemnities, the ILOAT stated that there is no acquired right to the amount and method of calculation of an indemnity.[118] Even where there is a suppression of a particular indemnity, such as the suppression of the invalidity lump sum in the European Patent Organisation (EPO), the Tribunal found that acquired rights were not breached.[119] Also, when the executive head of an organization claimed an acquired right to be reappointed, the Tribunal rejected this argument.[120]

3.2 Duty to Ensure a Safe and Adequate Environment for the Staff Members

As a general rule, international organizations have a duty to provide a safe and adequate environment for their staff, and they in turn have the right to insist on appropriate measures to protect their health and safety.[121] This general principle has become even more important recently, as it is of crucial importance in the context of harassment cases. Already in 2006, the ILOAT recognized that harassment and mobbing are extreme examples of the breach of the duties to provide a safe and secure workplace and, also, to ensure that an employee is treated fairly and with dignity.[122]

What organizations sometime fail to remember, and incorrectly draft their rules accordingly, is that harassment claims are directed to the employer and

116 Judgment 4990, consid 3.
117 Judgment 2632, consid 13.
118 Judgment 368, consid 7.
119 Judgment 4898, consid 10.
120 Judgment 4737, consid 13.
121 Judgment 2706, consid 5. See also Judgment 3689, consid 5; Judgment 3025, consid 2; and Judgment 2403, consid 16.
122 Judgment 2524, consid 6.

not to the alleged harasser. Although an underlying personal conflict may be in origin of the feeling of being harassed, it is ultimately the organization that is liable for unacceptable behavior of the alleged harasser, being a supervisor acting in the course of their duties, or a colleague when the victim is subjected to treatment that is an affront to their dignity, and for all injuries caused to a staff member.[123] As the Tribunal stated in a landmark Judgment 4207, "[a] claim of harassment is a claim addressed to the organization the resolution of which only involves two parties, the organization and the reporter of the harassment".[124]

As most organizations proclaim 'zero tolerance' for harassment and require all officials to report harassment that they may be aware of, the organizations have an obligation to initiate the investigation themselves,[125] even in the absence of a formal harassment complaint. Of course, it is easier where there is a formal complaint which needs to be examined, since the alleged victim must provide some evidence. In organizations requiring a preliminary assessment, there is no obligation to open a full investigation into allegations of harassment if the allegations are insufficiently substantiated at the stage of the preliminary assessment[126] or there is no *prima facie* finding that the complaint was genuine.[127] However, if there are enough elements, the investigation must be initiated promptly, conducted thoroughly and the facts must be determined objectively and in their overall context.[128] The organization has to ensure that an internal body competent for investigating and reporting on claims of harassment is properly functioning.[129]

When the investigation on the alleged harassment is completed, the complainant is entitled to a response from the organization regarding their claim

123 Judgment 4217, consid 9; Judgment 3170, consid 33; Judgment 2706, consid 5; Judgment 1875, consid 32; and Judgment 1609, consid 16. In Judgment 1609, consideration 16, the Tribunal explained that "[a[n organisation will of course not be liable for private misconduct of an employee that has no link with the performance of duty. But misconduct in the context of employment is another matter. When someone whom the organisation has appointed to act as supervisor or director commits an abuse of authority, the subordinate who suffers injury thereby is entitled to damages".

124 Judgment 4207, consid 14.

125 Judgment 3347, consid 14.

126 Judgment 4746, consid 9.

127 Judgment 4900, consid 27; and Judgment 4883, consid 7.

128 Judgment 4207, consid 15. See also Judgment 4961, consideration 6, for a more detailed explanation on what are obligations of those involved in the harassment complaint.

129 Judgment 3069, consid 12.

of harassment.[130] The victim does not have to wait until the investigation is completed regarding the alleged harasser. This is frequently neglected by organizations, as they immediately focus on the investigation aimed at establishing elements regarding the alleged harasser. According to the Tribunal, "there is no need to prove that the perpetrator intended to engage in harassment, the main factor being the perception that the person concerned may reasonably and objectively have of acts or remarks liable to demean or humiliate [them]".[131] If the organization determined, based on a standard of proof which is 'less onerous'[132] than the 'beyond reasonable doubt' standard required to impose disciplinary measures on an individual charged with misconduct,[133] that the victim of harassment had objective reasons to feel harassed, the organization must take proper actions to protect that official[134] and compensate them for any damage that the victim may have incurred.[135] The punishment of the alleged harasser is not a remedy to which the victim is entitled.[136] If the organization concludes that the harassment did not happen or could not be proven, the alleged victim must be notified by a properly motivated decision, and such a decision can be challenged by the official concerned in the internal procedure and before the Tribunal.[137]

If the organization considers that the investigation collected sufficient evidence that disciplinary charges may be brought against the alleged harasser[138]

---

130 Judgment 4207, consid 15.

131 Judgment 4900, consid 18, referring to Judgment 4808, consid 17; Judgment 4663, consid 3; Judgment 4541, consid 8, and Judgment 3318, consid 7.

132 Judgment 4839, consid 6, and the case law cited therein. The Tribunal has also referred to the "balance of probabilities" concept when referring to the "less onerous" standard of proof (see Judgment 4839, consid 8).

133 Judgment 4839, consid 6; Judgment 4663, consid 12; Judgment 4289, consid 10; and Judgment 4207, consid 20.

134 Ibid.

135 See Section 3.3.

136 Judgment 4944, consid 8; and Judgment 4512, consid 6.

137 For more detailed analysis of recent case law, see Dražen Petrović, 'How Should Harassment Cases Be Dealt with in International Organizations? A Concise Guide Through the Case Law of the Administrative Tribunal of the International Labour Organization' in *НОВЫЕ ВЫзоВЫ ИНТЕГРАЦИИ ЕАЭС: ПРАВОВОЕ ИЗМЕРНIЕ* (*New Challenges of EAEU Integration: the Legal Dimension*), Acts of international conference organised by the Court of Justice of the Eurasian Economic Union (Minsk, 25–27 November 2020) (2021), 183–195. See also Donata Rugarabamu, 'Milestones in the Jurisprudence of the International Labour Organization Administrative Tribunal: Guiding International Organizations and Their Personnel in Addressing Harassment', in Petrović (ed), *90 Years of Contribution of the ILOAT* (note 25), 137–152.

138 As the Tribunal stated in Judgment 4900, consideration 31: "it is useful to recall that a finding of harassment can sometimes be made in the victim's favour without the perpet-

and concludes that the charges may be ultimately proven beyond reasonable doubt, it may – and this is within its discretionary power – initiate disciplinary proceedings against them. In those proceedings the parties are the organization and the alleged harasser in question, while the reporter of the misconduct, the presumed victim, becomes a witness and not a party in the proceedings.[139] Thus, it is not for the victim to bring sufficient evidence against the alleged harasser, but for the organization to do that.

The duty to provide a safe and adequate environment is obviously not limited to harassment. In Judgment 3994, the ILOAT recalled that its case law obliged international organizations to take appropriate measures to protect their officials' health and safety, but stated that the measures requested must be reasonable and based on objective evidence of their necessity.[140] In that specific case, the Tribunal found that the complainant's request that, in order to limit her exposure to electromagnetic fields, the organization should move her into an office with concrete walls and deactivating the Wi-Fi hotspot for a whole sector, represented an excessive burden on the organization's resources.[141]

In another case, the complainant fractured her ankle on the organization's premises while climbing the steps to a podium set up for a seminar that she was to lead. She lost her balance when she stepped into a hole, approximately 7 centimetres long and 1 centimetre deep, that was concealed under the carpet on the floor. The Tribunal found that the floor of the podium set up for the seminar was defective and should have been repaired or, at least, signposted, and that the organization, which had ordered the construction of the podium in which the hole was found, should have ensured that this work was properly carried out. Accordingly, the Tribunal found that the organization breached its duty to provide a safe and adequate environment for its staff and awarded 15,000 euros for moral damages.[142]

International organizations must be particularly vigilant when sending officials on missions or to various duty stations worldwide. For example, when four officials of the International Criminal Court (ICC) were detained in Libya and charged with various criminal offences on the basis they had committed or been complicit in acts endangering national security, the Tribunal

rator necessarily having to undergo disciplinary measures as a result (see, for example, Judgment 4601, consideration 8)".

139 Judgment 4207, consid 14.

140 Judgment 3994, consid 8. See also Judgment 3689, consid 5; Judgment 3025, consid 2; and Judgment 2706, consid 5.

141 Ibid.

142 Judgment 4222, consid 17.

found, in the case filed by two of them, that their ordeal in Libya was a direct result of the ICC's failure to properly prepare for the mission. Specifically, this comprised the ICC's failure to: (i) establish a diplomatic basis by ensuring that a Memorandum of Understanding was established or *Notes Verbales* were exchanged, or both, with the Libyan authorities prior to the mission's initiation; (ii) establish a mission plan which identified the objectives of the mission, the locations to visit and persons to be met, as well as naming the head of mission and clarifying the specific responsibilities of the team members; and (iii) ensure that all security protocols were followed and advice was implemented to guarantee the safety and security of the staff members on mission. For these failures, the Tribunal awarded moral damages in the amount of 140,000 euros to each of them.[143]

We should also not forget an old case, dealt with in Judgment 402, which triggered the need for contracting the malicious act insurance by the organizations. The complainant was a WHO employee who was injured in his head and spine in a bomb explosion while he was on a mission to Dacca in 1971. Before dealing with remedies, as will be presented below, the ILOAT made several statements of general interest. It first stated that:

> It is a fundamental principle of every contract of employment that the employer will not require the employee to work in a place which he knows or ought to know to be unsafe. […] If there is doubt about the safety of a place of work, it is the duty of the employer to make the necessary inquiries and to arrive at a reasonable and careful judgment, and the employee is entitled to rely upon his judgment.[144]

It, however, explained that:

> This principle is to be applied with due regard to the nature of the employment. In some employments there are unavoidable risks. A doctor may have to risk infection and a soldier or a policeman to risk bombs. The question in each case is whether the risk is abnormal having regard to the nature of the employment.[145]

In this particular case, the Tribunal concluded that the risk was abnormal: the complainant was employed in the branch concerned with malaria eradication

143 Judgment 4003, consid 16.
144 Judgment 402, consid 1.
145 Ibid, consid 2.

and did not therefore by the nature of his employment accept the risk of hostilities in an area of civil war; the dependents of the United Nations staff were not authorized to stay in Dacca and the fact that their return was not authorized was sufficient by itself to show that the risk was abnormal, because the risk of injury by hostile action was no greater for the complainant's dependents than it was for himself. As a result, the Tribunal found that the organization bore full responsibility for the ensuing injuries.

3.3 Duty to Provide Remedies When Non-compliance with the Rules Caused Damage to the Staff Members

If the organization has caused injury to its officials by violating its obligations, damages are, in principle, due.[146] Many organizations' rules contain provisions regarding compensation to be paid for 'no fault' service-incurred injuries or illnesses or for damage to personal property in relation to the performance of official duties. The compensation in those cases may be limited to, for example, full medical expenses or a ceiling amount for the property loss, and such a risk is normally covered by insurance.

However, the case law reveals that there are situations in which the internal rules are incomplete, and the organization is liable to pay compensation for actions or omissions that are not mentioned in the internal rules. For example, in one of the early cases, the ILOAT, after having found that the claimed damages to personal effects arose out of and in the course of employment, concluded that "[w]hether or not the claim for compensation was allowable under the organization's baggage insurance policy, the organization was directly liable for compensation".[147] Therefore, although the insurance is a good way of making a loss predicable and contained, the insurance coverage cannot limit the liability of the organization towards its officials.[148] The amount due will, therefore, be only partly covered by the insurance and the rest will be paid out of the financial resources of the organization.

The organization may be liable to pay damage for a moral injury resulting from an unlawful act. In this case, "[t]he amount of compensation must be the subject of a specific examination, which takes into account all relevant factors, such as the seriousness, nature and duration of the damage suffered and also

146 Judgment 196, consid 6.

147 Judgment 53, consid 9.

148 In Judgment 2533, consideration 26, it was stated that "the Tribunal asserts unequivocally that the defendant's obligation to pay the complainant reasonable compensation for the results of his workplace injury is a continuing one and is not affected or diminished by the terms of an insurance policy to which the complainant is not a party".

whether or not the organization withdrew the irregular decision and rectified the irregularity".[149]

The organization is also fully liable for injuries resulting from its *negligence*. For example, in Judgment 2843, as a result of slipping on liquid in the organization's underground car park, the complainant suffered a fracture of the leg. He asked for compensation beyond what was foreseen in the rules for service-incurred injuries. The ILOAT affirmed that "[i]t is well settled that in order to extend an organisation's liability beyond its liability under its no-fault regime, a claimant must prove negligence or the intentional breach of a duty".[150] It then went on to quote Judgment 2804, under 25: "Negligence is the failure to take reasonable steps to prevent a foreseeable risk of injury. Liability in negligence is occasioned when the failure to take such steps causes an injury which was foreseeable."[151]

It must also be emphasized that a person seeking damages for negligence bears the burden of establishing the factual foundation on which their claim is based.[152] However, in this specific case, the Tribunal found that, even if additional measures had been taken, they would not have eliminated the risk of injury. Accordingly, it concluded that there was no negligence. In contrast, in the above-mentioned case of injury resulting from the defective podium for a seminar,[153] the ILOAT, having found that the complainant's injury was caused by the organization's negligence, determined that the complainant was entitled to compensation for injuries not already compensated under the applicable rules.[154]

In the case of *harassment*, the victim of harassment is entitled to compensation regardless of whether the rules of the organization foresee such compensation. In Judgment 4602, the Tribunal rejected argument of the organization that no provision in the internal regulations, rules or policies directly provides for the possibility of compensation to the individuals who filed a harassment complaint. It recalled not only its plenary Judgment 4207, but also its case law before[155] and after that judgment.[156]

149 Judgment 4156, consid 6.

150 Judgment 2843, consid 3. See also Judgment 3215, consid 12; and Judgment 3733, consid 12.

151 Ibid.

152 Judgment 3215, consid 12.

153 See Section 3.2 above.

154 Judgment 4222, consid 16.

155 Judgment 3995, consid 9; and Judgment 3965, consids 9–10.

156 Judgment 4547, consid 3; and Judgment 4541, consid 4.

Even if harassment was act of an individual, and not the administration of an international organization, the organization is liable for the damage caused by it, because it failed to prevent it. In Judgment 1609 it was affirmed:

> [A]n international organisation is liable for the injury a staff member may cause in the performance of duty, and that includes injury to other members of staff. [...] An organisation will of course not be liable for private misconduct of an employee that has no link with the performance of duty. But misconduct in the context of employment is another matter. When someone whom the organisation has appointed to act as supervisor or director commits an abuse of authority, the subordinate who suffers injury thereby is entitled to damages.[157]

This liability generally entitles the staff member to the payment of monetary compensation for the moral injury suffered because of harassment and the resultant affront to their dignity.[158] However, redress for injury suffered by the victim of harassment may, in certain cases, take forms other than monetary compensation.[159]

There may be some situations in which compensation should be provided even if the claim of harassment fails:

> Save where a claim is so specific that it must either succeed or fail according to its terms, the material advanced in support of a claim of harassment may disclose some other form of harassment, or some lesser breach of one or other of those duties entitling the person in question to an award of damages even though the claim of harassment must fail.[160]

Organizations may be liable for other financial losses suffered during employment. For example, when dealing with a transfer of the pension rights of an official, in Judgment 2403, the Tribunal put the financial loss at the same level as loss resulting from a physical injury or personal property loss:

> It is not in doubt that an international organisation is under an obligation to take proper measures to protect its staff members from physical injury occurring in the course of their employment. The same is true with respect to loss of

157 Judgment 1609, consid 16.

158 Judgment 4808, consid 17, referring to Judgment 4663, consids 17 and 20; Judgment 4241, consids 24–25, Judgment 4217, consid 9; and Judgment 3995, consid 9.

159 Ibid. One should not underestimate the importance of an apology, as a form of satisfaction.

160 Judgment 2524, consid 6.

> or damage to their personal property. As a matter of principle, the same must be true of financial loss suffered in the course of their employment. Particularly is that so where, as here, the loss is directly associated with compulsory participation in a fund established by the organisation and managed in accordance with rules which limit the participants' rights with respect to that fund.[161]

Organizations may also be liable to pay damage caused by an inordinate delay in the internal appeal process. The ILOAT summarized its case law on this issue in Judgment 4891:

> An organisation is indeed expected to process internal appeals with the requisite promptness and diligence, and it has a positive obligation to see to it that such procedures move forward with reasonable speed [...]. Under the Tribunal's case law, the amount of compensation for unreasonable delay is ordinarily influenced by two considerations, one being the length of the delay and the other the effect of the delay [...]. In Judgment 4799, consideration 7, the Tribunal recalled that its recent case law holds that an unreasonable delay in an internal appeal is not sufficient in itself to award moral damages. The complainant must also articulate the adverse effects which the delay has caused [...]. Furthermore, the Tribunal has regularly stated that, in terms of damages, a complainant seeking compensation must provide clear evidence of the alleged unlawful act, of the injury suffered and of the causal link between the unlawful act and the injury, and that she or he bears the burden of proof in this regard [...].[162]

Compensation for damage normally covers actual loss. However, in exceptional circumstances, for instance where an organization's conduct has been in gross breach of its obligation to act in good faith, it may be subject to punitive or exemplary damages, namely, compensation exceeding the material and moral injury actually suffered by the complainant.[163] By a recently adopted judgment, the Tribunal considered:

> [I]n view of the evidence on file, that the number and gravity of the various unlawful acts committed by [the European Organisation for the Safety of Air

161 Judgment 2403, consid 16.

162 Judgment 4891, consid 17.

163 Judgment 2935, consid 5. See also Judgment 4963, consid 23; Judgment 4961, consid 25; Judgment 4954, consid 10; Judgment 4391, consid 14; Judgment 4385, consid 7; Judgment 2720, consid 16; and Judgment 2418, consid 15.

> Navigation (Eurocontrol)] in the present case constitute[d] a flagrant breach of its obligation to act in good faith and a seriously disrespectful treatment of the complainant, which warrant[ed] ordering the Organization to pay punitive damages [...] at 20,000 euros.[164]

Organizations may also, in assessing material damage, need to take into consideration the case law of the Tribunal in awarding damages for a loss of valuable opportunity (for instance, to be appointed, to be promoted, to be reassigned, to have a contract extended or confirmed, to continue career with the organization).[165]

3.4 Duty to Provide Social Protection to Staff Members

The two main fields we have identified in which international organizations do have specific duties towards their officials are the medical sphere and the pension area, which we will deal with in turn. But before doing so, one observation is warranted: while specific obligations in these fields are usually (if not invariably) expressly set out in the organization's internal rules, the Tribunal's case law serves to play a 'fill in the gaps' role by completing and clarifying the statutory and regulatory provisions and interpreting the legality of the decisions taken following the rules outlined in Section 2.1 above.

3.4.1 Medical Coverage[166]

The main obligation of international organizations in the field of health care is to ensure adequate coverage and fair treatment for their officials or even their dependents.[167] This obligation applies throughout the entire period of employment but may also extend beyond the officials' separation from service. In this regard, the Tribunal has relevantly stated that "[i]nternational civil servants' social protection forms an integral part of their terms of employment, which are the responsibility of the organisation for which they work".[168]

---

164 Judgment 4819, consid 22. Prior to Judgment 4819, the Tribunal awarded punitive or exemplary damages on only three occasions (see Judgment 4385, consid 7; Judgment 2720, consid 16; and Judgment 2418, consid 15).

165 See, for example, Judgments 4845, 4670, 4668, 4622, 4583, 4540, 4490, 4481, 4149 and 4019.

166 See also cases cited by Germond (note 9), 137–138.

167 See, in this regard, Judgment 3019, consid 7; and Judgment 1176, consid 12.

168 Judgment 3506, consid 9, citing Judgment 3031, consids 14, 18–19; and Judgment 2063, consid 8.

Most of the time, the obligation to provide medical insurance coverage (including reimbursement of medical expenses, hospitalizations, dental and vision care) is stipulated in the officials' terms of appointment and flows directly from the organizations' internal rules and policies. Once again, the *tu patere legem quam ipse fecisti* principle (namely, any authority is bound by the rules it has itself issued) applies. Organizations are required to provide a comprehensive coverage and to ensure that the processes for claiming medical insurance are fair, transparent and accessible.[169] Moreover, there is an obligation to process and reimburse medical claims in a timely manner, failing which the organizations may be sanctioned by the Tribunal.[170]

Many organizations outsourced their medical insurance scheme to an insurance company. However, this does not absolve the organizations from their responsibility in relation to their officials. Indeed, organizations have "a duty to ensure that the insurer correctly processes the claims submitted by insured persons" and, as such, they are in fact liable for the acts of their insurer.[171] Thus, it is incumbent upon organizations to ensure the proper examination of a claim for the reimbursement of medical expenses.[172] As organizations are liable for the acts of their insurer, they can be ordered by the Tribunal to reimburse the disputed expenses, which they may then seek to recover from the insurance company.[173] In the event of an error in the calculation of medical contributions, organizations should rectify it. However, an organization cannot be held responsible for additional services offered by the insurer to staff on an optional basis. Indeed, "[t]hese additional services stem from individual contracts and in this respect a dispute between a staff member (or a former staff member) and the insurance company is a private dispute which is outside the purview of the organization and of the Tribunal".[174]

Sometimes, organizations can rely on the social protection system in the host State. In several cases involving the International Criminal Police Organization (Interpol), the complainants sought the restitution of amounts wrongly deducted from their salaries in respect of sickness insurance contributions.[175] The Tribunal noted that Interpol had decided to affiliate its officials stationed in France to the French social security scheme, thus making French

169 See, for example, Judgment 4818.

170 See, for example, Judgments 4162 and 4060.

171 Judgment 3506, consid 9. See also Judgment 2063, consid 8; or Judgment 3031, consids 14, 18–19.

172 Judgment 3506, consid 9.

173 Judgment 4932, consid 4; and Judgment 3506, consid 19.

174 Judgment 4932, consid 6.

175 Judgments 4671, 4670, 4669, 4668 and 4667.

law applicable to their employment relationship regarding social protection. Since January 1999, French legislation had stipulated that those affiliated to the social security system in France who were exempt from all or part of direct income tax must pay an 'enhanced sickness insurance contribution' (ESC). Interpol levied this contribution, set at 5.5% of the salaries of the civil servants concerned, on behalf of the *Union de recouvrement des cotisations de sécurité sociale et d'allocations familiales* (URSSAF), a non-market, private body with a public service remit that formed part of the 'collection' arm of the general social security scheme. On 13 December 2012 the French Constitutional Council declared unconstitutional the provision that provided for the ESC levy. However, unaware of this decision, Interpol continued to levy the ESC on salaries paid after 13 December 2012. The case before the Tribunal involved the extent to which Interpol should reimburse the staff.

The Tribunal ruled that Interpol's decision to affiliate its officials to the French social security scheme did not in any way release it from its obligations towards them. It found that, "[w]hile it [was] true that the Organization only deducted the ESC following what it believed, wrongly, to be the applicable French law on the matter, it [could not] take refuge behind the fact that it acted only as an intermediary, nor behind its status as an international organisation with no responsibility of its own for the application of that law". The Tribunal observed that, in view of its obligations towards its officials, Interpol was not entitled to make the refund of the contributions at issue conditional on reimbursement of the amount of those contributions by URSSAF or the host State. It concluded that Interpol was negligent in several respect: it did not take the necessary measures to ensure that it kept itself informed of changes to the French Social Security Code; it was unaware of the possibility of obtaining a retroactive refund of the unduly paid contributions provided for by the same Code; and, even when it approached URSSAF and the host State's authorities with a view to obtaining a refund of the amounts deducted from its officials' salaries in respect of the ESC, it failed to include in its requests the amounts corresponding to the sums deducted for the period preceding 2013. The Tribunal thus sanctioned Interpol for having been negligent, which resulted in the complainants being denied a valuable opportunity to receive a refund of the amounts of ESC deducted from their salaries for the period preceding 2013.[176]

Recent Judgment 4818 also addresses an important issue regarding the social security entitlements of officials. In this case, involving the Green Climate Fund (GCF), the complainant challenged the decision denying her and

176 See, for example, Judgment 4667, consids 9–17.

her dependents an individual medical insurance plan following her separation from service. She mainly based her arguments on the grounds that the organization breached its duty of care by failing to facilitate her request for conversion from the GCF's Group Medical Insurance Plan (GMIP) into the Individual Medical Insurance Plan (IMIP) and breached the principle of good faith. The Tribunal found that:

> [T[he fact that the organisation was not able to then facilitate the insurance sought since it was not available, did not relieve it of its obligation to facilitate the requested conversion in accordance with its own rules […]. [The GCF] was bound to negotiate a framework or similar agreement with an insurer, setting out the terms and conditions, and potentially the rates, to be applied to individual agreements between the insurer and departing staff members availing themselves of the conversion option from the GMIP to the IMIP […]. [The GCF was] expected to act diligently and in good faith to rectify its omission by exploring all viable solutions, such as engaging suitable insurers to ensure the availability of the conversion or implementing appropriate measures to meet its obligations and mitigate the adverse impact on its staff. […] [T]he organisation in fact did not act in good faith in securing an agreement with any insurer which had the potential for the complainant to be offered a comparable alternative.[177]

The Tribunal decided to award material damages to the complainant in this respect. Financial viability and solvency of the medical insurance funds is a problem present worldwide. Many organizations also struggle with this problem and the way it has been addressed is twofold: either to limit the reimbursement or to increase contributions. Concerning the ceilings in the reimbursement for certain medical expenses, the Tribunal considered that such a practice was neither unlawful nor unreasonable:

> According to precedent […], coverage at the rate of 100 per cent does not mean that in all circumstances an insured person is entitled to full repayment of expenses incurred. […] To allow the [sickness fund] not to reimburse the part of the expenses deemed to be excessive is in keeping with the purpose of sickness insurance and it is a means of ensuring sound financing and comparable coverage for the beneficiaries, and as such falls within the authority delegated to the Director General. The reimbursement of expenses can be restricted by

177 Judgment 4818, consids 21–22.

> setting maximum limits or ceilings for certain types of expenditure or by reckoning limits for each case on the basis of costs incurred.[178]

As for the contributions, they are normally shared between the employer organizations and the staff. Normally, the contribution of the staff is determined as a percentage of their income, be it the salary or the pension. Medical insurance is thus established in accordance with the idea of mutual aid and solidarity.[179] Therefore, in cases where contributions of the retirees[180] or acting staff[181] were modified, the Tribunal concluded that there was no violation of acquired rights.

3.4.2 Pension Entitlements

As for the medical insurance coverage, pension entitlements are often stipulated in the officials' terms of appointment and flow directly from the organizations' internal policies and rules which, when they give rise to a dispute, may be complemented and specified by the Tribunal's case law. In this respect, officials offering their services to an organization are expected to give "decisive importance to the provisions on [their] pension rights" and, as such, "[a]ny curtailment should [...] be regarded as affecting an acquired right".[182]

In relation to pension benefits, international organizations have a duty of care towards their officials and must provide clear rules and regulations as well as clarifications of such when requested, even though they cannot be solely responsible for every situation stemming from confusion regarding the said rules.[183] In this respect, their duty of care encompasses a general duty of information, which is reinforced when "the applicable rules [are] so complex that a mere perusal of the documentation would not enable employees to understand them fully".[184]

The Tribunal has defined pensions as being "deferred pay" and has stated that, because "pensions are subject to the same basic rules as pay, a method establishing the terms of adjusting the pensions paid to the retirees of an organisation is to be considered as being governed by the same require-

178 Judgment 1880, consid 8.
179 Judgment 1241, consid 22.
180 See, for example, Judgments 1186 and 1226.
181 See, for example, Judgment 4195.
182 Judgment 366, consid 10.
183 See, for example, Judgment 3213, consid 7, citing Judgment 2997, consid 6.
184 Judgment 2768, consids 4–5.

ments",[185] meaning notably that the Noblemaire principle, which is part of the principles governing the adjustments to salary, also applies to pension benefits.[186] The Tribunal has also specified that the right to a pension constitutes "a fundamental and essential term of the complainants' conditions of appointment", which is an acquired right that, if impaired by the organization, may lead to a sanction.[187]

However, some adjustments, such as downward adjustments or an increase in the pension contributions by the individuals concerned, may be acceptable and do not necessarily represent a breach of acquired rights.[188] In this regard, the Tribunal has observed:

> [W]hereas the right to a pension is no doubt inviolable, a pension contribution is by its very nature subject to variation [...]. Far from infringing any acquired right a rise in contribution that is warranted for sound actuarial reasons [...] actually affords the best safeguard against the threat that lack of foresight may pose to the future value of pension benefits".[189]

The question of the sustainability of pension schemes must be a primary concern to organizations and, as such, may naturally require adjustments to be made to the norm regulating pension schemes over time. Hence, pension contributions may be modified throughout the years, provided that: (i) amendments be reasonable; (ii) the changes made balance the interests of the officials against that of the organization concerned; and (iii) the interests of current and future employees, who are not currently affected by the changes but shall be in the future, are taken into account by the organization.[190] Moreover, any alteration in a pension scheme must represent "a *bona fide* attempt to secure the pension scheme into the future and is based on what appears to be properly reasoned actuarial advice",[191] and the methodology chosen by the organization to set adjustments must ensure "stable, foreseeable and clearly understood" results.[192]

---

185 Judgment 2793, consid 20.
186 Judgment 4057, consid 5; and Judgment 986, consid 7.
187 Judgment 2632, consid 13, referring to Judgment 2089, and the case law cited therein.
188 See, for example, Judgments 4422, 3538 and 3346.
189 Judgment 4580, consid 13, and the case law cited therein.
190 Judgment 4563, consid 12.
191 Judgment 4277, consid 20; and Judgment 3538, consid 15.
192 Judgment 4277, consid 17, and the case law cited therein.

In Judgment 4057 in which the complainant challenged WTO's decision to reduce her pension based on a reduction of the consumer price index, the Tribunal has held the following:

> The Tribunal's case law does not establish a principle that there can never be a downward adjustment of pensions (that there can be such downward adjustments is apparently accepted by the complainant in her rejoinder) and indeed there is a theme in the case law that it is entirely appropriate to have, in the rules governing pension funds, a provision to preserve the purchasing power of the pension, to protect staff members from "the adverse repercussions of a rise in the cost of living on their purchasing power and hence in theory to maintain the standard of living their pension initially secured for them" (see Judgment 2615, consideration 6). As a matter of logic and fairness, this approach would justify a reduction in pensions in the face of falling costs of living.[193]

With regard more specifically to acquired rights stemming from a practice within the organization, "a practice of salary and pension adjustment, even where repeated, does not bind the Organisation that adopted it, which is at liberty to abandon it provided that it does so lawfully".[194] International organizations may also introduce an entirely new pension scheme. For example, in the 1950s, several organizations abandoned their Provident Funds to join the United Nations Joint Staff Pension Fund (UNJSPF). Where such a decision is taken based on financial reasons, such as the need to address the rising cost of pensions, the new pension scheme cannot be considered to be invalid merely because it leads to a situation that is less favourable to employees.[195]

As to the functioning itself of a pension scheme, organizations must: (i) ensure that pensions be paid "punctually and in full, if only on account of the precise commitments which beneficiaries may have to honour on a daily basis";[196] (ii) ensure the regular monitoring of their scheme so as to prevent and avoid losses for themselves and their officials,[197] even if it means establishing an effective system to monitor the performance of their pension fund;[198] and (iii) respect the principle of equal treatment.[199] Moreover, even if it is admitted that an organization may try by all legal means to recover any

193 Judgment 4057, consid 6.
194 Judgment 2632, consid 13, referring to Judgment 2089.
195 Judgment 2633, consid 7.
196 Judgment 2721, consid 3, citing Judgment 2381, consid 3.
197 Judgment 2403, consid 23.
198 Judgment 2403, consid 25.
199 Judgment 2292, consid 11.

money an official may owe it when they leave service, that does not entitle it to suspend or block consideration of the official's pension entitlements.[200]

4 Complying with Procedural Requirements

Complying with the procedural requirements is an essential element of legality. As the ILOAT exercises control over the lawfulness of the organizations' actions, it inevitably checks whether the required procedure was followed. The ILOAT does not, except in very limited circumstances, put in question the discretionary powers of the organizations, for example in the area of performance appraisal or the need to restructure the organization. However, procedural aspects of the decision-making in those areas are always important and many organizations neglect them, giving precedence to the substance of decisions over the way they were adopted. In this section, we deal with six duties: (i) the duty to take individual administrative decisions in a transparent and lawful manner; (ii) the duty to respond to officials' queries and do it in a timely manner; (iii) the duty to assess performance of officials in a transparent and fair manner; (iv) the duty to comply with basic rules and principles applicable in the case of restructuring; (v) the duty to guarantee due process rights in disciplinary proceedings; and (vi) the duty of assistance with respect to host States.

4.1 Duty to Take Individual Administrative Decisions in a Transparent and Lawful Manner

As part of their day-to-day functioning, international organizations take systematically decisions concerning their officials. These decisions – whether of a general nature, applying to all or a group of officials, or of an individual nature, directed at a particular official – must be based on valid grounds.[201] Moreover, consistent within their general duty of care and the concomitant principle of good faith, organizations have a specific duty to take decisions with respect to their officials in a transparent and lawful manner so as to avoid causing them undue injury. Consequently, they must inform officials in advance of any action that may imperil their rights or harm their rightful interests.[202]

---

200 Judgment 2103, consid 7.

201 See, for example, Judgment 4658, consid 6; Judgment 4437, consid 19; and Judgment 4108, consid 3.

202 Judgment 3861, consid 9, referring to Judgment 3024, consid 12.

4.1.1 Duty of Transparency in Decision-Making

As regards transparency – a principle regularly invoked and upheld by the Tribunal – the main objective is to ensure clarity, confidence and accountability in the legal system and to leave no room for arbitrariness. From our point of view, transparency comes in two forms.

(a) Transparency in the context of access to information

We have identified two specific examples where the principle of transparency must be scrupulously observed by international organizations towards their officials, while respecting confidentiality of personal data in relation to third parties.

First, organizations do have a duty of transparency with respect to officials' full and unfettered access to their medical file. In this regard, the Tribunal has relevantly stated the following:

> Regarding a staff member's request for the disclosure of their medical file, the Tribunal recalls that [...] the principle of transparency as well as the individual's right to access personal data concerning them mean that a staff member must be allowed full and unfettered access to their medical file and be provided with copies of the full file when requested (paying the associated costs as necessary). The only situation in which this rule does not apply is where specific circumstances temporarily prevent such access. However, a decision to deny a staff member full access to their medical file temporarily must be fully justified and reasonable [...]. The Tribunal also relevantly stated, in Judgment 3120, consideration 6, that in the absence of specific rules or regulations governing the right of a staff member to access their own medical file, that right must be considered to comprehend the right to view and obtain copies of all records and notes in the file, and to add relevant notes to correct any part of the file considered wrong or incomplete, and that, so stated, the right to access one's own medical file gives effect to the organisation's duty of transparency.[203]

Added to these requirements is the additional need for organizations to gather and process their officials' medical information on a fully confidential basis to preserve their right to privacy.[204] In principle, such information should never

203 Judgment 4260, consid 2.

204 Judgment 2271, consid 7. See also Judgment 2045, consid 11.

be communicated to third parties without the explicit consent of the person concerned.[205]

Second, organizations do have a quasi-identical duty of transparency with respect to officials' access to their personnel file, which should be guaranteed at any time.[206] Such file should be kept updated (i) to keep track of developments in the officials' professional situation and career and (ii) in the manner required by the rules.[207] Consistent precedent requires that "a staff member should be notified of any document that is placed on her or his file and be given an opportunity to respond to it".[208] Moreover, because personnel files are by nature confidential, all reasonable precautions should be taken to ensure that access to officials' personnel files by third parties remains within the bounds of what is required, that any unjustified disclosure or dissemination of personal information is avoided and that the officials concerned be informed without delay of any disclosure.[209]

(b) Transparency in the context of decision-making

Decision-making transparency means that organizations must provide the reasons underpinning the decisions they take and explain the process followed to reach those decisions or even the issues at stake leading up to the said decisions. How extensive the reasons need to be will depend on the circumstances of each case, based on a case-specific assessment,[210] and also taking into account any requirement for confidentiality or legal privilege set out in the applicable internal rules.

It follows from the principle of transparency that organizations have a general duty to motivate their decisions. Motivation serves several purposes for each party involved in the litigation process, irrespective of the field in which a decision is taken. In Judgment 1817, which has been confirmed and reaffirmed to this day, the Tribunal has stated that "[a] staff member needs to know the reasons for a decision so that [she or] he can act on it, for example by challenging it or filing an appeal. A review body must also know the reasons so as to tell whether it is lawful".[211] The Tribunal, in turn, if seized, also needs to know the rationale behind a decision in order to assess its soundness and legality

205 Judgment 2271, consid 7.

206 See, in this regard, Judgment 256, consid 4.

207 Judgment 4642, consid 8.

208 Judgment 3487, consid 9; and Judgment 3239, consid 10.

209 See, in this regard, Judgment 3852, consid 9.

210 See, in particular, Judgment 4164, consid 11; Judgment 4081, consid 5; Judgment 4037, consid 7; and Judgment 1817, consid 6.

211 Judgment 1817, consid 6.

when exercising its power of review.[212] The reasons for an administrative decision do not need to be set out in the decision itself; they may be provided in other documents or even orally,[213] during a meeting for example.[214] However, when providing reasons for their decisions, organizations should avoid using "generic formula" which, in the absence of any other explanation, is "meaningless".[215] The breach of the duty to substantiate a decision may lead to its quashing by the Tribunal.[216]

As to the scope of the motivation, the Tribunal has held that:

> How ample the explanation need be will turn on circumstances. It may be just a reference, express or implied, to some other document that does give the why and wherefore. If little or no explanation has yet been forthcoming, the omission may be repaired in the course of appeal proceedings, provided that the staff member is given [their] full say.[217]

A specific situation in which the motivation is indispensable is when the executive head of an organization takes a final decision at the end of an internal appeal process. When the executive head accepts the recommendation and endorses the findings and conclusions of an internal appeal body, a mere reference to its report is sufficient to motivate the final decision and, hence, the executive head is under no obligation to give any further reasons in their decision than those given by the internal appeal body itself.[218] However, the executive head is not bound to follow the recommendation of an internal appeal body, or to adopt the reasoning of that body. In this situation, they must state the reasons for disregarding it and must motivate the decision eventually reached.[219] In Judgment 3161, the Tribunal has recalled that it is necessary for the executive head of an organization to explain the basis on which they arrived at a different conclusion than that of the internal appeal

212 See, for example, Judgment 4467, consid 7; and Judgment 4081, consid 5.

213 Judgment 4885, consid 9; Judgment 4880, consid 9; Judgment 4451, consid 11; Judgment 3662, consid 3; and Judgment 1590, consid 7.

214 Judgment 4877, consid 8; and Judgment 3914, consid 15.

215 Judgment 4658, consid 6.

216 Judgment 2347, consid 11; and Judgment 2261, consid 15.

217 Judgment 1817, consid 6. See also Judgment 4903, consid 7; Judgment 4683, consid 12; Judgment 4467, consid 7; and Judgment 2978, consid 4.

218 See, for example, Judgment 4877, consid 12; Judgment 4865, consid 7; or Judgment 4147, consid 10.

219 See, for example, Judgment 4062, consid 3; Judgment 3830, consid 6 and 8; Judgment 3695, consid 9; Judgment 3208, consid 11; Judgment 2699, consid 24; or Judgment 2339, consid 5.

body.[220] In this regard, it is not enough to simply identify flaws in the reasoning or procedures of that body, but reasons must be provided for the opposite conclusion reached by the executive head.[221]

4.1.2 Duty to Take Decisions in a Lawful Manner

As regards the duty to take decisions in a lawful manner – which is both a procedural and substantive obligation for international organizations when taking decisions that may affect the legal status and situation of their officials – it is intrinsically linked to the *tu patere legem quam ipse fecisti* principle (namely, any authority is bound by the rules it has itself issued). It follows that decisions must be taken in compliance with the rules and provisions of the organizations, but also while respecting any existing practices (insofar as they are lawful) and the general principles of law. Failing this, the Tribunal may set aside the decision concerned and award damages to the complainants.

The duty to take decisions in a lawful manner encompasses several significant aspects, which may be grouped as follows.

(i) International organizations must ensure that the person taking and signing the contested decisions is competent to do so, even if it means having a delegation of authority for this purpose,[222] or even a subdelegation.[223] The decision of the executive head of an organization may be communicated to the official concerned by means of a letter signed by another official, "provided that it is clear from the terms of that letter, or, at least, from consideration of the documents in the file, that the decision in question was indeed taken by the executive head [themselves]".[224] It is for the organizations to prove that whoever issues a decision is authorized to take that decision, either by virtue of a statutory provision, or by virtue of a lawful delegation by the person in whom such authority is vested under that provision.[225]

---

220 Judgment 3161, consid 7.

221 Judgment 4832, consid 32.

222 Judgment 4809, consid 4; Judgment 4291, consids 17 and 18; Judgment 3352, consid 7; and Judgment 2836, consid 7.

223 See, for example, Judgment 4594, consid 6, and the case law cited therein.

224 Judgment 4831, consid 9, citing Judgment 4506, consid 4.

225 Judgment 4506, consid 4; and Judgment 2028, consids 8(3) and 11.

(ii) Where the internal rules and regulations provide for a specific consultation of a person or a body before adopting a decision, such consultation must take place, or the Tribunal may set it aside.[226]

(iii) Conflict of interest – that is, a situation that gives rise to an objective partiality – may invalidate any decision.[227] It is a general rule of law that "an official who is called upon to take a decision affecting the rights or duties of other persons subject to her or his jurisdiction must withdraw in cases in which her or his impartiality may be open to question on reasonable grounds".[228] Officials bear the burden to prove a conflict of interest.[229] However, it is incumbent upon organizations to ensure that decisions are taken free from partiality, bias and conflict of interest.

(iv) Decisions must not be tainted by abuse or misuse of authority, which occurs when an organization acts for reasons that are extraneous to the organization's best interests and seeks some objective other than those which the authority vested in it is intended to serve.[230]

(v) Decisions should be taken in good faith and for a proper motive.[231]

The most telling examples in the case law in which the Tribunal has simultaneously condemned several international organizations for failing to comply with their duty to take decisions in a transparent and lawful manner concern the decisions to apply a post adjustment multiplier to their salaries, which was determined by the ICSC based on a 2016 cost-of-living survey for Geneva. This adjustment resulted in reduced salaries. In Judgments 4134-4138, the Tribunal first recalled that:

> [B]y incorporating the standards of the common system in its own rules the [organizations] ha[d] assumed responsibility towards [their] staff for any unlawful elements that those standards may contain or entail. Insofar as such standards are found to be flawed they may not be imposed on the staff and [the organizations] must if need be replace them with provisions that comply with the law of the international civil service. That is an essential feature of the

226 See, for example, Judgment 4797, consid 10.

227 Judgment 4915, consids 5–6.

228 Judgment 4891, consid 11, and the case law cited therein.

229 See, for example, Judgment 4963, consid 15; Judgment 4962, consid 13; Judgment 4915, consid 5; Judgment 4679, consid 3; Judgment 4617, consid 9; and Judgment 4616, consid 6.

230 Judgment 4437, consid 23, and the case law cited therein.

231 Judgment 4688, consid 10; Judgment 4524, consid 15; Judgment 4467, consid 17; Judgment 4146, consid 10; Judgment 3939, consid 10; Judgment 2264, consid 7(a); and Judgment 2163, consid 11.

> principles governing the international legal system the Tribunal is called upon to safeguard".[232]

Secondly, the Tribunal found that the ICSC's methodology and decisions, while not binding, were adopted by the organizations, impacting staff salaries.[233] It then emphasized the importance of stable, foreseeable and transparent salary adjustment methodologies[234] and recalled its previous case law according to which, if an organization is relying on an external body for advice and assistance, "[it] has the duty of checking the lawfulness of any decision by another body on which it bases its own decision".[235] It finally decided to order all the organizations to compensate affected staff members for the salary differences, including interest, thus underscoring the need for organizations to adhere to fair, transparent and legally sound salary adjustment methodologies.

4.2 Duty to Address Officials' Claims in a Timely Manner

Sometimes organizations do not take initiative in taking individual decisions but are called to act based on a specific request from a staff member. Some examples are requests for annual leave, requests to recognize an illness or injury as service-incurred, requests for education grant or other staff allowances, claims of harassment. According to the Tribunal:

> The concept of a claim involves the assertion of an unsatisfied right to a benefit or entitlement under the terms of appointment or the staff rules and regulations and its rejection entails the refusal to pay the benefit or grant the entitlement either in whole or in part.[236]

Underpinning the general duty of care is the organizations' duty to respond to requests from their staff members and to do it within a reasonable time,[237] especially when it comes to a matter in which delays can cause significant

232 Judgment 4134, consid 8 (citing Judgment 1266, consid 24), reiterated in Judgments 4135 to 4138.
233 Ibid, consid 9, reiterated in Judgments 4135 to 4138.
234 Ibid, consids 26 and 49, reiterated in Judgments 4135 to 4138.
235 Ibid, consid 28, reiterated in Judgments 4135 to 4138.
236 Judgment 4693, consid 8.
237 Judgment 4606, consid 14; and Judgment 3188, consid 5.

harm to the complainants, including distress and feeling of isolation.[238] This is especially true in cases involving harassment or misconduct where procedural fairness plays a key role and includes the right of complainants to be informed and to receive a decision within a reasonable period. An organizations' failure to respond in a timely manner amounts to a procedural flaw which is most often sanctioned by the Tribunal. In Judgment 3188, the Tribunal has relevantly stated that:

> [A] failure to respond to a legitimate request of a staff member within a reasonable time may be deemed to be a refusal of the request if the staff member elects to accept that refusal. Additionally, egregious delay in responding to a reasonable request may involve a breach of the obligation to deal with the staff member in good faith.[239]

Moreover, the failure to respond to an official's query may be considered, pursuant to the applicable internal rules, as a rejection of the claim entitling the official to appeal it. If the rules do not contain such a provision, the failure to answer the claim within 60 days entitles an official to submit a complaint directly to the Tribunal in accordance with Article VII, paragraph 3, of its Statute. Resorting to implicit rejections is not a good practice, since such decisions, by definition, lack motivation[240] and may unnecessarily generate disputes.

4.3 Duty to Assess Performance of Officials in a Transparent and Fair Manner

Another crucial obligation of international organizations – and bearing in mind that discretion may play a key role in this matter – concerns the assessment of officials' performance. The jurisprudence in this area is abundant. It is possible to distinguish between what we would call 'general obligations', which concern the duties of organizations in all circumstances and even before a decision is made, and 'specific obligations', which we consider are reinforced when it comes to adverse decisions having an impact on the legal status and situation of officials.

238 See Laurence Fauth, 'Proving He Said/She Said Sexual Harassment Claims: Lessons From ILOAT Judgment No. 4207' (2020) <https://www.unattorney.com/2020/09/10/sexual-harassment-claims-lessons-from-iloat-judgment-no-4207/> accessed 13 December 2025.

239 Judgment 3188, consid 5.

240 Judgment 3884, consid 6.

The general obligations we have identified are the following:

(i) Organizations must abide by their own policies and procedures according to the *tu patere legem quam ipse fecisti* principle. In other words, they must comply with the procedures they have established for evaluating performance.[241] *A fortiori* (with even stronger reason), in the absence of specific statutory or regulatory provisions, organizations may not establish an assessment system parallel to that which existed officially by, for example, commissioning an extraneous body to undertake a task which entailed interfering in the assessment of staff members' suitability for the available positions and which, moreover, did not offer staff members the safeguards inherent in the official system.[242]

(ii) In the event of a change in the applicable regulatory framework of an appraisal procedure, organizations may not amend the framework by a provision adopted after the beginning of the reporting period concerned:

> [T]hat approach, which applies first and foremost to the setting of the criteria on the basis of which the assessment is performed, is justified by the need to observe both the principle of the non-retroactivity of administrative acts and the requirements of good faith, transparency and fairness that are incumbent [on international organizations] in the matter of staff appraisals.[243]

By virtue of the non-retroactivity rule, organizations are prevented from altering definitively established legal situations, for example by calling into question a performance appraisal rendered during an evaluation period prior to the adoption of new rules.[244]

(iii) Performance evaluations should be made objectively. Staff reports should be free from personal, subjective and emotional remarks. No room must be left for arbitrariness and bias or partiality, meaning that the organization's discretionary power must not be exceeded.[245] In the same vein, performance assessment should be conducted fairly and transparently. The officials' rights should be protected, and the integrity of the evaluation process must be maintained throughout the whole

241 Judgment 3932, consid 21; Judgment 3252, consid 8; and Judgment 3240, consid 20, and the case law cited therein.

242 Judgment 3437, consid 9.

243 Judgment 4897, consid 14, and the case law cited therein.

244 Judgment 3185, consid 7(b).

245 See Judgment 4981, consid 7; Judgment 4978, consid 6; Judgment 4977, consid 2; Judgment 4962, consid 7, and the case law cited therein.

procedure. In Judgment 3692, the Tribunal has provided some interesting clarifications on how objectivity may be ensured when there may be a conflictual situation between the official and their supervisor:

> [I]f the rules of an organization require that an appraisal form must be signed not only by the direct supervisor of the staff member concerned but also by [their] second-level supervisor, this is designed to guarantee oversight, at least *prima facie*, of the objectivity of the report. The purpose of such a rule is to ensure that responsibilities are shared between these two authorities and that the staff member who is being appraised is shielded from a biased assessment by a supervisor, who should not be the only person issuing an opinion on the staff member's skills and performance. It is therefore of the utmost importance that the competent second-level supervisor should take care to ascertain that the assessment submitted for [their] approval does not require modification [...]. Of course, this check must be carried out with particular vigilance when the assessment occurs in a context where it is especially to be feared that the supervisor making it might lack objectivity and, *a fortiori* [with even stronger reason], when it takes place, as it did in the instant case, in a situation of overt antagonism.[246]

(iv) In making an assessment, organizations must establish clear objectives against which performance will be assessed, provide the necessary guidance for the performance of the duties, identify in a timely manner the unsatisfactory aspects of the performance so that remedial steps may be taken, and give a specific warning where continued employment is in jeopardy.[247]

(v) Organizations have an obvious duty to consider factors that may affect officials' performance. That would be the case for a fragile medical situation[248] or in cases in which officials may act as staff representatives.[249]

(vi) The burden of proof is always on the pleading party. Accordingly, it is for the organization to prove that a staff member is not performing in a satisfactory manner before any adverse decisions may be taken as a result of the performance assessment process, and not for the staff member to prove the contrary.[250]

---

246 Judgment 3692, consid 14, and the case law cited therein.

247 Judgment 4930, consid 2; Judgment 4748, consid 8; Judgment 4450, consid 3; and Judgment 4282, consid 3.

248 Judgment 4793, consid 9.

249 Judgment 4794, consid 13, and the case law cited therein.

250 See, in this regard, Judgment 4840, consid 31.

As to the reinforced obligations that are incumbent upon organizations and which are related to adverse decisions, such as non-renewal or termination of contracts due to unsatisfactory performance or underperformance, we have identified the following:

(i) Organizations cannot base an adverse decision on a staff member's unsatisfactory performance if they have not complied with the rules established to evaluate that performance.[251] This is all the more true in cases in which organizations have decided to terminate or not to renew a contract for unsatisfactory performance.[252] As regards particularly a non-renewal decision, the Tribunal aptly stated that "[a]n examination of a staff member's assessment report before taking any decision not to renew that person's contract on the basis of unsatisfactory performance is a fundamental obligation, non-compliance with which constitutes a procedural flaw that has the effect of an essential fact being overlooked".[253] In Judgment 3417, the Tribunal went one step further by stating:

> [W]hile there is an undoubted right of an organisation to decide not to renew a fixed-term contract, it does not follow that an organisation is, additionally, immune from any liability if it has failed to follow its own procedures designed to monitor, assess and evaluate staff performance and progress. The fundamental purpose of such procedures is to explicitly alert a staff member to identified deficiencies in her or his performance and thus give the staff member an opportunity to address those deficiencies and improve performance.[254]

This is equally true regarding officials who are perceived to be difficult to deal with and who are perceived to have been performing unsatisfactorily in fairly fundamental ways.[255]

(ii) As regards decisions to terminate an official's appointment at the end of their probationary period for unsatisfactory performance, the Tribunal has held that, since the purpose of probation is to permit an organization to assess the probationer's suitability for a position, in the course of making its assessment, an organization must establish clear objectives, provide the necessary guidance for the performance of the duties, iden-

251 Judgment 3932, consid 21; Judgment 3252, consid 8; and Judgment 3240, consid 20, and the case law cited therein.

252 Judgment 4840, consid 10.

253 Judgment 4666, consid 4, and the case law cited therein.

254 Judgment 3417, consid 6.

255 Judgment 3286, consid 25.

tify the unsatisfactory aspects of the performance in a timely manner so that remedial steps may be taken, and give a specific warning where continued employment is in jeopardy. Moreover, a probationer is entitled to have objectives set in advance.[256]

(iii) In the same vein and reasoning, organizations must provide adequate time for a staff member to improve their performance. In terms of alleged unsatisfactory performance, a staff member should not only be warned but also given an opportunity to improve and correct the alleged poor or unsatisfactory performance: "an organisation may not in good faith end someone's appointment for poor performance without first warning him and giving him an opportunity to do better".[257] Similarly, in Judgment 3026, the Tribunal recalled that "[a]n opportunity to improve requires not only that the staff member be made aware of the matters requiring improvement, but, also, that he or she be given a reasonable time for that improvement to occur."[258]

4.4 Duty to Comply with Basic Rules and Principles in the Case of Restructuring

Restructuring of secretariats of international organizations is a frequent phenomenon. It may be motivated by the appointment of a new executive head, by financial or operational needs. It often responds to the calls of member States to implement reforms which, although not always specific and well-articulated, impose on the organization an impetus to change and adapt. As a result of the restructuring, some staff positions may be abolished, leading to staff reductions, some positions may be transferred to other organizational units, leading to reassignment, and some positions may be redefined, triggering the need to adjust their terms of reference.

As a matter of principle, the Tribunal recognizes the right of international organizations to restructure.[259] It has also been specifically recognized that

256 See, for example, Judgment 4930, consid 2; Judgment 4450, consids 3 and 6; and Judgment 3085, consid 23, and the case law cited therein.

257 Judgment 3282, consid 5, citing Judgment 2196, consid 4.

258 Judgment 3026, consid 8.

259 Judgment 4935, consid 4; Judgment 4599, consids 11–12; Judgment 4353, consid 7; Judgment 3908, consid 16, Judgment 3437, consid 5; Judgment 3238, consid 7; and Judgment 3169, consid 7. In Judgment 4841, considerations 4–6, the ILOAT made a comprehensive restatement of its previous case law.

the legitimate reasons for restructuring may be budgetary, in order to achieve better efficiency or budgetary restrictions.[260]

The restructuring may lead to the abolition of certain posts and the officials holding those posts are directly and adversely affected by this process. While the restructuring may validly justify the abolition of posts,[261] it should not amount to a disguised attempt to get rid of an unwanted staff member,[262] as this would constitute abuse of authority.[263] The Tribunal has specifically put in relation the right to abolish posts with an obligation "to deal fairly" with the officials concerned.[264] Each restructuring exercise is implemented through individual administrative decisions that may be challenged and that "must respect all the applicable legal rules and in particular the fundamental rights of the staff concerned".[265] This triggers the general rules applicable to the abolition of posts, regardless of what is actually written in the organization's rules.[266] As a part of the duty to treat officials concerned with dignity and respect, there is an obligation to make reasonable efforts to find for them another suitable position, that is to say to reassign them.[267] The Tribunal even said that there must be "proper institutional support mechanisms in place to assist the staff member concerned in finding a new assignment".[268]

The search for adequate posts should not be limited to the same organizational unit, but should be broader.[269] Offering a position at a lower grade should also be considered.[270] This protection is particularly important for offi-

---

260 Judgment 4937, consid 2; Judgment 4935, consid 4; Judgment 3437, consid 5; Judgment 3238, consid 7; Judgment 2907, consid 13; Judgment 2510, consid 10; and Judgment 2156, consid 8.

261 Judgment 4009, consid 15; and Judgment 4008, consid 15: "as the Tribunal has consistently held, although job abolitions may arise from a restructuring, they must be justified by real needs and not be immediately followed by the creation of equivalent posts (see Judgments 3422, under 2, and 2156, under 8)".

262 Judgment 4599, consid 11; Judgment 4353, consid 6; Judgment 2830, consid 6(b); and Judgment 1231, consid 26.

263 Judgment 4935, consid 4.

264 Judgment 3908, consid 16.

265 Judgment 3437, consid 5, and the case law cited therein. See also Judgment 4935, consid 4; and Judgment 2907.

266 Judgment 4097, consid 9: "normative legal documents promulgated within an organization cannot alone circumscribe the obligation of the organization to explore other employment options within the organization for staff whose positions have been abolished".

267 Judgment 3903, consid 15.

268 Judgment 3041, consid 8, reiterated in Judgment 3928, consid 15.

269 Judgment 3903, consid 15.

270 Judgment 3290, consid 30; and Judgment 2830, consid 9.

cials holding a long-term employment (without a limit of time, indefinite or permanent). In Judgment 3436, the Tribunal stated:

> [W]hen an organisation has to abolish a post held by a staff member who, like the complainant in the instant case, holds a contract for an indefinite period of time, it has a duty to do all that it can to reassign that person as a matter of priority to another post matching his or her abilities and grade. Furthermore, if the attempt to find such a post proves fruitless, it is up to the organisation, if the staff member concerned agrees, to try to place him or her in duties at a lower grade and to widen its search accordingly (see Judgments 1782, under 11, or 2830, under 9).[271]

However, the reference to contracts of indefinite period is not necessarily limitative anymore. Noting that "[t]here is, presently, a greater mix of staff of differing status in international organizations", the Tribunal affirmed that "simply because some staff are not permanent, it does not follow that those other classes of staff of differing status should be afforded no protection by principles developed by the Tribunal in circumstances where their post is abolished and attempts are being made to reassign them".[272]

The organization must do "its utmost" to find another position[273] and must be ready to prove that the affected staff member was not able to remain in the organization's service.[274] The search for reassignment should start before the decision to abolish post is taken.[275] The Tribunal said that "an organization has a duty to apply processes biased in favour of the staff member whose position has been abolished and which are likely to promote appointment to another position"[276] and "an organization has an obligation to deal fairly with staff who occupy an abolished position which ordinarily extends to finding, if they exist, other positions within the organization for which those staff have the experience and qualifications".[277] This last proposition should be qualified not only with the number of available posts, but also with the specific terms of appointment, such as officials recruited locally, which limits the opportunities

271 Judgment 3436, consid 6. See also Judgment 3917, consid 6, and the case law cited therein.
272 Judgment 4097, consid 10.
273 See Judgment 3754, consid 16, citing Judgment 2830, consid 9.
274 See Judgment 4097, consid 13; Judgment 3755, consid 19; Judgment 3238, consid 14; Judgment 3169, consid 14; and Judgment 2830, consid 9.
275 See Judgment 3900, consid 4; Judgment 3238, consid 13; Judgment 3169, consid 10 and 13; and Judgment 2294, consid 9.
276 Judgment 4097, consid 9.
277 Ibid.

for their mobility to a particular country.[278] In recent Judgment 4935, the Tribunal explained that it generally considered the extent of an organization's duty to reassign staff members whose positions were abolished mainly in relation to the type of contract they held, the nature of the post and the role to which they were assigned, and their length of service with the organization.[279]

As the Tribunal explained:

> The right which the Tribunal must uphold is the right to remain in employment, not the right to termination thereof. The Tribunal considers that termination of employment must be an *ultima ratio* measure to which recourse may be had only after all other alternatives have been examined and found to be impracticable (see Judgment 2830, under 8(a)). At all events, continued employment must be preferred to redundancy.[280]

Another obligation is to give proper notice of abolition of post. In Judgment 3041, the Tribunal has noted:

> The decision to abolish a post must be communicated to the staff person occupying the post in a manner that safeguards that individual's rights. These rights are safeguarded by giving proper notice of the decision, reasons for the decision and an opportunity to contest the decision.[281]

---

278 In Judgment 4097, the complainant was a National Professional Officer. The Tribunal acknowledged, in consideration 10, that "[t]he extent of WHO's obligations in relation to the complainant's reassignment is plainly influenced by the fact that she had been appointed to a National Professional Officer post on the basis of local recruitment. It could not be expected that WHO assess whether within the entire Organization there was any available position for which the complainant was qualified and suitable". The legitimacy of a differentiated treatment was already recognized by the Tribunal in Judgment 1196, consideration 19.

279 Judgment 4935, consid 21, referring to Judgment 3754, consid 16.

280 Judgment 3902, consid 11.

281 Judgment 3041, consid 8, reiterated in Judgment 4935, consid 4; Judgment 4609, consid 8; Judgment 4451, consid 11; Judgment 3928, consid 15; Judgment 3755, consid 6; Judgment 3662, consid 5; Judgment 3234, consid 7. See also Judgment 1556, consids 10 and 12; and Judgment 810, consid 7. However, in Judgment 4935, consideration 10, it was explained that "the Tribunal does not impose on international organizations a duty to provide staff members whose positions are abolished with the full set of internal documents used as a basis for such decision".

The organization is "under a positive duty to communicate" with the staff concerned "in a way that promotes the likelihood of reassignment".[282] Also, when the restructuring leads to a transfer, the case law of the Tribunal becomes directly relevant and applicable:

(i) A staff member who is to be transferred should be informed in advance of the nature of the post proposed for them and, in particular, of the duties involved, so that they are able to comment on those new duties.[283] The organization must show due regard, in both form and substance, for the dignity of the official concerned,[284] particularly by providing them with work of the same level of responsibilities as they performed in the previous post and matching their qualifications.[285] It is not enough for the person concerned to retain their grade and remuneration.[286]

(ii) When the transfer involves a change in duty station, the organization must ensure that the implementation of that measure is preceded by proper notice enabling the staff member to make the necessary arrangements for the change to their duty station.[287]

(iii) When the interests of the organization and the official concerned differ:

> [E]very international organization is bound by a duty of care to treat its staff members with dignity and avoid causing them undue and unnecessary injury (see, for example, Judgment 4253, under 3). While the head of an international organization must take into account the organization's interests as well as the staff member's abilities and interests in the exercise of the discretion to transfer a staff member, in cases where the two are at odds, greater weight may be accorded by the decision-maker to the interests of the organization (see Judgment 2635, under 6).[288]

The restructuring not resulting in abolition of posts or transfers may nevertheless lead to a change in the existing administrative unit and its methods of work. This is found acceptable in principle and does not necessarily violate acquired rights. The Tribunal specifically stated that "a particular model of

---

282 Judgment 3918, consid 9, citing Judgment 2902, consid 14; Judgment 3439, consid 9; and Judgment 3755, consid 9.

283 Judgment 4830, consid 15, and the case law cited therein.

284 Judgment 4595, consid 2; and Judgment 4427, consid 11.

285 Judgment 5001, consid 2, referring to Judgment 4599, consid 19.

286 Judgment 4599, consid 19 and the case law cited therein.

287 Judgment 4609, consid 10, citing Judgment 1556, consid 12; Judgment 1496, consid 11 and 13; and Judgment 810, consid 7.

288 Judgment 4687, consid 5. See also Judgment 5001, consid 2.

organising a service, such as the one previously in force in this case, cannot constitute an acquired right".[289] Another acceptable example is the assignment of new or different shift work patterns.[290]

4.5 Duty to Respect Due Process Rights in Disciplinary Proceedings

Due process rights in disciplinary proceedings are essential to ensure fairness and justice. This is particularly important given the significant repercussions (namely on a financial, moral, physical and reputational level) such proceedings can have on an international civil servant, especially if they lead to a disciplinary sanction.

A careful reading of the many judgments delivered in this area reveals several elements in which due process rights must be guaranteed by the organizations. The starting points are to be found in (i) Judgment 3944, in which the Tribunal has found that, since disciplinary proceedings are, in essence, adversarial, they begin only once the official concerned has been notified of them;[291] and (ii) Judgment 2786, in which the Tribunal has stated:

> Due process requires that a staff member accused of misconduct be given an opportunity to test the evidence relied upon and, if he or she so wishes, to produce evidence to the contrary. The right to make a defence is necessarily a right to defend oneself before an adverse decision is made, whether by a disciplinary body or the deciding authority.[292]

4.5.1 Investigation

The decision to open disciplinary proceedings is usually preceded by an investigation, the purpose of which is "not to gather evidence which can be used against the person concerned, but to provide the competent authority with information enabling it to determine whether the opening of a disciplinary procedure is warranted",[293] while scrupulously safeguarding the rights of defence.[294]

---

289 Judgment 3373, consid 8.
290 Judgment 2972, consids 7–8.
291 Judgment 3944, consid 4. See also Judgment 4583, consid 4.
292 Judgment 2786, consid 13. See also Judgment 5003, consid 5; Judgment 4343, consid 13; and Judgment 2496, consid 7.
293 Judgment 4038, consid 3; and Judgment 4039, consid 3.
294 Judgment 4038, consid 6.

Although it is normally not part of the disciplinary proceedings, an investigation is generally conducted prior to those proceedings in compliance with certain procedural standards. Several duties incumbent upon organizations may be deduced from the case law:

(i) The decision to open an investigation lies at the discretion of the competent authority of the organization, based on sufficient *prima facie* (at first sight) evidence of misconduct, but must not be arbitrary.[295] Where the competent authority considers that there is no *prima facie* evidence of misconduct, the decision to close the complaint can be justified in a relatively summary manner.[296]

(ii) An organization has an obligation to initiate the investigation "in a timely manner" and "the corollary obligation of ensuring that the internal body responsible for investigating and reporting on the allegations has the necessary resources to carry out that responsibility".[297]

(iii) Once the investigation is initiated, the organization is under an obligation to provide the person concerned with an opportunity to explain their conduct and to present any information on their behalf. This opportunity should preferably be afforded before rather than during the interview.[298]

(iv) Investigations must be objective, rigorous and thorough in that "they must be conducted in a manner designed to ascertain all relevant facts without compromising the good name of the employee and that the employee be given an opportunity to test the evidence put against him or her and to answer the charge made".[299] At least that is so where no procedure is prescribed. Where there is a prescribed procedure, that procedure must be observed.[300] In this regard, the investigation should be fair in the sense that there must be an opportunity to answer the evidence and the charges.[301]

(v) Because due process rights apply in a less scrupulous way during the investigation, the Tribunal has held that, while it is preferable to notify the person concerned that they are to be the subject of an

295 Judgment 4967, consid 9; Judgment 4038, consid 4; and Judgment 4039, consid 3.
296 Judgment 4923, consid 10.
297 Judgment 4038, consid 11; and Judgment 3347, consid 14.
298 Judgment 4038, consid 6; and Judgment 2771, consid 18.
299 Judgment 4961, consid 6; Judgment 4343, consid 13; and Judgment 2475, consid 7.
300 Judgment 4011, consid 9, citing Judgment 2771, consid 15.
301 Judgment 4011, consid 9; and Judgment 2475, consid 7.

investigation, except where this would be liable to compromise the outcome of the investigation, such notification is not a requisite element of due process.[302]

(vi) During the investigation, allegations against a staff member should not be altered unless new facts discovered during the investigation establishes adequate link between the original allegations and the altered allegations. New allegations should be investigated separately in the absence of such link.[303]

(vii) On the possibility for officials to be accompanied during the investigation – which, in the Tribunal's view, is certainly preferable – the case law has it that "no general principle obliges an international organisation to make provision for staff members under investigation to be assisted by a staff representative when they are interviewed".[304]

(viii) Moreover, unless otherwise specified in the organizations' internal rules, officials may be given the opportunity to request the presence of an interpreter should they have an issue with the language used during the interview. The organizations may refuse the request, provided that they justify their refusal.[305]

(ix) For the rights of defence to be guaranteed, it is sufficient for an official to know the content of the statements made by witnesses during the investigation and it is not necessary for them to know the witnesses' names.[306]

4.5.2 Provisional Administrative Measures

It is quite common for organizations' internal rules to provide for interim measures concerning the legal position and status of an official charged with misconduct – and even more so if serious misconduct is at issue – pending the outcome of the investigation. The aim of such measures is generally to preserve the integrity of the investigation and to avoid that evidence be compromised or destroyed or that witnesses be placed under pressure.[307] Although provisional measures are not disciplinary sanctions, they must

302 Judgment 4038, consid 6; Judgment 3295, consid 8; and Judgment 2589, consid 7.
303 See, in this sense, Judgment 4038, consid 9.
304 Judgment 4038, consids 3 and 7; and Judgment 2589, consid 7.
305 See, in this sense, Judgment 4038, consid 8.
306 Judgment 4814, consid 14; and Judgment 4615, consid 22.
307 Judgment 4519, consid 6.

have a legal basis, be justified by the needs of the organization and be taken with due regard to the principle of proportionality.[308]

One of the most frequently used interim measures is suspension, whether with or without pay. The Tribunal recognizes the validity of such a measure, provided that the organizations comply with certain principles and rules. The following has recently been stated:

> [A] measure of suspension decided in the context of disciplinary proceedings, with or without pay, is an interim measure which in no way prejudges the decision to be taken on the merits as to whether a disciplinary sanction should be imposed on the official concerned. However, since it imposes a constraint on the official, it must be legally founded, justified by the requirements of the organisation and in accordance with the principle of proportionality. A measure of suspension will not be ordered except in cases of misconduct [...]. Such a decision lies at the discretion of the organisation's executive head. [...] In order to assess whether a measure of suspension is lawful, the Tribunal must determine whether the conditions required to take such a measure were met at the time it was ordered, all subsequent facts being irrelevant [...]. Where a measure of suspension has been extended, the Tribunal must also determine whether the conditions for each extension decision were met at the time that decision was taken [...]. Lastly, while an authority may adopt a measure of suspension if it considers, on the basis of the evidence before it and at its own discretion, that the charge of misconduct against an official is reasonable, there is no need at this stage to prove that the accusations are well founded [...].[309]

The main lessons to be learned from these statements are that, even though suspension is a discretionary decision, if the executive head of an organization decides to apply it to a staff member pending the investigation, several principles are to be respected since suspension has, by itself, an immediate, material, legal and adverse effect on the person concerned,[310] especially when it comes to suspension without pay.[311] In this regard, the Tribunal has stated that, when a staff member is suspended, the damage already inevitably done

308 See, with respect to suspension, Judgment 4612, consid 3; Judgment 4586, consid 8; Judgment 4515, consid 4; and Judgment 2698, consid 9. The same reasoning seems to apply *mutatis mutandis* to other provisional measures.

309 Judgment 4658, consid 2. See also Judgment 4948, consids 9 and 15.

310 Judgment 3958, consid 14.

311 Judgment 4519, consid 6.

to their professional reputation arises primarily from the very fact that they are removed from duty.[312]

The following principles do apply in all circumstances:

(i) Organizations must at all times comply with the *tu patere legem quam ipse fecisti* principle (namely, any authority is bound by the rules it has itself issued).

(ii) Concerning in particular the duration of suspension which is, by its very nature, a 'short-term' measure,[313] when there is a specific reference in the internal rules to the possibility of suspending an official until the end of the investigation into the facts of which they are suspected, this cannot be interpreted as "authorising an extension of that suspension beyond the end of the investigation in question and, in particular, during any disciplinary proceedings subsequently instituted against the official concerned."[314] An egregious duration of suspension, especially when the staff member is deprived of any professional income for an unreasonably long time, will be sanctioned by the Tribunal.[315]

(iii) Suspension must not be an arbitrary measure nor an act of bias or prejudice, retaliation or abuse of authority, equating to a hidden disciplinary measure or a clear constructive dismissal.[316]

(iv) When suspension comes with the ejection of the staff member from the workplace, the organization must strictly comply with their duty of care. In this regard, the Tribunal has noted that, by its very nature, being escorted out of the workplace is a humiliating experience, and can be even characterized as "brutal".[317] As such, according to the Tribunal, "unless there is a justified need, the use of such procedures is strongly condemned in its case law."[318] As to the disabling of a staff member's

312 Judgment 4519, consid 14.

313 Ibid, consid 9.

314 Judgment 4519, consid 5; Judgment 4515, consid 8; and Judgment 3880, consid 20.

315 Judgment 4519, consid 9.

316 Ibid, consids 6 and 11.

317 Judgment 3169, consid 21.

318 Judgment 4457, consid 27, referring to its previous Judgment 3169, consid 21; and Judgment 2892, consid 26. However, the case law on this issue appears to be contradictory. In recent Judgment 4948, in consideration 19, the Tribunal has reiterated a statement which it made previously in Judgment 4831, consideration 10, and Judgment 3649, consideration 13, according to which: "although, by its very nature, a staff member being escorted from [their] office by officers and being escorted out of the workplace is a humiliating experience, such a course of action is admissible in the absence of any conduct of the officers that would exacerbate the humiliation [and is simply a matter of sound business practice on the part of an organisation]". This is quite surprising as being escorted out of

email account and the denial of access to certain floors and facilities, these are simply "matters of sound business practice" on the part of the organizations, which are acceptable, provided that they are lawful.[319]

(v) Staff members do not have a right to be heard before a decision to suspend is made.[320]

(vi) Also, it is for the organizations to palliate any defect in their provisions to prevent any difficulty that the return to duty of a staff member after their provisional suspension may cause.[321]

Another example of provisional measure is the executive head's decision to place a staff member on special leave pending an investigation into allegations of misconduct. If such a measure is disciplinary in nature, procedural guarantees must be provided before imposing it.[322] The rules must provide specifically that an official could be placed on special leave as an interim measure. As most of staff rules describe special leave as a privilege for the benefit of staff members, it is an error of law and an abuse of authority to unilaterally "place" an official on special leave, since it is for a purpose which was extraneous to the rule.[323]

4.5.3 Disciplinary Proceedings

Once the investigative stage is over and it has been considered that the opening of a disciplinary procedure is warranted, the organization is not obliged to

the office is surely humiliating and denigrating, and creates an obvious psychological shock to the official concerned which, according to the 'but for' test, may even be considered as service-incurred. Except under exceptional specific circumstances in which the organization can prove the existence of a real danger for it and its staff, the use of such measures should be strongly discouraged. In today's situation, in which all the organizations can monitor the move of the staff member out of the building by video equipment and electronically deactivate the access badge once the person passes the gate, it is difficult to see why physical escorting of a staff member out of the premises would be necessary. How something that affects the officials' dignity and causes them unnecessary personal distress and disappointment where this could be avoided, which the Tribunal found unacceptable in consideration 14 of Judgment 4178, could be considered a sound business practice? How to prove that the conduct of the officers exacerbated the humiliation? Faced with two lines of the case law, we express our strong preference for what is stated in Judgment 4457, consideration 27.

319 Judgment 3649, consid 13.

320 Judgment 4612, consid 3; and Judgment 4361, consid 12.

321 Judgment 4519, consid 6.

322 Judgment 2661, consid 16.

323 Judgment 4231, consids 13–14.

repeat all the investigative steps recorded in the investigation report but must ensure that the person concerned is given the opportunity to reply to the findings it contains so as to respect the rights of defence.[324] Due process rights – which must be observed at all stages of disciplinary proceedings – require that the staff member accused of misconduct be given an opportunity to defend themselves before an adverse decision is made, whether by a disciplinary body or the deciding authority.[325]

Most of the obligations incumbent upon organizations during the investigation stage (which are listed above) are reiterated – and even reinforced – during the disciplinary proceedings. Those we consider most important are the following:

(i) Respect for the principle of presumption of innocence.[326]

(ii) Disclosure of evidence – which is a corollary of the organizations' duty to inform their officials – resulting from the Tribunal's consistent case law that:

> [A] staff member must, as a general rule, have access to all the evidence on which an authority bases (or intends to base) a decision that adversely affects [them] [...]. Under normal circumstances, such evidence cannot be withheld on grounds of confidentiality unless there is some special case in which a higher interest stands in the way of the disclosure of certain documents. But such disclosure may not be refused merely in order to strengthen the position of the [organization] or one of its officers.[327]

Concerning more precisely an investigation report, the Tribunal has considered that the document in question is generally "of vital importance having regard to the subject matter of the dispute",[328] meaning that it has to be disclosed to the official concerned even, if necessary, in a redacted version.[329]

(iii) Respect for the rules according to the *tu patere legem quam ipse fecisti* principle (namely, any authority is bound by the rules it has itself issued). Recently, the Tribunal has sanctioned an organization for hav-

324 Judgment 4311, consid 4; Judgment 3640, consid 16; and Judgment 2773, consid 9.

325 Judgment 4832, consid 28; Judgment 4343, consid 13; and Judgment 2496, consid 7.

326 Judgment 2741, consid 4(a), and the case law cited therein.

327 Judgment 4839, consid 9, and the case law cited therein.

328 Judgment 3995, consid 5. See also Judgment 4900, consid 42; and Judgment 4820, consid 10.

329 Judgment 4954, consid 5.

ing added another layer of investigation in the disciplinary process, which was not contemplated by the internal rules, coupled with the failure to share with the complainant the new evidence gathered during this process before a final decision on the disciplinary measure was reached. It considered that this amounted to gross procedural irregularities that violated the complainant's right of defence and entitlement to due process.[330]

(iv) Respect for the official's right to be heard who must be given the opportunity to state their case before the final decision to impose a disciplinary measure is taken.[331] This includes that the official be given the opportunity to provide additional information if invited to submit their observations on the proposal for a sanction.[332]

(v) Impartiality of the decision-maker, excluding bias, partiality or lack of independence from the official concerned. This necessarily implies that in the event of a conflict of interest, the decision-maker must recuse themselves.[333]

4.5.4 Disciplinary Sanction

Four main obligations can be identified as regards the disciplinary measures. First, the choice of the appropriate disciplinary measure falls within the discretion of an organization, provided that the discretion is exercised in observance of the rule of law, particularly the principle of proportionality:[334]

> Lack of proportionality is to be treated as an error of law warranting the setting aside of a disciplinary measure even though a decision in that regard is discretionary in nature. In determining whether disciplinary action is disproportionate to the offence, both objective and subjective features are to be taken into account.[335]

---

330 Judgment 4832, consid 29.

331 Judgment 5003, consid 5, and the case law cited therein.

332 See, in this sense, Judgment 4697, consid 11; and Judgment 4310, consid 10. See also Judgment 2261, consid 13; and Judgment 2014, consid 17.

333 Judgment 4915, consid 5.

334 Judgment 4949, consid 20–21; Judgment 4859, consid 28; Judgment 4660, consid 16; Judgment 4504, consid 11; Judgment 4247, consid 7; Judgment 3640, consid 29; and Judgment 1984, consid 7.

335 Judgment 4697, consid 24, referring to Judgment 4478, consid 11, and the case law cited therein; and Judgment 4504, consid 11.

Case law gives examples of what can and cannot be taken into account as mitigating factors (such as health, long service and service record).[336] Second, there is a duty to motivate the final decision imposing a disciplinary sanction. Reference is made here to the application of the correct standard of proof in case of misconduct. In this regard, the Tribunal has long established that the burden of proof rests on an organization to prove allegations of misconduct "beyond reasonable doubt" before a disciplinary sanction can be imposed.[337] In Judgment 3875, the Tribunal explained that:

> In disciplinary matters, the burden of proof lies with the employer, which must demonstrate that the employee did indeed engage in the conduct of which she or he is accused. If the facts are disputed and there is no persuasive material evidence, the facts of the dispute must be appraised on the basis of conclusive circumstantial evidence. Thus, the facts may be held to be established when a set of precise presumptions and concurring circumstantial evidence enable the decision-making authority to conclude beyond reasonable doubt that the person concerned is guilty [...].[338]

Common law lawyers criticized this standard of proof as too high, referring to their own national laws. These critics are simply wrong for referring to the disciplinary procedure as following a 'criminal' standard as in some domestic legal systems. As the Tribunal explained in Judgment 4749:

> The standard of proof of beyond reasonable doubt does not exist to create an insuperable barrier for organisations to successfully prosecute disciplinary proceedings against staff members. Indeed, it should not have that effect. What is required is discussed in many judgments of the Tribunal. Rather the standard involves the recognition that often disciplinary proceedings can have severe consequences for the affected staff member, including dismissal and potentially serious adverse consequences on the reputation of the staff member and [their] career as an international civil servant, and in these circumstances it is appropriate to require a high level of satisfaction on the part of the organisation that the disciplinary measure is justified because the misconduct has been proved.

---

336 Judgment 4859, consid 28; Judgment 4856, consid 19; Judgment 4779, consid 16; Judgment 4749, consid 12; Judgment 4745, consid 11; Judgment 4453, consid 15; and Judgment 4415, consid 12.

337 Judgment 4971, consid 5; Judgment 4936, consid 6; and Judgment 4934, consids 7–8. See also Judgment 4832, consid 31, referring to Judgment 3969, consid 10; and Judgment 3862, consid 20. See also Judgment 4697, consid 12.

338 Judgment 3875, consid 8.

> The likelihood of misconduct having occurred is insufficient and does not afford appropriate protection to international civil servants. It is fundamentally unproductive to say, critically, this standard is the 'criminal' standard in some domestic legal systems and a more appropriate standard is the 'civil' standard in the same systems involving the assessment of evidence and proof on the balance of probabilities. The standard of beyond reasonable doubt derived from the Tribunal's case law as it has evolved over the decades, serves a purpose peculiar to the law of the international civil service.[339]

Third, there can be no double jeopardy. The double jeopardy rule precludes the imposition of further disciplinary measures for acts which have already attracted a disciplinary measure.[340] Fourth, while, ordinarily, a final decision maker can refer to other documents which, when taken together with such reasons for decision as are given by the decision maker, can constitute the reasons for decision, the aggregation of reasons from multiple sources is not recognized as appropriate in relation to disciplinary decisions.[341]

4.6 Duty of Assistance with Respect to Host States

Many of the international organizations having recognized the Tribunal's jurisdiction have concluded agreements relating to their presence in a given country. These agreements are crucial in defining the legal framework within which the organizations operate.[342] Nonetheless, in order to preserve independent functioning and autonomy of the organizations, host States' laws do not, in principle, have to interfere with the internal regulations and rules of the organizations who enjoy immunity from jurisdiction of national courts.[343] This has been recently confirmed by the Tribunal which has recalled that "as a rule, the conditions of employment of staff of an international organisation are subject exclusively to that organisation's own Staff Rules and Regulations

---

339 Judgment 4749, consid 5, citing Judgment 4362, consid 7. See also Judgment 4478, consid 10; and Judgment 4360, consid 10.

340 Judgment 4817, consid 7.

341 Judgment 4373, consid 10; Judgment 4081, consid 5; and Judgment 2112, consid 5.

342 See the definition of 'Headquarters Agreement' given by Judge Rondón De Sansó in her dissenting opinion in Judgment 2193.

343 See, in this regard, A.S. Muller, *International Organizations and Their Host States – Aspects of their Legal Relationship* (Kluwer Law International 1995) <https://books.google.ch/books?hl=en&lr=&id=jMf7EAAAQBAJ&oi=fnd&pg=PR3&dq=relationship+between+international+organizations+and+host+states&ots=TVxgOWeE_m&sig=qTq3JZimabMx7mGQVJuK2UHBqmg#v=onepage&q=relationship%20between%20international%20organizations%20and%20host%20states&f=false> accessed 13 December 2025.

and to the general principles of the international civil service, and national laws – such as those of the organisation's host State – apply only where there is express reference thereto".[344]

While international organizations are generally not bound by national laws in the States in which they operate, there may be some situations in which those laws may be relevant. Firstly, as stated by the Tribunal, when the organization's internal rules or the officials' terms of appointment specifically refer to national laws, they may be relied on. Secondly, national laws may develop general principles of law, and as such, can be applicable 'by ricochet'. And thirdly, in situations where the organizations' internal rules do not contain clear provisions or no provisions at all, domestic law may be applied to interpret and provide adequate guidance on a specific issue or even to 'fill in the gaps'.[345]

Coming back to the duties incumbent upon organizations with respect to their host States when dealing with the situation of their officials, we have identified the following ones based on some practical examples. It is incumbent upon international organizations to properly manage their officials' status and the related administrative processes in order to ensure that the officials' situation complies with the laws of the host State, failing which they may be held to have abused the privileges and immunities conferred upon them and upon their staff members[346] or to be accused of "great negligence".[347] This duty already arises at the outset of a contractual relationship as organizations must carry out any checks to ascertain the officials' status when recruiting them,[348] and even later when their appointment is extended.[349] Failing this, organizations may be sanctioned for having been negligent by causing significant negative harm to their officials.[350]

Also, organizations do have a duty of assistance and a duty to act in good faith towards their officials in order to protect their dignity.[351] Inappropriate behaviour, negligence in monitoring the progress of a case, excessive deliberate delays or even the taking of steps which may influence the host country's

344 Judgment 4882, consid 2; and Judgment 4878, consid 3, and the case law cited therein.

345 For example, to determine what the marriage is and what could be considered as divorce, since the internal rules generally do not define these notions. See, in this regard, Petrović, 'Domestic Law and International Administrative Tribunal' (note 4), 619–626.

346 Judgment 3141, consid 36.

347 Ibid, consid 37.

348 Ibid, consid 53.

349 Ibid, consid 37.

350 Ibid, consid 39.

351 Judgment 3510, consid 12, and the case law cited therein.

decisions is proscribed.[352] From this perspective, the duty of assistance encompasses a requirement of diligence. Organizations are expected to facilitate procedures for obtaining official documents, to forward relevant information to the national authorities and, whenever necessary, to obtain information from the competent authorities in the matters concerned, to take the relevant steps aiming at helping their officials to have their requests granted, to keep their officials regularly informed of the progress made in processing their requests and to answer any query they may have.[353] When the Tribunal is seized of disputes involving procedures with host States, it verifies whether the organization concerned has displayed the necessary diligence to persuade the host country's authorities to grant a complainant's request.[354] By way of example, in Judgment 4727 involving the EPO, the complainant had asserted that the EPO failed to assist him in his attempts to obtain corrected identity cards for his children. The Tribunal has relevantly stated:

> [T]he issuing of identity documents or visas to persons enjoying the privileges and immunities conferred by the seat agreement of an international organisation is the prerogative of the host State. The only duty on the organisation in question in that regard is to provide its officials with the necessary assistance to ensure that the rights inherent in their status as members of staff of that organisation are complied with by that State. Furthermore, the organisation is free to choose how it approaches the authorities in order to discharge that duty. As a result, the organisation can only be liable for delays in a suitable visa or identity document being issued if it has acted in bad faith, behaved inappropriately in its relations with the host State or been negligent in monitoring the progress of the case.[355]

5 Concluding Remarks

Although the ILOAT case law may appear to be very complex, it is possible to identify several very stable lines of jurisprudence, which may help orient the organizations in a proper exercise of the authority conferred on them by the constituent instruments and general rules of the organizations. While the ILOAT case law may sometimes be perceived as contradictory, this may not

352 Judgment 3510, consid 14.
353 Ibid, consids 17–19.
354 Ibid, consids 17–20.
355 Judgment 4727, consid 6.

necessarily be the case, and one must bear in mind several important elements when analysing it. The first is that the ILOAT does not have the general mandate to control the legality of the functioning of an organization. It is not a constitutional court. It is a tribunal with a limited mandate which consists of dealing with complaints. Therefore, the Tribunal reviews the arguments of the parties, and its judgments are based on what was pleaded before it. The Tribunal cannot make arguments for the parties at the risk of ruling *ultra petita* (namely, beyond what the parties requested). Accordingly, the judgments may be silent on some aspects of the issue under review simply because the parties did not invoke them or did not make an argument on them.

The second important element is that the ILOAT relies on some 60 applicable laws, namely, the internal rules of the organizations under its jurisdiction. Accordingly, the judgments rely on the content and terminology of those rules. Only when referring to its precedents and general principles of law may the Tribunal repeat general statements given in the context of judgments involving different parties.

Thirdly, the ILOAT does frequently clarify, refine and even modify its case law. This may be necessary not only in light of modifications in the internal rules and new arguments of the parties, but also because the current composition of the judges may decide that an old case law should not be pursued or that some judgements are "at odds"[356] with a general line of other judgments. The modifications in the case law are normally done by the plenary judgments, adopted by all seven judges of the Tribunal.[357]

There is a long tradition in the ILO that all the seven judges of the ILOAT must be professional judges with a long experience in judicial organs, mostly supreme courts, of the States of their nationality. Hence, they join the ILOAT with an extensive knowledge of their national jurisprudence and legal tradition. They cannot be accused of favouring staff members or the organizations, as they do not have any interest in doing that. By their profile, they offer equivalent guarantees to the officials and the organizations as they would have if the immunity of jurisdiction would be lifted and the disputes would be brought before national courts of justice. That is why their judgments do not generally come as surprise. That is also why their judgments are often quoted by other international administrative tribunals. We hope that with this manual we assist the better understanding of the present state of this rich, interesting and comprehensive case law.

---

356 See Judgment 3515, consid 3.

357 See Judgment 3450.

PART 3

YLPIO Interview

'There's a Liberian Expression: If You Mind the Noise of the Market You Will Not Buy Your Fish.'

*Rhoda Weeks-Brown and Peter Quayle**

Abstract The inaugural YLPIO Interview with Rhoda Weeks-Brown, former General Counsel of the International Monetary Fund (IMF), explores the professional trajectory, leadership philosophy, and institutional practice of one of the most influential legal advisers in contemporary international financial governance. Organized across four thematic sections – Introductions, Legal, Practices, and Conclusions – the conversation traces Rhoda's path from Liberia to a pioneering leadership role at the IMF, reflecting on an experience as the first woman, first person of colour, and first General Counsel from a developing country to hold the position. Rhoda discusses formative career influences, including mentorship, resilience and a commitment to international public service, whilst also recounting pivotal institutional moments in which

* Rhoda Weeks-Brown served as General Counsel and Director of the Legal Department (LEG) of the International Monetary Fund (IMF) from 2018 to 2024, and also served in a number of other senior roles, including Special Advisor to the IMF's Managing Director, Deputy General Counsel and Deputy Director of the IMF's Communications Department (COM). During her over 27-year career at the IMF, Rhoda advised the IMF's Executive Board, management, staff and country membership on all legal aspects of the IMF's operations and on IMF strategic communications; lectured and wrote numerous journal and other articles on the law of the IMF; and led the work of LEG and COM on a wide range of significant country, policy and administrative matters. Since leaving the IMF, she has been engaged in a number of pursuits, including launching and serving as Chair and President of The Aurelia & Edith Breast Cancer Foundation, which focuses on improving access to breast cancer care for women in low-income countries, starting with Liberia. A graduate of Howard University (*summa cum laude*) and Harvard Law School, Rhoda is a member of the Committee on International Monetary Law of the International Law Association (MOCOMILA), the Leadership Council of the World Justice Project, and the Panel of Recognized International Market Experts in Finance (P.R.I.M.E. Finance), and serves on the Boards of Results for America and TalentNomics, Inc.. She was named one of the *Financial Times*' top 27 Global General Counsels (2020) and one of the top five General Counsels for Promoting Ethical Standards. During her tenure, the IMF's Legal Department was also short-listed for two FT Awards: Innovation in Strategic and Risk Advice and Most Innovative In-House Legal Team in North America. Rhoda is admitted to the practice of law in New York, Massachusetts and the District of Columbia and a member of the US Supreme Court Bar. Peter Quayle is Editor-in-Chief of the Yearbook of Legal Practices and International Organizations (Brill Nijhoff), peterquayle.ylpio@gmail.com. The views expressed in this interview are solely those of the author. They do not necessarily reflect the views of, and should not be attributed to, any institution with which the author is, or has been, affiliated.

 | HTTPS://DOI.ORG/10.1163/9789004765672-009

legal innovation proved critical to IMF operations, including responses to major financial crises, debt relief initiatives, governance reforms, and the creation of new financing mechanisms. Beyond institutional history, the interview examines the evolving role of legal departments within international organizations, emphasizing the importance of strategic vision, collaboration, clear communication and principled problem-solving. Rhoda also reflects on the ethical and professional responsibilities of General Counsel as an independent guardian of a multilateral institution's legal framework, highlighting trust, integrity and institutional loyalty as foundational elements of effective legal leadership in international organizations.

> The interviewee's expression of views and opinions are in their personal capacity and not attributable to any institution, including the International Monetary Fund (IMF or Fund), nor YLPIO. The interview has been edited for clarity and concision. Footnoting by YLPIO.

1 Introduction

Peter Quayle (PQ): Rhoda, you were the first General Counsel of the IMF from a developing country background. What shaped your awareness of being a pioneer in that role?

Rhoda Weeks-Brown (RWB): Thanks, Peter. Yes, I have been first in many contexts: not only as the first General Counsel of the IMF from a developing country (and also the first woman and first person of colour to be IMF General Counsel), but also well before that. In private practice, I was the first Black woman and first African woman lawyer in the Washington, DC office of the large law firm where I worked. When I joined the IMF, I was the first Black woman lawyer in the Legal Department, along with another colleague who joined the Legal Department on the same day; so the number went from zero to two overnight! I was also the first Black person to reach managerial level in the Legal Department, and later the first to serve as Deputy General Counsel (first woman in that role as well). When I moved to the Communications Department, I was once again a first in that role. So it really has been a series of firsts in my professional career. A different angle is that I am also the first General Counsel that is a breast cancer survivor – and, indeed, one of my main areas of focus in retirement has been launching a breast cancer foundation focused on raising awareness and increasing access to breast cancer screening, diagnosis, treatment and care for women in low-income countries starting with Liberia. The options in countries like the US are vast and improving constantly, whereas in places like Liberia, late-stage diagnosis is the norm and the available treatment options are both limited and unaffordable for most women.

To be honest, none of the professional 'first' experiences felt like a big deal to me at the time. In large part, I believe, that was because I had grown up in a place (Liberia) where it was the norm that people who looked like me were in myriad leadership roles (including close family members). Growing up in that ecosystem, there was nothing unusual about being a Black leader, or even a Black woman leader. Once in the US, however, I quickly became accustomed to what I now characterize as the 'idiosyncratic' reactions I sometimes received. People would be surprised to see me in a particular role, or would assume I must be in a different (less significant) role.

I remember one instance from private practice vividly. I had spent sleepless nights working on a major project. When the clients arrived, I walked into the conference room to start the discussion with them before the partner in charge arrived, and I was asked upon entering the room to make photocopies of some documents. I politely said I'd pass the request to our administrative assistant colleague working on the matter. They were mortified and apologized profusely; I told them not to worry about it. I simply refused, then and now, to let experiences like that bother me.

What mattered more to me was the responsibility that I felt came with being a first. I knew I would be seen as representing an entire race, gender, geography, and so forth. So I had to work harder than most, not only for myself, but for those who would come after me. I was in some ways creating a playbook, and I wanted to ensure that others that came later who looked like me would not be presented with the same assumptions and doubts. There's a saying: once you break the glass ceiling, the next person coming through gets fewer cuts. It was important that those who followed me would get no cuts at all, if possible.

That said, I should also note that I had tremendous support along the way. In every role where I was a 'first' and encountered challenges, I also had mentors, supporters, collaborators and friends – many of whom didn't look like me. They made the journey easier and less lonely. And now, I try to do the same for others. I mentor, coach, and guide – not just within the IMF, but beyond. It's not only about paying it forward; I really genuinely enjoy it. I share my experiences and lessons I've learned along the way in the hope that others can learn from that.

PQ: You mentioned those 'idiosyncratic reactions'. Was your decision to interpret them in that way a conscious strategy – something you adopted as a form of self-protection?

RWB: Yes. It was clear to me that letting those moments affect me too deeply would be counter-productive. And again, I think growing up in a country where almost everyone looked like me helped shape my attitude. I often say I didn't realize I was Black until I came to the United States! In Liberia, it had no consequence, no assumed implications. Suddenly, in the race-consciousness of the US, that characteristic seemed to carry weight for some. That struck me as odd – and I simply refused to allow it to bother me.

So when that client asked me to make photocopies, I didn't take it personally. It wasn't about me – it was about his assumptions and mind bugs. He apologized, and we moved on. My formative years gave me a resilience that I've never taken for granted.

PQ: You also spoke about the importance of mentorship. From your perspective, does a mentor need to share your background or identity?

RWB: Not at all. As I noted, when I was starting out, there were practically no senior people in the spaces I worked in that shared my specific identity – and indeed, terms like 'mentor' and 'sponsor' weren't really a part of the standard work conversation. But this support was still there. At my law firm, for example, there was one senior woman in my practice area who guided and looked out for me and showed me the ropes – what to do and what to avoid. She was a wonderful source of wisdom. Similarly, in those early days at the IMF, we had no formal labels, but I was given great advice and opportunities – including pivotal assignments that provided visibility and allowed me to show what I could do. That, in turn, led to more opportunities.

PQ: Do you think today's language – mentor, mentee, sponsor – can sometimes get in the way?

RWB: I was lucky that I had mentors, sponsors and champions at key points in my early career when we barely had labels, let alone institutional programs, for these arrangements. This is not to suggest, however, that institutional programs are not necessary. To the contrary, it is critically important in an institutional setting to be deliberate and persistent about fostering mentorship and sponsorship, not least to ensure that all employees have an opportunity to benefit. I was fortunate that it happened spontaneously in my case, but this is too important to be left to chance!

PQ: Your father was a government attorney in Liberia and argued before the International Court of Justice. What influence did he have on your legal career?

RWB: My father – Daddy as we all even now refer to him – was a force of nature. He was one of Liberia's great public servants and legal minds, playing a number of key roles. These included serving as Secretary of Liberia's delegation to the United Nations General Assembly; Assistant Attorney General of Liberia; and a member of Liberia's delegation to the first Law of the Sea Conference. He was also the first Liberian to serve as President of the University of Liberia. And even while in that role he remained engaged in international affairs, including leading the Liberian delegation to the First Assembly of the Inter-Governmental Maritime Consultative Organization, serving as Rapporteur General of the UNESCO Conference on the Development of Higher Education in Africa, and finding time to argue before the ICJ.

He went on to serve as Secretary of State of Liberia and later as Liberia's Senior Maritime Representative to the United States – which was his final official role. But beyond the impressive résumé, what influenced me most was his deep and abiding commitment to public service and international cooperation and his firm belief in the role of law as a powerful tool for positive transformation. Sadly, he passed away in his early sixties, but his legacy left a lasting impression on me and many.

PQ: You initially studied economics before turning to law. Was that decision influenced by your father's legal career?

RWB: In very large part, yes. Practically speaking, I also couldn't go straight into law since in Liberia (as in the US) law is offered only at the graduate level. So I needed to pursue another field first. Economics was a good one, in part to understand better why some countries fare so well economically while others like Liberia did not, despite vast resources. Let me be clear, however, what I truly wanted at that time was to be an astronaut and explore the cosmos! I've always loved science fiction – and still do. But alas, there were no classes towards that path at the University of Liberia – so I had to settle for economics!

PQ: What's your favorite sci-fi?

RWB: Oh, *Star Trek*, of course.

PQ: So you're *Star Trek* over *Star Wars*?

RWB: Absolutely! *Star Wars* is fine, but *Star Trek* was extra special, with its vision of a federation of planets where diverse species came together to search for new worlds and new forms of life. They pursued peace and multilateral cooperation to make things better for all – a lot like our earthly international cooperation, but at a celestial level. What could be more exciting?

So I started with economics. But then the political situation in Liberia began to worsen and, eventually, soldiers were sent to the University of Liberia campus to attack students. It was terrible. After that, my mother did all she could to get me out of Liberia (my father had passed away by then). So I moved to Washington, DC to attend Howard University where I continued my economics focus (my father had received his LLB from Howard decades earlier).

I had to assess whether to pursue economics or law for graduate school – though economics probably had little chance, given my father's known views. I went to law school and entered private practice with a Big Law firm, focusing on financial sector regulation and mergers and acquisitions. But I knew I wanted a job with an international public service focus; to work in an international organization that brought people together to solve global problems. After six years of private practice, I combined my legal and economic training and my interest in international public service by joining the Fund's Legal Department – which was in many ways my dream job.

PQ: When people ask you to reflect on being the first woman to serve as General Counsel at the IMF, do you see that as distinct – or inseparable – from being a pioneering General Counsel more broadly?

RWB: Being selected as General Counsel was both an honor and a huge responsibility. By being the first in such a position – whether as a woman, an African, or a person from a developing country – you are in essence a pioneer paving the way for others, as I noted earlier. It is therefore critical to excel; lack of success is not an option. So I committed to doing the most outstanding job I could, in the hope that it would make the path easier for those who would follow.

Let me also emphasize, though, that you simply cannot do the job if you're constantly preoccupied with the symbolism of being first – or with the 'idiosyncratic' reactions that others may have to seeing you in that role.

There's a great Liberian expression: "If you mind the noise of the market, you will not buy your fish." That's exactly it. You cannot let the views and expectations of others – or lack thereof – distract you from doing what you need to do.

PQ: The move to Washington, entering private practice, and then joining the IMF – these were all pivotal moments. What were other pivotal moments in your career? Once you were at the Fund, was there a point when you thought, "Maybe I'll be General Counsel one day"?

RWB: On the last part: no – I never spent time thinking about becoming General Counsel. In fact, I was not entirely sure I should even apply for the job after my predecessor announced his retirement, as I was worried that the work pressures of the role would be more than I wanted.

Your question on pivotal moments is a good one, as I have been fortunate over my IMF career to have been involved in a series of high-impact assignments and initiatives.

I joined the IMF in September 1997, a few months after the start of the Asian financial crisis,[1] and Indonesia was an early assignment. The Fund had major financing programs across the region – including in Korea, Indonesia, and Thailand, in a context where there were significant local currency depreciation and widespread bank and corporate sector distress stemming from large unhedged foreign currency borrowing. Traditional macroeconomic tools – for example, monetary and fiscal policy – weren't enough to resolve the crisis. So we had first-ever IMF-supported financing in which corporate debt resolution and related legal and institutional reforms were assessed to be critical for resolving the balance of payments problem and restoring macroeconomic and financial stability. The specific measures varied, but included insolvency law reforms, designing out of court restructuring frameworks to expedite corporate sector restructuring, strengthening key institutions including insolvency practitioners and the judiciary, and even establishing an anti-corruption commission. The Fund needed to take a new approach, to address the corporate sector issues impacting financial institutions.

---

1 Asian financial crisis was a financial crisis that started in Thailand in July 1997 and spread across East Asia, wreaking havoc on economies in the region and leading to spillover effects in Latin America and Eastern Europe in 1998. See Michael Carson and John Clark, 'Asian Financial Crisis' (*Federal Reserve History*, 22 November 2013) <https://www.federalreservehistory.org/essays/asian-financial-crisis> accessed 10 December 2025.

We had not previously focused on these kinds of legal and institutional reforms as a critical part of ensuring success in IMF-supported economic programs, but the economic case was strong – and suddenly we had to delve into those issues, partnering closely with others. I was deeply involved in that work and must have traveled to Indonesia alone over a dozen times in a relatively short period. The pace was relentless.

After that, I worked on the Argentina currency crisis of the early 2000s where too there was a need for targeted legal and institutional reforms to help resolve the balance of payments problem and restore stability, including reforms to improve confidence. Then came the Multilateral Debt Relief Initiative (MDRI),[2] a major donor country-led effort that provided post-Highly Indebted Poor Countries (HIPC) debt relief to qualifying countries. The initial idea raised issues that required creative modifications to ensure consistency with the Fund's legal framework. Another significant and unique undertaking in which I was involved was the development of a new income model for the IMF in the mid-2000s, which was intended to supplement the IMF's then greatly reduced income from lending and involved complex legal aspects, including amendment of the Fund's Articles of Agreement and the sale of IMF gold to create an endowment. That work had just wrapped up when the Global Financial Crisis[3] hit, and then the eurozone crisis. In addition to working on the crisis-affected countries, there were also a large number of very high-impact policy reforms to strengthen the system, including the creation of innovative new IMF financing instruments, new policies for IMF engagement on financial sector issues, IMF quota and voice reforms, and an overhaul of the Fund's policies on bilateral and multilateral surveillance.

---

2 The Multilateral Debt Relief Initiative (MDRI) is a program that provides 100% debt relief to eligible, heavily indebted poor countries (HIPCs) for debts owed to the International Monetary Fund, the International Development Association of the World Bank, and the African Development Fund. It was proposed by G8 finance ministers and implemented by the IMF. See IMF, 'Multilateral Debt Relief Initiative—Questions and Answers' (21 November 2025) <https://www.imf.org/external/np/exr/mdri/eng/index.htm> accessed 10 December 2025.

3 The Global Financial Crisis (2007–2010) was a severe worldwide economic downturn that began in the US and quickly spread to other countries. It was triggered by a collapse in the housing market, exacerbated by high-risk mortgage lending practices, particularly subprime mortgages. The crisis led to a global recession, significant losses for financial institutions, and ultimately, a period of great recession. See Michael P. Auerbach, 'The Global Financial Crisis of 2007–2010' (EBSCO, 2021) <https://www.ebsco.com/research-starters/business-and-management/global-financial-crisis-2007-2010#:~:text=The%20Global%20Financial%20Crisis%20of%202007%2D2010%20was%20a%20severe,lending%20practices%2C%20particularly%20subprime%20mortgages> accessed 10 December 2025.

After all that non-stop action, I simply needed a break from the law. So I made another 'unprecedented' move, from being an IMF Deputy General Counsel to being a Deputy Director in the Communications Department (COM). It was a great opportunity to serve in a different and very critical area for the Fund. And an exciting time also to be in COM, as that was the period when the institution began to emphasize communications as a critical policy tool to improve the traction of IMF policy advice and ultimately the Fund's effectiveness. I oversaw a number of key areas there as well, including communications in Africa, Asia and Europe, as well as Annual and Spring Meetings communications.

That pivotal experience continued after I returned to the Legal Department as General Counsel, including, among many others, a wave of major policy and operational reforms to better meet member country needs in response to the COVID-19 pandemic; creation of the ground-breaking Resilience and Sustainability Trust to help countries strengthen resilience and longer-term balance of payments stability including by implementing reforms to address climate change risks; major reforms to the Fund's financing policies including to enhance lending to low-income countries; new strategies for IMF engagement on climate and gender; the largest Special Drawing Rights allocation in IMF history; and a far-ranging Institutional Safeguards Review that resulted in strengthening significant aspects of the Fund's administration and internal safeguards, including an update of the Executive Board's Code of Conduct.

All very exciting, maybe too much so. By Summer 2024, it was clear to me that after more than a quarter century at the IMF, it was time to begin the transition to new adventures.

PQ: So pivotal moments for the institution were also pivotal moments for you. Being thrown into a crisis, being part of a team solving problems – those experiences propelled your career?

RWB: Yes, I think that's a fair statement. The work kept evolving, and I evolved with it. I also had – and seized – opportunities to make important contributions.

PQ: What would you say to lawyers who are fearful about having to adapt to crisis or institutional change? You seem to have navigated those moments with confidence. What's behind that?

RWB: I think that for those who are drawn to the kind of work that lawyers do at the Fund, those moments of crisis and major institutional change are quite meaningful, as that is when the IMF is needed the most and also when what we do can be most impactful.

The work is substantively rich and demanding, requiring agility, creativity, resilience, and a lot of energy. But it can also be incredibly rewarding, for example, seeing member countries benefit as new IMF policies take hold; or seeing country-level legal and institutional reforms adopted during an economic crisis (often with the IMF team working closely with local reform champions) begin to yield results. This type of work is not every lawyer's cup of tea. But for me, it was exciting and energizing because it was exactly the kind of law practice I wanted.

2 Legal

PQ: Looking back on your path to becoming General Counsel, what professional skills do you think are essential for a lawyer aspiring to that role? We'd assume that mastering the 'Law of the Fund' is a prerequisite. But what other skills and attitudes should one develop or refine over the course of a career?

RWB: Yes, General Counsels must possess in-depth knowledge of the key legal and institutional frameworks relevant for their roles, as well as the broader institutional and historical context of their institutions. The General Counsel role increasingly requires strategic vision and advice, which in turn – and counter-intuitively – requires a deep substantive foundation. You're absolutely right that for the Fund General Counsel, deep knowledge and understanding of the internal 'Law of the Fund' is critical, and this includes the Articles of Agreement and related legislative history, Board of Governors Resolutions and related materials, and Executive Board general and country-specific decisions. It also includes some knowledge of external legal frameworks relevant for the work of the IMF, including in areas such as central banking, financial sector regulation, tax and fiscal laws, anti-corruption and rule of law, AML/CFT and insolvency law and corporate restructuring. Also, knowledge of international administrative law is particularly relevant for the Fund's relations with its staff.

In terms of other skills and attitudes, I would put excellent communications skills high on the list. In a context like the IMF's, a lot of the work of the General Counsel and other Legal Department colleagues involves advising non-lawyers on complex legal issues that sometimes can be, frankly, quite esoteric. The ability to explain those issues clearly, persuasively and accessibly is critical in ensuring understanding of – and ultimately buy-in for – a General Counsel's advice.

And communication isn't just about persuasion. It's also about collaboration – being able to engage effectively with colleagues and devise solutions, especially in high-stake or high-pressure settings.

It is very critical also for General Counsels to have a deep understanding of the broad strategic priorities facing the institution and how legal and related considerations guide, impact and can help to achieve those.

Lawyering is also fundamentally about problem-solving. If there is a proposal for the Fund to do something new, the General Counsel and legal team's job (among others) is to assess the issue and figure out how the desired objective can be achieved in a manner consistent with the relevant legal and institutional framework, and based solely on that framework, to provide the same independent and impartial advice to all: staff, management, the Executive Board, Board of Governors, and member countries alike. The institution is the ultimate client. I have noted that this institutional role is akin to that of the Lorax,[4] from Dr. Seuss: "I speak for the trees, for the trees have no tongues." That was an important aspect of how I saw the role of General Counsel – speaking for the institution, because the institution cannot speak for itself.

PQ: So it's a three-part skill set: first, mastery of the law; second, strategic vision and strong communication and persuasion abilities; and third, being both a problem-solver and a person of integrity?

RWB: That's a great summary. And I'd really emphasize the problem-solving aspect. A good example is the MDRI I mentioned earlier. The initial idea contemplated additional IMF-funded debt relief for all countries who had previously qualified for debt relief under the HIPC Initiative. But the Fund has a core principle of uniformity of treatment – we must treat similarly situated member countries similarly when we use IMF funding – and at the time of the MDRI, the group of previous HIPCs were no longer all similarly situated in terms of the relevant economic criteria such as income level.

So we had to find a way to resolve that. The solution was to create two MDRI trusts. One used IMF resources and applied objective and uniform criteria that did not limit assistance to being a former HIPC. The second trust used donor resources, which can be targeted as desired by the relevant donor,

4 Seuss, *The Lorax* (1971).

and thus provided more flexibility to cover the former HIPCs not meeting criteria for the first trust. That's what I mean by elegant solutions – alternatives that are legally sound and operationally effective.

PQ: What's your approach when you know your legal advice will be difficult to hear? Do you try to pair a 'no' with a constructive alternative?

RWB: Always, to the maximum extent possible, and there are many examples beyond the MDRI. You are not adding value if the only contribution is saying no.

So the first step is communication – explaining clearly what the legal issue is and why it matters. Then you work with your counterparts to design a path forward. That's where creativity comes in. Most of the time, there's a way to achieve the underlying objective. But sometimes the answer really is no. And in those cases, you have to be able to explain why.

PQ: You've described the legal function as a problem-solving one. But how did you reconcile that with your role as the IMF's chief legal adviser? In moments of institutional leadership, how do you balance being the legal conscience of the Fund with being part of its leadership team?

RWB: That's a great question. For me, the key is remembering that even in leadership discussions, my primary role and value-added is legal. Of course, I may express informed and useful views on non-legal issues, but this is not my paramount role.

And this is not necessarily as narrow as it may seem. In fact, I think lawyers in general often have a particularly deep understanding of an institution's mandate and guiding principles, which can be quite useful in strategic discussions. That's why it's so important to involve any institution's legal function early in the process. In the distant past, there was sometimes more of a silo mentality – people would develop proposals and then send them to Legal at the last minute, which ran a high risk of raising legal difficulties.

The standard practice in the Fund is now much more collaborative. Legal is at the table from the beginning, helping to shape proposals in a way that ensures potential issues are identified and resolved at an early stage. Consistent with this dynamic, the Fund's Legal Department is normally a co-author of papers that include proposals for the Executive Board's adoption. That's a much healthier and more institutionally effective model.

PQ: You're saying that if you have a collaborative working culture, you can avoid some of those extreme, standoff-style legal clashes?

RWB: Precisely. Those kinds of confrontations are infrequent nowadays. Legal is brought in early, and the vibe is more of a shared problem-solving exercise rather than a legal standoff or veto.

PQ: Let's talk about your time as Deputy Director in the IMF's Communications Department. It's not a typical path for a lawyer to move into a non-legal function. What did you take away from that experience?

RWB: As I mentioned earlier, that move to Communications came at a point in my career when I really needed to step away from the law. So in some ways, it was a sabbatical from law – although it was still a very busy and highly demanding role, just in a different way. The 'one big thing' was that I was not giving legal advice, and that shift was refreshing. The move pushed me out of my comfort zone – and I absolutely loved it.

My COM stint also deepened my understanding and appreciation of the reality that well-designed communications are absolutely critical for the effectiveness of institutions like the IMF. For example, in many countries, local support (or the lack thereof) for IMF recommended economic reforms will depend fundamentally on how effectively the *rationale and benefit* of those reforms have been communicated to and understood by the population at large. This requires being able to explain (without jargon) what is in it for ordinary citizens – while also preparing them candidly for any difficult interim period before the benefits materialize.

My COM experience was also helpful when I moved back to the Legal Department as General Counsel, as it made me appreciate better the importance of effective communications and engaging with a broad range of stakeholders for LEG's own effectiveness, particularly when handling difficult legal issues.

PQ: You mentioned being outside of your comfort zone. What made it uncomfortable? Was it the temperamental difference?

RWB: To some extent. Being in COM often required rapid responses to breaking news developments, not something common in LEG. But recall that I also see communication as one of the top skills a General Counsel needs. I had to develop it – and I have still not entirely perfected it! But it is important to recognize that any legal advice is only as effective as the number of people you can get to understand and buy-in to it. People may go along because LEG says so; but the best of all worlds is to be able to explain to them persuasively why something is an issue – and jointly design ways to resolve it. All of this puts a very high premium on effective communication for lawyers.

The comfort zone issue was more basic. Instead of advising on the Fund law and external legal issues that had been my bailiwick for over 15 years by the time I moved to COM, I was now advising on communications. But of course, the substance of communications matters greatly, and I think that was my key value added as part of the COM team. It was also an exciting time to be in COM as noted earlier, as that was the point at which the Fund began to emphasize the role of communications as a strategic policy tool to increase IMF's effectiveness and traction.

PQ: Would you recommend that kind of non-legal role to other lawyers? Would you encourage your mentees to step outside the legal function?

RWB: Absolutely. I encourage colleagues all the time to think expansively about their careers and not feel stuck in any one role, legal or otherwise. Especially in a context where promotion opportunities are limited (which is true for many institutions including the Fund), delving into other career streams can be intellectually stimulating and exciting; an opportunity to explore something different. And the benefits can be even greater, as we have had Legal Department colleagues move on to managerial roles in other departments, and even to head other departments. More attention is also being paid institutionally to non-traditional mobility initiatives.

PQ: In a place like the Fund, tradition and adaptation are often seen as opposites. But it sounds like your view is that adaptation is essential for relevance – and that lawyers, as part of a collaborative process, can help ensure that adaptation respects the institution's core principles. Is that right?

RWB: Yes, that's exactly right. It goes back to the Fund's unique mandate – international monetary cooperation; balance of payments, macroeconomic and financial stability. Over time, what's required to achieve those objectives has evolved. In the past, economic difficulties could often be resolved simply with currency valuation changes and fiscal responses. But economics has become more complex, and so have the solutions.

Take women's economic participation, for example. The number of countries that still have limits restricting what women can do economically is astounding. And even where discriminatory legal provisions have been repealed, de facto barriers remain. Remove those provisions and barriers, and suddenly more women can enter the workforce, bringing their skills and triggering increased economic growth, reducing inequality, improving financial sector outcomes, and a range of other measurable economic benefits that have been documented in the economic literature. The inclusion of women in the economy is thus clearly macroeconomically critical for many countries.

Remember also the point I made earlier about how some of the countries affected by the 1990s Asian crisis had IMF supported crisis response programs that focused on a range of then non-traditional areas, including insolvency law reforms, out-of-court corporate restructuring frameworks, and even anti-corruption measures and reforms to strengthen the judiciary. All of these were assessed to be critical for resolving the balance of payments problem and restoring macroeconomic and financial stability in the context of that crisis. So areas such as anti-corruption, often characterized as 'new', were actually part of the toolkit a quarter of a century ago – even if the more detailed IMF policies for addressing these issues are of more recent vintage.

Ultimately, the question as I see it is not tradition versus adaptation. It's about prioritization, institutional focus and resource allocation among competing areas that are macrocritical, but that potentially cannot all be pursued given limited resources. Choices need to be made that take into account both the assessment of criticality and available resources. But what is not negotiable is that in all cases we stay true to the Fund's mandate.

3 Practices

PQ: Returning to the core legal functions – particularly the role of General Counsel and leading a legal department – what's your view on legal department strategy? Is it a good thing? Should it be written down?

RWB: As with any other organizational unit, there is definitely a need for a well thought out strategy on how a legal department sees its evolution over time and how it will address key issues of interest or concern. There does not need to be a formal document labeled 'Legal Department Strategy', but it is critical to have a game plan that reflects all relevant input and views and lays out clearly the key issues and how to address them. Importantly, I do not see a strategy as something that the General Counsel goes up to the mountain top and comes down with! Rather, it needs to include views and input from the team (and where relevant, from other key stakeholders as well).

During my time as General Counsel, we spent a considerable amount of time discussing, designing and implementing measures to address a range of issues relevant for the department, including workplace and well-being initiatives, particularly during COVID and in its aftermath. I always viewed my first priority as addressing team members' wellbeing in the workplace, and a significant focus was on strategies to manage work pressures and workloads and improve work conditions. Another important set of discussions related to enhancing career development, especially considering that most staff in the legal function are specialized and thus tend to stay in the same roles for most, if not all, of their tenure. Ways to improve inclusion and belonging for all team members was a further priority area.

Retreats, town halls and other forms of active team engagement are critical mechanisms to carry forward these discussions. And while the key issues were not resolved overnight, the broad team engagement and shared vision were critical and very impactful.

PQ: Is information and knowledge management central to legal department strategy?

RWB: Knowledge management is critical. Especially for a legal department that, like the IMF's, strives to ensure that consistent legal advice is provided across time and countries on all issues.

You cannot answer legal questions responsibly without knowing what's been said before on that issue. Fortunately, knowledge management has already come a very long way from the physical 'green files' that were in vogue when I joined the Fund – you'd put the relevant files on a cart and wheel them back to your office to review! Now that we're dealing with eight decades of increasingly complex institutional history, the scope and complexity is such that you can no longer simply glance at a few paper files, pick the brain of the most senior lawyer and view your research as complete. Moving from green files to searchable digital records was transformative. AI overlays are now at the next frontier. The latter will undoubtedly be game-changing and make it a very exciting time to look at these issues.

PQ: You've spoken about the importance of career conversations – talking to people about their ambitions and direction. Do you see that as a contributor to high performance?

RWB: Absolutely. Most people at the Fund are here because they believe in the mission and vision – international public service. So part of encouraging high performance is reminding people of how what they do links to that mission and vision. It's easy to get lost in the technical details, but the big picture matters. I often reminded the team that what we did was ultimately about the people in IMF member countries. If we get it right, we can make a real and significant difference in improving their lives. That perspective comes also from my own experience growing up in Liberia.

But mission alone isn't always enough. If someone has been doing the same thing year after year, they may need more. So it is important to think about how to keep careers interesting and rewarding. Compensation matters, of course. But so does autonomy – giving people space to shape how they work. And visibility. I still remember being invited to attend important meetings with management or department heads as a young lawyer. That mattered. It showed someone believed in me and saw me as an integral part of the team.

It is also very important for all managers, not only the General Counsel, to hear what team members want for their own careers. Some might be interested in mobility to a different part of the legal function or to another department, while others might simply want an opportunity to delve into a different workstream within their organizational unit.

Fortunately, the Fund and most departments are now much more deliberate about issues like career conversations, visibility, mobility and inclusion. These may seem to be not a big deal, but they make a big difference. People need to see that they matter – not just in words, but in actions.

PQ: Especially early in your career, it's how you remember every single meeting you had with the Managing Director or the head of the organization?

RWB: Totally. Those moments are etched in your memory.

PQ: What advice would you give to someone new to the age-old dynamic between management and a board of directors? What helps a General Counsel navigate that dynamic effectively?

RWB: It all comes down to trust. And the thing about trust is that it has to be developed and nurtured and the work never really ceases to keep it alive. At the Fund, we have a new Executive Board term every two years. In the past, many Executive Directors stayed on for successive terms and sometimes very long tenures, so there were more continuity and institutional memory, and Executive Directors and staff knew each other better. Now, tenures are shorter, and you have to regularly re-establish relationships – and trust.

That often means explaining the legal framework from the ground up – what the Articles say, how the Fund operates, and fundamentally, explaining the independence of the General Counsel's role. I've even shared my *Lorax* analogy with Executive Directors, noting that I speak for the trees, and for the institution itself, rather than for management or the Board. My experience is that everyone understands the role conceptually and fully supports it; though having trust is ultimately what makes the role work in practice.

PQ: And how do you build that trust?

RWB: You have to be accessible; stakeholders need to know you. In the Fund, that would include Executive Directors, management, other senior staff and colleagues at all levels. And you have to be clear about the role. Yes, I'm a staff member, and I report to the Managing Director. But my responsibilities go beyond that. I have a fiduciary duty to the institution itself. That's a difficult concept to explain – especially to people coming from settings where the legal advisor's role is different. In my Big Law days, identifying the client took a nanosecond. At the Fund, explaining that your client is the institution can take longer.

PQ: Let's talk about delegation. When does the General Counsel need to take the papers home and do the preparation personally?

RWB: It's all about balance. We talked earlier about autonomy – empowering your team. That means saying: "Here's the objective. Go achieve it. If you get stuck, come back to me." But it's not a hands-off approach. You don't say, "Go off and do no harm." You say, "Come back, update me, let's discuss it, and then I'll come on board."

The reality is that the days when the Legal Department wrote one Board paper every few months are long gone. Things moved more slowly then, and the scope was narrower. Now, we have multiple specialized legal divisions, each producing or reviewing critical Board papers, country papers, discussion notes, technical assistance reports – you name it. The work is diffuse. There's simply no way for a General Counsel to do it all personally. So delegation isn't optional – it's mandatory.

PQ: So the question is – how do you do it? How do you retain control while delegating so much?

RWB: There is no universal approach; leaders, organizations and scope of work differ. When I was General Counsel, I stayed engaged, including through regular updates and team discussions, to get my views and inputs, along with an understanding that important or tricky issues must be discussed in more detail. In practice, if there is a major issue, you read everything including every footnote; in other cases, quick eyeballing does the trick. Delegation is an art, not a science!

Ultimately, this is about risk management – prioritizing and diverting maximum attention to what's critical and doing less for the less critical. You have to trust your team and allocate your time strategically.

4 Conclusions

PQ: To wrap up, a few rapid-fire questions. What's the one thing you think holds organizations back the most?

RWB: This is not specific to the IMF, but my answer would be groupthink and, relatedly, fear of rocking the boat. You can sit in a meeting sometimes and see everyone converging towards the same line of thinking even where there is scope to ask questions or even challenge some aspects. And related to that, a fear of taking risks – even calculated ones; a reluctance to be too different.

PQ: What's the one professional trait you rely on more than any other?

RWB: The ability to connect – to understand where people are coming from and try to meet them where they are. And I think that's helped by genuinely caring about the work and the people, both in the Fund and those that the Fund serves in its member countries.

PQ: What's something you've changed your mind about over the course of your career?

RWB: The importance of personal relationships. As I became more senior, I realized how critical it is to have networks you can connect with both on substance and for moral support. These relationships can provide strength and support when difficult issues arise, but their foundations must be set in advance.

PQ: What's your greatest insight about being General Counsel?

RWB: I may give more than one insight! First, trust matters: your legal advice, especially on difficult issues, gets maximum traction and support if there is trust – and that trust has to be built over time. Second, integrity is non-negotiable: you have to give the best legal analysis and advice you can, guided solely by the relevant legal considerations. This includes, of course, offering alternatives wherever possible, but also being clear on the redlines if there are no viable alternatives. Third, the job can be difficult – and sometimes lonely. Despite all the delegation and teamwork, there may be some issues sufficiently sensitive that you handle alone; and only you can make the final call on really tough issues.

Final insight: it really is a great job! And the impact makes the job more than worth the challenges. For me, that was the ultimate motivation: if we can make a meaningful and lasting difference for some people, somewhere in our member countries, then it's worth it. That's what kept me going for over 27 years!

www.ingramcontent.com/pod-product-compliance
Ingram Content Group UK Ltd.
Pitfield, Milton Keynes, MK11 3LW, UK
UKHW020846290926
15470UKWH00004B/1585